My Shriners Diary

Our Mission, Our Members and Me

Gyp Bergenske

PROCEEDS BENEFIT SHRINERS HOSPITALS FOR CHILDREN
AND SHRINERS INTERNATIONAL EDUCATION FOUNDATION

A Year as the Imperial Potentate of Shriners International

My Shriners Diary

OUR MISSION, OUR MEMBERS AND ME

PROCEEDS BENEFIT SHRINERS HOSPITALS FOR CHILDREN
AND SHRINERS INTERNATIONAL EDUCATION FOUNDATION

GARY J. BERGENSKE

A Year as the Imperial Potentate of Shriners International

My SHRINERS DIARY - *Our Mission, Our Members, and Me*
by Gary J. Bergenske
Copyright 2019 by Gary J. Bergenske
All Rights Reserved
ISBN: 978-1-59755-506-7

Published By: **ADVANTAGE BOOKS**
                       Longwood, Florida, USA
                       www.advboostore.com

This book and parts thereof may not be reproduced in any form, stored in a retrieval system, or transmitted in any form by any means (electronic, mechanical, photocopy, recording, or otherwise) without prior written permission from the author, except as provided by the United States of America copyright law.

Library of Congress Control Number: 2019941587
1. Biographies and Memoirs: Memoir
2. Travel: Specialty Travel

Photographs by: Jon Thomas and Kathy Gumina, Harry Reiter, and Gary Bergenske

All of the pictures in this book can be seen in full color by purchasing the E-book version at AdvBookstore.com

Pin designs by; Tony Rossi

Shriners Diary is available in Hardcover, Paperback and E-book versions. Videos of some of the events in this book can be seen on YouTube by searching Gary Bergenske.

Watch Gary Bergenske - "One Man's Dream" on YouTube

First Printing: July 2019
19 20 21 22 23 24 25   10 9 8 7 6 5 4 3 2 1
Printed in the United States of America

Proceeds from "My Shriners Diary" support Shriners Hospitals For Children and Shriners International Education Foundation.

Shriners Hospitals for Children has a mission to Provide the highest quality care to children with neuromusculoskeletal conditions, burn injuries and other special healthcare needs within a compassionate, family-centered and collaborative care environment.

Provide for the education of physicians and other healthcare professionals.

Conduct research to discover new knowledge that improves the quality of care and quality of life of children and families.

This mission is carried out without regard to race, color, creed, sex or sect, disability, national origin, or ability of a patient or family to pay.

and...

Shriners International Education Foundation

Shriners International Educational Foundation has a mission to:

Provide information and knowledge and develop necessary skills of aspiring leaders of nonprofit organizations.

Engage in and provide neutral analysis and study of the effectiveness of nonprofit organizations' leadership skills and successes.

Underwrite, sponsor and support studies and conferences in effective leadership of nonprofit organizations.

At the heart of both Shriners International and Shriners Hospitals for Children is a strong desire to strengthen and improve lives and abilities, and to make the world a better place. As nonprofit organizations, all tax-deductible gifts and donations to the Hospitals or the Foundation are greatly needed and sincerely appreciated.

A Year as the Imperial Potentate of Shriners International

Be sure to read other books by Gary Bergenske

"Campaign for a Better Life"
20 Tools to Enrich Your Life and Everyone Around You

"Campaign to be a Better Leader"
12 Essential Keys for Unlocking Leadership Excellence

"Quotes for Leadership Success"
365 Little Quotes for Optimizing BIG Opportunity

A Special thank you to members of the Joint Boards of Shriners International and Shriners Hospitals for Children for their commitment and passion during the 2017-2018 Imperial year. Your time, talents, and efforts are recognized and greatly appreciated for the fine volunteer work you do every day.

It was my honor to have each of you as part of the team while serving as the Imperial Potentate.

Gary Bergenske

Members of the 2017-2018 Shriners Joint Boards; Gary Bergenske, Jim Cain, Jeffery Sowder, James R. Smith, William Bailey, Brad Koehn, Randy Rudge, Kenny Craven, Ed Stolze, Richard Burke, Kevin Costello, Larry Leib, Bobby Simmons, Jerry Gantt, Peter Diaz MD, Skip Stanaway, Anthony West, Jim Doel, Brandt Bede MD, Chuck Pittman, and Chris Smith.

Endorsements

I visited a Shriners Hospitals for Children in 2007, my rookie season in the NASCAR Cup Series. I immediately saw that this was no normal hospital. Children were happy, smiling, and in good spirits. Not only do the Shriners Hospitals for Children treat all their patients' physical needs, they also provide the encouragement that allows kids to be confident in who they are. This is why I joined the Shriners International Fraternity and chose the Hospitals as my charity of choice in 2007. It was an honor to work with Imperial Sir Gary Bergenske on a number of projects to help raise awareness for the Hospitals. Gary set a great example of what it means to be a Shriner and I enjoyed getting to know him and his family.

David Ragan
NASCAR Driver

****

If children are the soul of Shriners Hospitals for Children, Shriners are its heart. Physicians and nurses help heal while Shriners give compassionately. This story takes you on a journey of an Imperial Potentate's servant leadership and dedication to helping children take their first steps.

Mahealani Richardson
Anchor/Reporter - Hawaii News Now
Former Communications and Marketing Director
Shriners Hospitals for Children - Honolulu

****

I had the privilege of meeting Gary through a mutual friend. In June 2018, Gary came to my house in Plains, GA to present President Carter with the **Shriners Hospitals for Children Humanitarian Award**. I found both Gary and Anne to be wonderful people and was enthralled with his service. I had the opportunity to read his manuscript when he sent a copy to Andrea. I really enjoyed his stories and found his work throughout the year very special. As you read, you will be reminded of what the good people in this world do.

Jill Stuckey

Gary and I met at Oriental Guide school when my late husband was elected to the HASAN Shrine Divan. He and Gary had many great adventures including the privilege of awarding Former President Jimmy Carter as an Honorary Shriner and a Hospital Ambassador. After my husband passed away during his Potentate year, Gary and I remained friends while I helped Gary complete a project with President Carter. After completing his Potentate year, Gary sent me a transcript of his memoirs. Gary really embraced his year as Imperial Potentate. His memoirs were a joy to read. As a past First Lady of the Shrine, it really warms my heart to know others that care so much.

Andrea Walker
HASAN Shrine, First Lady 2017.

****

Around 1963 or so, I came to the realization of just how much the Shriner's Hospitals for Children did for the care and health for needy children. As a result of this realization, I resolved to become a Shriner as soon as I had the means to do so. I was in law school at the time and was living hand to mouth. I became a Shriner in 1972 and the Shriner's Hospitals have been one of my passions in life ever since. The Shriners are unparalleled in their loving care for children. Please read these pages carefully and you will be impressed as I was with all that the Shriners do for children. God bless the Shriners and their "kids".

Gordon H. "Stumpy" Harris, Esq.
Director General
2017 and 2018 Imperial Conventions

****

Being Imperial Potentate requires many qualities, total dedication and love. One of the highest qualities is communications including sharing information with various media outlets, the membership of the fraternity and our hospital system. Gary and Anne were able to follow their dreams to enhance Shriners International and Shriners Hospitals for Children in every visit, in fact sometimes you felt that you were even traveling with them. As a Bahia Shriner I am very proud of Gary and Anne and all the time and hard work they contributed during their year. Thank you, Gary and Anne.

Bob Wagner, Chairman Public Relations Committee
2017-18 Sessions Committee

The Springfield Shriners Hospitals for Children has been collaborating with the George & Thelma Paraskevaides Foundation in Cyprus for over 38 years and the charitable help provided is immense. Over 3500 children from Cyprus, Greece and other countries in the region have been admitted to the Shriners Hospital in Springfield, Massachusetts for treatment. In addition, 12,000 children have been examined on the annual Shriners outreach clinic in Cyprus.

In October 2017 for the first time after 38 years of cooperation the Imperial Potentate, Imperial Sir Gary and Lady Anne Bergenske visited Cyprus together with the team of doctors from the Springfield Shriners Hospital. Their visit gave a new dimension to the cooperation of Shriners International with Cyprus by signing agreements with the Cyprus Ministry of Health and the Medical School of the University of Nicosia. The Imperial Sirs visit gave inspiration to the Nobles of Alasia Shrine Club of Cyprus to consider the possibility of establishing a new Local Shrine Chapter in order to expand Shriners work all over the Middle East.

Costas Paraskevaides, Executive Director
George and Thelma Paraskevaides Foundation

****

Shriners International is a fraternity of men who have the desire to serve their community. As Shrine Masons we have committed to this with other members throughout the world. We try to make the countries that we live in a better place and have fun with a purpose. Shriners Hospitals for Children is our philanthropy and the back bone of the drive in all of us to be better. Taking care of children that need our services is the main focal point in our organization. The Imperial Potentate is the number one Shriner who leads us in the direction to accomplish the needs of these children. In this book you will live the life of serving in this position. This book will give you an insight on the drive, dedication and sacrifices it takes to accomplish and provide the care for those in need.

Robert Amico
Deputy Director General 2017 - 2018

Inside the pages of this manuscript, the reader will gain insight and enlightenment into what it takes to run Shriners International, including the "World's Greatest Philanthropy." Along this journey one may also experience the unselfishness of Shriner's from all over the world. Understand how their equally combined efforts, personal sacrifices, and penchant for fun help to fulfill our purpose of helping children by supporting Shriners Hospitals for Children.

Although I consider the author as a close personal friend, a fraternal brother of over twenty years, and even though he has requested that there be no accolades for himself in this writing, it will become clear to the reader how much recognition he truly deserves. As evidenced by the monumental greatness of effort, deep personal commitment, and the mantle of sacrifice Gary, with the unyielding support of his wife Anne, have made for his year of stewardship as the Imperial Potentate (President) of Shriners International. Those and much more will speak louder than any words I can pen in this endorsement. One of my favorite lines of this book which resolves his selfless dedication to the duties and responsibilities of his position in my mind is where Gary alights, sleeping in his own bed for two days in a row is a luxury. For me, that sums it up nicely. Enjoy your read.

Dr. Ken Vehec, Shriner
Chairman of Special Events
Imperial Sessions 2017 & 2018

****

As Shrine Imperial Divan members move thru the line there is nothing to guide them for when they become the Imperial Potentate. This day to day recollection of events will give the future Potentates an insight of what they need to prepare for. This is priceless to all of them. People have no idea of the time required to serve as an Imperial Potentate, the travel commitments, the social events, the business meeting presentations, staff meetings and all the planning that is involved. All this on top of the regular scheduled committee meetings, board meetings, and every day dealings with issues that arise from the membership.

I was privileged to be part of some of the activities during Gary's year as Imperial Potentate and can say that he represented all of the Shriner's in the World with dignity and grandeur during his tenure. From the Bolivian Andes to the Temples in the Philippines you made us all proud to be Shriners.

Peter Diaz MD
Shriners Hospitals for Children, Trustee

Gary Bergenske's Shriners Diary - Our Mission – Our Members – and Me

In a world of go go go and me me me, Gary Bergenske and the Shriner organization slows the world down so you can see the true beauty that surrounds us all. In a magical way Gary and Anne brought that beauty to the doorstep of Daytona Beach and enriched all our lives.

Linda McMahon
Daytona Beach area CVB
Director of Group Sales
Meetings/Conventions
Travel Trade

To Gary Bergenske – I believe you will find the rough diary to be valuable to you and your family as the years go by, as a reminder of the many interesting and delightful experiences and as a source of help to you if you ever decide to share with others your times as the Imperial Potentate of Shriners International, perhaps in an intriguing book. Thank you for giving me the opportunity to share some of your experiences and fine work in this way. Your friend,

Jimmy Carter
39th President of the United States of America

****

GARY BERGENSKE
Motivations

GaryMotivations.com

A Year as the Imperial Potentate of Shriners International

Dedication

The pencil drawing of Gary and Anne Bergenske was a gift from former First Lady of Bahia Shriners, Renee Snapp.

I dedicate this book to the many Shriners, past, present and future. These men of integrity and character enjoy fun and fellowship together. Their special mission is to assist in the care of children who become patients in the Shriners Healthcare for Children System worldwide. It has been my privilege to work alongside these men who are so willing to give of their time, talents and money.

MAY GOD BLESS EACH OF THEM!

Gary Bergenske's Shriners Diary - Our Mission – Our Members – and Me

Gary Bergenske Giving Thanks

From the day I became a Shriner in 1994, to becoming the Potentate of Bahia Shriners in 2005, then being elected to the Imperial Divan in 2007, and ultimately being elected Imperial Potentate in 2017, it's been a DREAM for me all the way. How can I ever give enough thanks? I'm sure I can't.

I will never forget the excitement of becoming a Shriner, my first Shriners Hospitals for Children visit, the tears that ran down my face as that first mother hugged me and thanked me for helping her child. Nor will I forget the friends I made from all over the world and the help each gave me so I could live out my dream. We have many memories we will share for the rest of my life. It's been an incredible ride.

Even after all of these memories, it will be the patients and the Shriners who made serving as Imperial Potentate so special. The patients provided the daily fuel to keep me going, and our members provided me with the confidence and respect to keep me focused.

I want to thank the people who work in our Home Office, the staff in our hospitals and the Shrine members and their families in each of our Shrine locations throughout the world. You are people who can move mountains and in fact perform miracles every day. Your efforts and the difference you make in the world are so great they are unmeasurable. You make me so proud and have inspired my every effort.

To my family, you not only helped enhance my dream, you were so understanding of my time commitment it took away from each of you. You supported me and became my biggest fans; I hope I continue to make you proud.

To my wife Anne, you kept us on track, you provided much needed advice and became the guiding light as you built relationships with people we worked beside every step of the way. You are so good at that; it made a big difference in our efforts. And Anne, your program, **"Loves Grow's Miracles"** and the reason you chose it, makes our whole family so PROUD. I love you.

In the end, I can promise you, every day I served as Imperial Potentate, I gave you all I had. Every day, no matter where I was, I gave it 100%. It was an honor to put that Five

Star Fez on each day and represent all of you. I thank you from the bottom of my heart for the privilege you afforded me, I am your grateful servant.

Inevitably, a one-year term goes by so quickly. All good things must come to an end. But this is not the end of the story, just the end of this chapter. There are many more Imperial Potentates to come who will continue the tradition of the Shriners.

"Today we are doing yesteryears impossibilities; we are doing them routinely, daily, and without a second thought."
GARY BERGENSKE

Table of Contents

Endorsements 7

Dedication 12

Foreword 18

Introduction 21

Acknowledgements 24

Preface 26

Chapter One: July 2017 28

Imperial Session In Daytona Beach, Hadji Visit, Demolay Visit In Jacksonville, Meetings At Tampa Home Office, Kansas Shrine Bowl

Chapter Two: August 2017 42

Almas Visit, Boumi Visit, Fort Mchenry, Medical Advisory Board, Shc Canada Golf Tournament, Midwest Shrine Association, Scottish Rite Southern Biennial Meeting, Research Board, Joint Board Workshop – Stone Mountain Retreat, Jimmy Carter Presidential Library Visit

Chapter Three: September 2017 60

Canada 150th Anniversary At Philae Shriners; Halifax And Prince Island Visit, Shc Strategic Planning Meeting, South Atlantic Association, Press Conference In Daytona Beach, Greenville Hospital 90th Anniversary Visit, Imperial Session Executive Meeting, Shrine Guilds Of America Visit.

Chapter Four: October 2017 76

Governance Workshop, Membership Seminar, Shc Clinic In Cyprus, Emirat Shriners Ceremonial In Cyprus, Shc Northern California 20th Anniversary, Committee Meetings, Shriners Hospitals For Children Pga Golf Tournament In Las Vegas.

Chapter Five: November 2017 .... **99**

SHC PGA OPEN IN LAS VEGAS, WREATH LAYING AT THE TOMB OF THE UNKNOWN IN WASHINGTON DC, CONGRESSIONAL MEETINGS ON THE HILL IN WASHINGTON DC, JOINT BOARD MEETING IN TAMPA, BOLIVIA SHRINERS VISIT AND CEREMONIAL, IMPERIAL SESSION EXECUTIVE MEETINGS, HEADQUARTERS MEETINGS.

Chapter Six: December 2017 .... **119**

Zor Shriners, Wisconsin For Ceremonial, Mabuhay And Agilia Shriners In The Philippines Visit, Philippines Hospitals Visit, Tim Tebow Cure Hospital Visit, Henry Rifle Meeting, Shrine Headquarters Awards Banquet, Shrine Bowl Of The Carolinas, Shc Strategic Planning Meeting, Recognition By Eola Lodge, Arrival For The Rose Bowl Parade.

Chapter Seven: January 2018 .... **137**

Rose Bowl Parade And Game, Demolay International Headquarters Visit In Kansas City, Al Rai's Saleh Shriners, Puerto Rico Visit, East West Players Visit To Tampa Hospital, Leadership Conference, Attend Texas Grand Lodge, East West Shrine Game Banquet And Game, Ewsg Hall Of Fame Induction, C. Victor Thorton Gala In Fort Worth, Mexico City Shc Visit, Pre-Con Meeting For Spring Board Meeting In Mexico City, Burn Summit.

Chapter Eight: February 2018 .... **157**

Mid West Shrine Association In Deadwood, Daytona Beach Cvb Meeting, Texas Shrine Association Meeting In Corpus Christi, Pacific Northwest Shrine Association Meeting In Coeur D' Alene, Conference Of Grand Masters Meeting, Murat Shriners Visit, Panama Clinic Visit, Abou Saad Shriners Visit In Panama.

Chapter Nine: March 2018 .... **175**

Shriners College Baseball Classic, Demolay Headquarters Meeting, Oriental Guide Conference, Assistant Rabban Conference, Imperial Potentates European Riverboat Cruise, Emirat Shriners Visit, Grand Encampment Of Knights Templar Easter Sunrise Service, George Washington Masonic Memorial.

Chapter Ten: April 2018 .... **196**

Committee Week, Pre-Con Meeting – Daytona Beach, Western Shrine Association, April Board Meeting – Mexico City, Shc Mexico City Visit, Mid Atlantic Shrine Association, Leah Foundation Golf Tournament, Atlanta

Chapter Eleven: May 2018 213

Mabuhay Ceremonial And Temple Visit– Manila, Philippines Grand Lodge And Demolay Visit, Ladies Oriental Shrine Annual Session – Honolulu, Strategic Planning, Murat Shriners Visit, Indy 500 Race.

Chapter Twelve: June 2018 234

Tunis Shriners – Wreath On Tomb Of Unknown Canadian Soldiers, Abou Saad Ceremonial – Panama, Panama Canal Trip, Plaque For Abou Saad 100th Anniversary And Celebration, Meetings – Tampa, Bahia Potentates Ball And Ceremonial, Shc-Springfield Ribbon Cutting, White House Visit To The Oval Office, President Jimmy Carter Plains, Ga Visit, Daughters Of The Nile Annual Meeting, Committee Meetings In Tampa.

Chapter Thirteen: July 2018 256

2018 Exec Meeting For Session Prep – Daytona Coke Zero Sugar 400, Daytona Int'l Speedway – Meeting With 3 Star General Tuck – Joint Board Meeting And Pre-Week Activities – Walk, Ride, Or Drive For Love -Imperial Church Service – 2018 Imperial Session – Presentation Of Shc Humanitarian Award And Impact Award – Presentation Of Imperial Potentate Awards Of Merit, Imperial Parade, Oak Ridge Boys Concert, Closing Session Of The 2018 Imperial Session.

Chapter Fourteen: Imperial Potentate Medallions 292

AWARDS AND THANK YOU- A COMPLETE LIST OF THE 37 IMPERIAL POTENTATE MEDALLIONS PRESENTED BY IMPERIAL POTENTATE GARY BERGENSKE DURING THE 2017 – 2018 SHRINE YEAR.

THANK YOU LETTER 296
ABOUT ANNE BERGENSKE 298
CONCLUSION 300
ABOUT THE AUTHOR 302
PICTURE INDEX 305

A Year as the Imperial Potentate of Shriners International

> "There is nothing like a dream,
> A dream can create the future.
> If you BELIEVE in it.
> A dream can take you anywhere."
>
> **GARY BERGENSKE**

Foreword

The world is changing faster than most of us can imagine. Daily, new programs, new people, new technology, and ways of doing business literally change our lives. But what about old traditions, history, relationships, and spending time face to face with people we admire, respect and love. There seems to be a shift of people spending more time working to accomplish great things with the modern tools they have and less time enjoying quality time with others. The character in each of us flourishes from the energy we get from others. Some old traditions never die, the human needs others around to inspire and motivate. A "**My Shriners Diary**" will take you on a journey of just how important these old traditions are.

These old traditions can be found in Shriners International. During the early part of the 20th century membership in Shriners International grew at a steady pace. By 1946, membership had jumped to 150,000 Nobles and another 250,000 had joined by 1958. In fact, Shriners International experienced one of its largest periods of growth in the years following World War II as returning soldiers looked for new ways to continue the camaraderie they had experienced with their fellow soldiers.

As the number of locations and nobles grew, so too did the hospitals. By 1958 the hospitals' endowment was valued at $125 million and growing. Today, there are nearly 200 Shrine Chapters, and hundreds of Shrine Clubs across North America, South America, Europe and Southeast Asia. With the number of Shrine locations growing around the world, men have found that old traditions and the value they bring are beneficial to their wellbeing. Their philanthropy, Shriners Hospitals for Children has flourished as well. With their endowment reaching into the billions of dollars they have treated over 1.4 million children regardless of their family's ability to pay. This unique healthcare system managed by volunteers of the Shriners organization and a professional staff have changed the lives of many families.

Shriners are a group of men, supported by their ladies and families who have made a tremendous impact on the world. They are a true example of what can be accomplished when many people work together, all pulling in the same direction, to make the world a better place. They enjoy life, respect each other, and their philanthropy. May some old traditions never die, as they are the spirit of the human soul.

Shriners were recently recognized by the 39th President of the United States, President Jimmy Carter. President Carter considered to be one of the world's finest

A Year as the Imperial Potentate of Shriners International

humanitarians, winning the Nobel Prize in 2002 **"for his decades of untiring effort to find peaceful solutions to international conflicts, to advance democracy and human rights, and to promote economic and social development."** President Carter has become an Ambassador for the Shriners organization's and provided the following letter that was published in the Shriners Program Book for their annual meeting in Daytona Beach in July of 2018. As you read **"My Shriners Diary"** you will take an inspiring trip around the world, enjoy...

JIMMY CARTER

July 15, 2018

To Shriners and their Ladies

    Rosalynn and I congratulate Gary and Anne Bergenske for their impressive work while serving as Imperial Potentate and First Lady of Shriners International. We are proud of the partnership between The Carter Center and the Shriners organizations, and we look forward to strengthening that relationship even further in the future.

    Thank you for everything you do to make the world a better place. Your work on behalf of children is inspiring, and thanks to your efforts, countless lives have been greatly improved. We are honored to work beside you in your important mission to provide hope and healing to children.

    I also would like to recognize Shriners Hospitals for Children's quick response and willingness to help after the recent volcanic eruption in Guatemala. I know that sending the "emergency medical go team" to Guatemala within 24 hours of the disaster was a challenge. Your efforts then brought six patients with complex severe burns back to the United States for treatment at the Galveston Shriners Hospital. We commend your commitment to children throughout the world, and thank you for helping to save these young, precious lives. Keep up the good work.

With best wishes,

Sincerely,

Jimmy Carter

Introduction

In the mid 1980's as a young man with a growing family and a business I had purchased, there was no time for anything other than family and work. I was in my early 30's, it took my full attention to grow our business to support our family. Although there was a lot of pressure building a company, they were wonderful years. Having young children in the home keeps you involved and happy.

Several years later as the business began to run smoother and the children were older, I began to open my eyes and look around outside my narrowly focused life. When we purchased the business, we had moved to a new city, and we arrived with no friends, and no social life. It was time to make some friends and reach out to others, after all this should promote a comfort in life and also help our business. So, I began to think in a different way, how do I enrich my life by being a part of something much bigger than myself?

In 1994 while attending a community parade with the family, I witnessed this group of men in the parade who appeared to be having the time of their life. They each were having a great time and were surrounded by others who all seemed to be their friends. Oh, what fun they were having. I thought to myself, wouldn't it be great to have friends and good times like that? Come to find out, they were the Shriners, I knew nothing about them. I did some investigating and found out a friend of the family actually belonged to the Shriners. After discussions with him, he soon had me in the Masonic Lodge to become a Mason and eventually a member of the Bahia Shriners in Orlando, Florida. Little did I know my life and the lives of my family would be changed forever.

I jumped right in, there were picnics, parades, parties, dances, specialized clubs, and formal events. All of these activities introduced us to new people; we were meeting people faster than the mind could keep track of the names. Then we learned there was another part to all of this, the Shriners have the world's greatest Philanthropy, Shriners Hospitals for Children. Suddenly the idea of making more friends was enhanced as these new friends were part of a healthcare system that changed children's lives through the expert pediatric care their hospitals provided. Again, my life was changed, I truly had become a part of something much bigger than myself.

My passion to become a bigger part of this was overwhelming me. I soon was a part of the leadership team of Bahia Shriners in Orlando. I proudly served as the chapters Illustrious Potentate (President) in 2005. This was an honor I could have never imagined in my life just a few short years ago. My circle of true friends had expanded throughout the entire community.

After completing the year as the Illustrious Potentate, I was still yearning for more. My wife and I began traveling the country campaigning for an international position with the Shriners. If successful we would embark on an eleven-year journey. In 2006 we were not successful, however in 2007 I was elected to the bottom of the progressive line that would place me in the top position of the Shriners fraternity and philanthropy in ten years. How exciting! This position comes with an extraordinary amount of responsibility and accountability. The commitment has to be unquestioned, your life now belongs to the future of the Shriners. Thank God, the business I had purchased years ago would support my efforts of participating at the highest level of leadership in one of the world's greatest organizations, where men are made better and children's lives are changed and saved.

As the years passed my circle of friends encompassed people from around the world. I tell people, **"As a child the world was my back yard, today my back yard is the world."** To think all of this was happening because I went to a parade and saw some men having a good time with their many friends. The opportunities and the doors that were opened were countless as we climbed the ladder to the top. Shriners Hospitals for Children is world renowned for the expert pediatric care they provide regardless of their family's ability to pay. The patients, the members, and the people you meet who are familiar with Shriners and their good work is incredible. A truly amazing reputation.

As a kid, growing up in a small town in Wisconsin, with a family that had little but knew the meaning of love and caring; stepping onto the stage to be installed as the top leader of Shriners worldwide in July of 2017 was unthinkable. It was a proud moment for our family as our real journey now began for a one-year term. We will be leading and serving our 240,000 Shrine members, our 6,000 Hospital employees, and our thousands of patients from around the world. This top position totally takes over your life for a year. I was only home about 30 days the entire year, Anne was home about 60.

I kept this diary, a **"Shriners Diary"** from a few days prior to taking office until a few days after going out of office. I wrote daily notes on my iPad daily, mostly when flying. Every single day has from one to several paragraphs depending on the activity of the day. Each day has what we were so honored to participate in, often mentioning the people we were with. During the year we traveled through 19 countries and worked alongside Shriners and medical staff from around the world, changing lives every step of the way.

Keeping this diary has to be one of the best things I did during the year. Personally, as I read through it there are so many amazing events, I would have forgotten had I not had this diary to refresh my memory. But more importantly, the real value of this diary is having the ability to share what someone who holds this office does. The responsibility, the travel, the people you meet, and the emotions that overtake you as you move from day to day could never be shared like they are in this book. You simply could not remember everything that happened. I am so happy to share this with everyone.

So, sit down and begin reading of this great adventure. If you were a part of our travels or we visited you during the year, find that date in the diary and see what we had to say. I hope everyone we spent time with enjoyed our visit as much as we enjoyed being with you... Read and enjoy!

> *"People forget what you say,*
> *and forget what you do,*
> *but forever remember how you make them feel."*
> **GARY BERGENSKE**

Acknowledgements

Gary and Anne Bergenske

I am appreciative and grateful to my wife, Anne, who has gone above and beyond in all aspects of my dream to achieve the leadership position of the Office of the Imperial Potentate of Shriners International, the highest office in all of Shrine organizations worldwide. She not only supported my efforts, she became engaged and worked alongside of me. She herself made great contributions to the Shrine organizations and participated with Shriners and Ladies worldwide.

I thank each of our six children and their families for their patience as Anne and I chased this dream. Often, we were gone doing our volunteer work more than we were home; we missed many family activities and we thank you for your understanding.

To our many friends who supported our efforts by always helping and encouraging us. We made friends around the world and because of you there were always friendly faces to greet us everywhere we went. A special thanks to our Convention Executive Team for your extraordinary work.

To the many Shriners Hospitals for Children patients we met along the way, you were the fuel that inspired us to keep going. It's because of you every day we served in the top office of Shriners, there was a reason to forge on.

Many thanks to President Jimmy Carter who inspired me to keep this journal one evening in Plains, GA when we had dinner together. Thank you, President Carter, for your encouragement.

"As a child the world was my back yard, today my back yard is the world."
GARY BERGENSKE

A Year as the Imperial Potentate of Shriners International

Preface

The journey started in Anaheim, California in July of 2007. It was here that I was elected Shriners Imperial Outer Guard after running for two consecutive years. After losing in 2006 in Tampa, and now winning, we could finally take a deep breath and relax, the campaigning was over. It was now time to go to work for the next eleven years as a member of the Board of Directors of Shriners International and a member of the Board of Directors for Shriners Hospitals for Children.

I desired this position with passion as I loved what both organizations represented. I had a deep hunger to be able to contribute to them, knowing the positive difference they made in so many lives. Fortunately, my wife Anne, fully supported me in this venture that would literally change our lives and the way we looked at the world. We came to look at things differently, we became humanitarians, looking for ways to improve the lives of others. In doing so, we gave up time with family and many commitments we had prior to be able to make a difference.

The journey found us traveling near and far, working both with the fraternity and the philanthropy. We met many wonderful people within and because of being a part of Shriners. We as well, were introduced to wonderful Doctors and medical staff who attended to the children we served in our Shriners Hospitals for Children health care system. We were most inspired though, by the children we met along the way who were patients of ours. Regardless of what they were facing, these children remained brave and continued to take on the challenges they had been handed. Having the opportunity to meet and be a part of the lives of so many of these children, made us work harder and caused us to appreciate them and what we were doing even more. They were motivating and inspiring, they kept our fuel tanks full, keeping us forging forward

As we closed in on our preparations of our final year as a part of this eleven-year journey we had many decisions to make. This would be the year Anne and I would serve as the top Shrine couple in the world. We would be responsible for a tremendous amount of planning and implementation. We would represent both organizations and become the face of top leadership for a year. We took this responsibility seriously, we gave it 100%.

During these final planning stages, Anne and I had an occasion to have dinner with President Jimmy Carter and the former First Lady, Rosalynn Carter in Albany, Georgia. During this dinner President Carter had many questions about what our role would be as the Imperial Potentate and First Lady of Shriners; where our travels would take us, and how much time would we be expected to spend in this capacity. He was amazed with what was involved. He also was amazed by many of the places we would go and of the many things we would do. He expressed we would be doing some of the same things he did while serving as President.

These discussions with President Carter lead to a recommendation from him. He expressed the best thing we could do for ourselves is to keep a daily diary of our year in office. As President he did it for every day he was in office, I know, he signed a copy of his book, WHITE HOUSE DIARY for me at a dinner we had a couple of years earlier. I took his recommendation seriously and committed to doing it.

A few days before I was sworn into office, I began this journal, it was typed on an I-Pad. Most of the work was done on an airplane during our many travels. Every single day is described with anywhere from one to several paragraphs depending on the day's activities. We traveled through nineteen countries, some only a layover at an airport, others for extended days and work. Although Anne spent a few more days at our home than I did during the year, I was only home about 30 days all year.

Reflecting back on this now, President Carter was correct, this was the BEST thing we could have done for ourselves. With our fast-paced agenda, we could have never remembered all that we have recorded in these notes. Every time I pick it up it brings back great memories, amazing people we met, and functions we will cherish forever.

Now, we are happy to share with you what it is like to have the honor and privilege to serve the members, employees, and patients of the world's finest fraternity and greatest philanthropy, ever, bar none. Enjoy your travel around the world as you read of our adventures.

Gary Bergenske
Imperial Potentate, Shriners International
Chairman, Board of Directors
Shriners Hospitals for Children - 2017 - 2018

A Year as the Imperial Potentate of Shriners International

July 2017

This is not your usual book, it's a diary or memoir of an extraordinary year my wife, Anne, and I experienced as the leading couple of the "World's Greatest Fraternity, **Shriners International** and it's Philanthropy, **Shriners Hospitals for Children**." It was my vision to share with as many as I could the tremendous work Shriners do, both in enriching the lives of their members and improving the lives of the children they are able to treat in their healthcare system. The daily diary I kept brings to you, the reader, the wonderful times and work that can be accomplished when people all pull together. Each month has its own chapter, making it easy to find certain events. If we spent time in your area during our tenure you will be able to read about it in this book. We had a wonderful year and enjoyed everyone we met and were able to work beside. So, travel with us, around the world, working to make a difference in the lives of others every step of the way.

July 9, 2017 - Sunday

Opening day of the 2017 Shriners Imperial Session in Daytona Beach, Florida. It was a busy morning with the Canadian Breakfast and then out to the Daytona International Speedway for the Walk, Ride, or Drive for LOVE. Then back to the hotel for a quick shower and off to the church service at the Peabody. Our entire family attended. Next up was the Opening Session of the 143rd Shriners Imperial Session. This was a wonderful start to a great week as the welcome messages from all of the local politicians and leaders were nice. A very good memorial video was played for Imperial Sir Jack Jones, a wonderful tribute to a great man. After the Opening, we attended the 2018 Session Reception and enjoyed our time there. Following that we went to the Ocean Center to practice for the pageant that will take place on Wednesday morning. Not enough time in the day, we got to dinner about 8:30 with our Executive Team.

July 10, 2017 - Monday

143rd Imperial Session opens for business and the Election of the 2017-18 Imperial Officers. I was honored to be elected as the Imperial Potentate for the 2017 – 2018 year on this day. It is hard for me to express how honored I feel. I, like many of you have my parents watching what I do from heaven. I know the representatives who entrusted me with this position made them very proud today.

I grew up in a small-town of 1300 people in Pardeeville, Wisconsin; my family really had very little. I say this because we lived in a small home without a lot of money. But I will also tell you that I had a rich childhood because of my parents. We were raised that richness was not in material things but rather richness was found in how you treated people and likewise how they treated you. As a young boy, I believed we had everything. When I would get into trouble as a boy, my father would say, " You're a Bergenske, act like it". It was his way of saying, do it right, keep your character high, respect others, accept nothing but the best, you are representing our family." Although at times his comment sounded harsh, it was always given with love and with an inspiration to do your best. I had no idea how little we had, yet how we had everything we needed and more.

The other newly elected Imperial Officers included Brad Koehn as Treasurer, Randy Rudge as Recorder, and Larry Lieb as Outer Guard. The remainder of all the officers moved up one spot on the progressive line. Business and legislation progressed nicely all day. There were 48 items of legislation on the call for this Session.

At the conclusion of the meeting a thank you celebration party was held at the Peabody for Bahia Shriners. This was a wonderful event with food and drink and gifts for Anne and me. A tremendous time to thank all those who helped us to accomplish this trip to the top of the Imperial line. After this it was back to the hotel to put on something comfortable and to head on down to the Band Shell for the Cigar Smoke Out and something to eat. This was a day to remember, being elected as the Imperial Potentate of Shriners International, who would have thought?

July 11, 2017 - Tuesday

Second day of the meetings, Imperial Sir Chris Smith did a great job of moving us through the 48 pieces of legislation, by the close of the day we were in good shape on time.

On this day, I received from the Grand Master of DeMolay the prestigious recognition of being installed into the Supreme Council of DeMolay. Then it was off to the Imperial Parade down A1A. It was a large parade with over 400 groups that lasted nearly 2 1/2 hours. The parade was led by Shriner and NASCAR Driver David Ragan. Zion and his family arrived and watched the parade from the grandstands. Zion, the first child ever to receive a double pediatric hand transplant has arrived to assist Anne with her program of *"Love Grows Miracles."* The evening ended with cocktails on our deck with fireworks. The members of the 2017 Exec Committee and CVB Staff joined us. Another wonderful day at the beach.

July 12, 2017 – Wednesday

This has to be right up there with one of the best days of my life. The pageant of being publicly installed as the Imperial Potentate and First Lady of Shriners International. The video, *"One Man's Dream"* of Anne and me and our family, illustrated what our dreams are for the coming year. (You can see this video on YouTube by searching Gary Bergenske.)

Then to be escorted in by Shriners Hospitals for Children patients to the Whitney Houston song, the "Greatest Love of All" how incredible to reach the stage of a room filled with love and applause. The installation by Imperial Sir Raoul Frevel was flawless on a stage set up by Aldis and team. It was a magical moment as Anne placed upon my head the five-star Fez of an Imperial Potentate. Then to have our family come across the stage, each member giving Anne a red rose, a statement of love and affection. Then Nobles from around the world came across the stage with gifts, what an honor for a small-time kid from Wisconsin.

Another highlight was Imperial Sir Ralph Semb and my son Jason making the **Presentation of an"Imperial Potentate Elect's personal flag":**

"Imperial Sir Gary, as you well know at the Imperial Potentate – Elect's Pageant he is presented with his personal Shrine flag. Today I have the distinct honor and pleasure on

behalf of Shriners International and Shriners everywhere to present your Imperial Potentate's flag, bearing the Shrines official seal, as well as your name and title.

The flag is of royal purple silk, embroidered in gold denoting the symbol of your authority and the importance of your high office. Imperial Sir, as you lead this great fraternity, may this flag stand with all of our other national flags as a reminder to our devotion to the principals of Freemasonry, our beliefs expressed in the Shriners Creed, and our commitment to serve mankind through the "World's Greatest Philanthropy, Shriners Hospitals for Children."

Imperial Sir, I present this flag to you with fraternal love, admiration, and best wishes from all of us for a very enjoyable and productive Shrine year. And, Imperial Sir, as you and Lady Anne embark upon your journey representing this great fraternity, may God bless, protect and keep you both safe."

Anne then took the stage to present her program to the 3000 people in the audience. She did an outstanding job presenting it and the video that supports it. At the conclusion, she introduced Zion, a Shriners patient from Philadelphia and that brought the house down. Eight year old Zion spoke to the crowd on why research is so important, it changed his life.

I then presented my membership program for the year, "I AM – RU Committed to Membership" along with clips, from the movie "Rudy." Pins were handed out to support the program and the excitement began.

That afternoon the Imperial Potentates Award of Merit awards were given along with a Donor Relations report. I had the opportunity to once again do one of the things I've enjoyed most, to give the Public Relations report. It was special this time as I was presenting the two new National Patient Ambassadors who would be working with Anne and me for the year to create awareness for Shriners Hospitals for Children. What an honor it was to present Isabella Rose and Emily Mellish.

The end of this fabulous day ended with a VIP dinner and a concert performed by the FAB FOUR, a Beatles tribute band. What a way to end a memorable day that will be remembered forever.

July 13, 2017 - Thursday

Thursday morning was the close of the 143 Imperial Session, I was officially installed as the Imperial Potentate. Following the meeting we had Joint Board photos done, lunch, and a Joint Board meeting where I presided officially as the Imperial Potentate of Shriners International and Chairman of the Board of Directors for Shriners Hospitals for Children for the first time.

One of the privileges of the Imperial Potentate is to appoint the Imperial Chaplain for the year. This is an honor to have the privilege to appoint and an even greater honor to be asked. I selected my friend, Illustrious Sir Bobby Simmons from Al Sihah Shriners in Macon, Georgia. Bobby served as Potentate of Al Sihah Shriners and also served as a Trustee for Shriners Hospitals for Children. He has held many other positions in other Masonic bodies as well. Bobby Brings with him his great character, integrity, and his faith in God. What a pleasure it is to have him join us today for our first meeting of the 2017-2018 year. I know he will make our fraternity proud.

That evening at the Shores Rooftop Restaurant overlooking the Atlantic Ocean we had the First Dinner of the new year. On this evening I recognized Linda McMahon and Lynn Miles of the Daytona Beach Convention and Visitors Bureau, I presented each of them with an Imperial Potentates MEDALLION.

July 14, 2017 - Friday

Packing up day and time to head home. Sadly, on this day we had to file a report with the hotel security and the Daytona Beach Police Department regarding jewelry that had been stolen from our room.

There was a lot to pack, and many people to say good bye to. We had lunch with many of our family members at the Deck Down Under on the way out of town. Then it was off to the house to unload and unpack. At this time, we were able to look closely at some of the many gifts we received. The task of the many thank you cards we needed to write was beginning to sink in, there were 100's of them.

July 15, 2017 - Saturday

I spent a good amount of time at my office catching up on work there. Jami and her family were at the house for a few days. It was good to be able to spend some time with the grandkids.

Anne and I went over her project, "Love Grows Miracles" and the product that we would need to carry around with us for the next year to sell. She had neckties, bowties, and 3 different types of lady's necklaces. Really some nice items. The following is a quick review of her project;

Lady Anne Bergenske, as the First Lady of Shriners International in 2017 - 2018, is promoting a program called *"Love Grows Miracles"* to raise money for research that is focused on Healthy Births. Bergenske, who lost a grandchild 7 1/2 months into the pregnancy knows the pain and sorrow a family feels in the loss of an unborn child. It was because of this loss she is spending her time and energy as First Lady to raise money to provide scholarships for medical students to research ways to give children healthier lives even before they are born.

"There are many people who have experienced the shock and sadness that comes with losing a child before birth," said Anne. "Research is developing ways to prevent and treat medical conditions that can cause such heartache."

"Many of us have experienced the joys of having a healthy newborn child. However, others experience the unbearable pain of losing a child or are coping with challenges some children are born with." Anne continued. "We are inspired and comforted by the fact that doctors and scientists at Shriners Hospitals for Children are developing innovative new ways to prevent and treat many medical conditions before children are born. The cutting-edge research in this area will prove to give many children healthier lives in the future."

July 16, 2017 - Sunday

Relaxed at home with family and cooked out. So much to do, but great to be home for a couple of days to prepare for the year ahead. A couple of calm days before the traveling begins.

As I sit here it's beginning to soak in; the honor that has been given to me, the responsibility that has been bestowed upon me, and the tremendous amount of accountability I am placing on myself to do a good job. I feel a strong duty to represent every Shriner, and every patient in a manner that will always make them proud of the organization I have been so blessed to represent. I am committed to do my very best, and to never cause any embarrassment for anyone. All this with the goal of building Shrine membership and a focus on how we can bring our expert pediatric medical care to children in the poorest of countries.

July 17, 2017 - Monday

Day at work at J&J Metro, worked on sending out thank you notes. We are so thankful for all that people did for us, it's incredible to think of the support we have been given. Feeling really grateful.

July 18, 2017 - Tuesday
Day at work at J&J Metro, preparing to be gone most of the year. Also, again, worked on sending out many thank you notes to all of the people who helped us and presented us wonderful gifts.

July 19, 2017 - Wednesday
Half day at work, then packed and prepared for our first trip as Imperial Potentate and First Lady to Hadji Shriners in Pensacola, FL.

A high goal of mine for the coming year is to promote building Shrine membership. As the Imperial Potentate, I hope to bring more awareness to our need to build membership than any previous Imperial Potentate has ever done before. This is a lofty goal as we have had many great leaders in the past. However, I have the advantage of modern social media technology, and tools to communicate better than anytime before. We also have a program we have developed to kick off and energize the nobility to seek out and enter qualified men into a system that will inform them of who we are and what we do to make the world a better place. It's called I AM – RU Committed to Membership.

The burden lies on my shoulders to promote this program and to endorse it as the top leader of Shriners. I'm ready for this with a plan to be transparent, and an effort to bring the nobility on each and every trip Anne and I go on through social media. If successful, we will bring our membership needs to top of mind. Just remember; I AM – RU.

July 20, 2017 - Thursday
Up early for the 6-hour drive to Pensacola. Upon arrival, we were taken to a really nice dinner at McGuires Irish Pub with the Hadji Divan and Past Potentates and their ladies. A really neat place and the food was great. Carlos and Karen Baxter were our escorts and what a fabulous job they did. Our room was full of goodies and they were so delightful to be with. They will serve as the 2018 Potentate foe Hadji Shriners.

July 21, 2017 - Friday
Up early to meet a group of Hadji Shriners and Ladies. Carlos and Karen were our escorts and what a wonderful job they did. We went to the Naval Air Museum. What a place with over 600 naval aircraft since the beginning of air traffic time. We spent 3 hours there and saw only a portion of what was there. Bet you could spend a week and not see it all. We had a nice lunch at a marina in Pensacola. The evening consisted of a great

event at Hadji Shrine. With 200 people for dinner it was fantastic. After dinner gifts and contribution to Anne's Project were made. During the evening Anne's project items were sold. (Total in contributions and sales approx. $4,000). Great evening.

July 22, 2017 – Saturday

Up early and off to Jacksonville, a 5-hour drive. Today we attend the Florida DeMolay Conclave. First, at 6PM a reception followed by their Opening Session. I was the first Imperial Potentate to attend their Conclave in their 84-year history. A proud moment. My unplanned escort into the room was by a DeMolay member who is a Shriners Hospitals for Children patient, this was extremely touching. When I spoke about it in my opening remarks, the room erupted in a standing ovation for the young

man. Following the opening session, Anne and I were back in the car for the 2 1/2-hour ride back home to our own bed.

July 23, 2017 - Sunday

A half day to unpack, wash, and repack. Plus, I was able to go to the office for a couple of hours. We then had to pack up and load the car with items for the Imperial Potentates office in Tampa and our travel clothes. Back on the road again. We checked in at the Doubletree Hotel in Tampa.

July 24, 2017 - Monday

We both arrived at Shrine Headquarters at 9AM and began working on the Imperial Potentates office. The highlight of the day was the two Town Hall Meetings we were having, one at 10AM and one at 2PM. These both went well as we shared the videos from the pageant, Anne's program, and the National Patient Ambassadors for 2017-2018. We also introduced the "I AM – RU Committed to Membership" program to all of the employee's, many who are already Shriners. We received good comments.

We then worked more on arranging the office. It was looking really good, defiantly going to be a great place to work out of for a year. We went to dinner at the Rusty Pelican. Then, after dinner Anne drove back to Orlando, I had two more days in Tampa.

July 25, 2017 - Tuesday

The day was spent at Shrine Headquarters organizing the office, meeting with staff and setting plans and goals. In the afternoon, I had an interesting conference call with Barry Smith and Daphne regarding the American Role Model program. This was very interesting and thought to be a way to promote Shriner awareness and to help our "I AM - RU M membership" program. More to come on this. Dinner out with the SHC Administrators.

July 26, 2017 - Wednesday

To start the day off I attended and welcomed the SHC Administrators to their 2-day Seminar. A great group with over 400 years of combined SHC service. Then I worked with Jessica on scheduled events and sending out "thank you" letters, a task I'm behind on. By 11 AM I was on the way back to Orlando. A couple of hours at work and then time to unpack and repack at home for Anne and my flight out in the morning.

July 27, 2017 - Thursday

Up and at it early. A quick trip to J&J Metro for an hour, then back home to pick Anne and the luggage and off to the airport. We had a problem finding a parking spot and visited 3 different lots to get a parking spot. We flew to Wichita, Kansas where Jeff and Cheryl picked us up for the Kansas EWSG Bowl. We had dinner and then back to their home for the night. We stayed up till midnight chatting and solving the world problems.

July 28, 2017 - Friday

A relaxed morning and homemade breakfast at the Sowders. I had another conference call with Daphne from American Role Models as we discussed how this could help the Shriners organizations. We agreed to meet the following week in Washington DC when we were going to be there. We drove off to El Dorado, Kansas where the football game was going to take place at and checked into our hotel. That evening was the banquet where 1200 people attended. An excellent event that really promoted the game and SHC. There were many speakers and I was one of them. I spoke on Lisa's college sports career and on Hero's and the importance of being a good citizen. After the event, it was off to the hospitality room. Anne and the ladies sold $1700 in First Ladies project items.

July 29, 2017 - Saturday

The day started off with breakfast and then off to the Kansas East West Shrine Game Parade. Many Shrine Parade Units were available for the parade and the local town had many people out to watch. After the parade, it was off to the hospitality room for lunch. Anne sold a bunch more First Lady's Project items. That evening was the big game and what a great turn out of spectators, the stadium was full. This was a wonderful event that raised good awareness for Shriners Hospitals.

July 30, 2017 - Sunday

It was up early and off to the airport. Jeff and Cheryl were great hosts as always and got us on our way. I have to say, Jeff is so committed to the success of Shriners International and Shriners Hospitals. He is a tremendous Board member.

Imperial Sir Jack Jones was to be Membership Chairman this year, he helped with the planning of the I AM - RU program and was extremely excited about leading this effort. His unexpected, untimely death shocked all of us and left an empty spot in all of our hearts. He was one of the finest Shriners we all came to know. Jeff stepped up to fill the vacancy on the Membership Committee and became the Chairman. He is a driving force assisting me promote membership, so thankful for his willingness to step it up.

Good flight home, Anne did up the laundry and I went to work at J&J Metro for a few hours.

July 31, 2017 - Monday

A day of work at J&J Metro catching up. The crew at work was all doing good in my absence. I'm very fortunate that they are all working hard to allow me to do my Shriner work. Things are all moving along well. I'm extremely proud of what is happening here, it allows me to focus on my Shriner responsibilities.

"Leaders who care are not threatened by others moving forward; they promote it for the betterment of the organization with influence."

GARY BERGENSKE

Chapter Two
August 2017

August 1, 2017 - Tuesday
A day of work at J&J Metro. Then off to reorder the Divans sport coats at Jos. A Banks for the Imperial Divan, the first batch wrinkled too much. The store made it good, thanks. I get to tell my Shrine story so often now, I'm impressed how many people know about Shriners but really don't know how much we do. I really enjoy telling people and watch their reaction, it's a powerful story we have. Anne and I then did the packing of our travel bags for our trip out the following day.

August 2, 2017 - Wednesday
Mid-day flight to Washington DC for a visit with Almas Shriners. We were picked up at the airport by Potentate Mike Gordon and taken to our hotel, a lovely Crown Plaza in downtown DC. The room was filled with goodies, wine and liquor. Dinner that evening was with the Potentate, Recorder and their wives and a Past Potentate at a nice restaurant. After dinner Anne went back to the hotel while I went to a Cigar Bar with the Potentate and Past Potentate. There we met a Past Grandmaster of DC for some great discussion and fellowship, and of course a good cigar.

August 3, 2017 - Thursday
Our day was spent in Washington DC with Almas Shriners. We started off with a tour of the White House, how amazing. We had a private tour by June, the wife of an Almas Past Potentate. June then took us over to the Eisenhower Office Building for a

private tour, again amazing to see this restored building that was built in the early 1800's.

The evening was a nice dinner that included Shriners from Almas, Keena, Acca, and Bolivia. A wonderful night! Gifts included a Capital Police 2017 Inaugural Badge, a flag flown over the U.S. Capital the day of my Public Installation, July 12th, a set of ten White House holiday ornaments to represent the ten years on the Imperial Divan, a custom handmade Shrine pen, a book, wine and more. Anne received a beautiful pearl necklace from Bolivia and had sales and donations to her project of $2800.00. Proud to say Almas Shriners are totally on board with the I AM - RU program.

August 4, 2017 - Friday

After a light breakfast Anne and I along with Mike Gordon met Daphne Boyd from America's Role Models for an opportunity to do some video clips for a documentary on Americas Role Models. The goal is to show that all Shriners are role models due to the work they do and the care they provide for children.

The first video clips were of Anne and Gary separately across the reflecting pond from the Jefferson Memorial. This was a great venue for the video that showed history and tradition. Anne did an excellent job talking about her First Lady's Project.

The second shots were of us walking with the White House and the Washington Monument in the background. We then moved to the Jefferson Monument, where video was done of us walking up and down the steps. The final video portion was more video with an interview of Anne and I together at the Jefferson Memorial. Upon completion, we had a nice lunch with Mike, and Daphne back at the Hotel.

After lunch, it was time to pack our bags and take them to Almas Shriners and to prepare for a membership evening. This turned out to be a good recruitment night. During the evening, I presented Past Potentate Don Holiday with an Imperial Potentates MEDALLION for the 522 trips he had made transporting children to the Philadelphia SHRINERS hospital. At 7PM we loaded up our bags in Potentate Mike Gordon's car, he then drove to Baltimore and handed us off to Illustrious Sir Mark Hartz and the Boumi Shiners. After a drink with them in the hospitality room and getting something to eat at the Tilted Kilt it was time for bed.

August 5, 2017 - Saturday

We were able to rest up a little in the morning. By 11AM we were at Boumi Shriners for a Tour and the Boumi Crab Feast. Talk about some good food, wow, outstanding. We received gifts from the many Mid Atlantic Shrine Association Potentates that were in attendance, shirts, aprons, key chains, etc. Anne sold First Lady's project items and did well. After lunch, it was back to the hotel to rest up for the evening event back at Boumi Shriners. For dinner, it was a NY Deli theme that was very good and was followed by a comedy show. Great night that concluded with a night cap in the hospitality room.

August 6, 2017 - Sunday

The day started off with breakfast at a local dinner with Raoul and Rosie, Mark and Kathy and their Chief Aide and wife. After that we were off to a marina where we met Ron Parker and his wife Sarah. we were all guests on their 60-foot Sea Ray yacht for the day. This was a beautiful yacht with all of the nice features. We motored around doing the Inner Harbor and then down the river to Nicks Restaurant where we docked and had lunch. We were able to view Fort McHenry from the water, what a sight, and to think what it must have been like in the War of 1812 there.

As we resumed our way back to the Marina, we were pulled over by the Coast Guard. They board the yacht and did a full inspection and checked out the boat vary carefully. Upon getting a clear inspection we spoke with the two officers about Shriners and Shriners Hospitals for Children. They commented on our commercials and Alec. We did pictures with them and they left. This made for an added event that was not planned, but all turned out ok and ended up being fun.

When we arrived back at the Marina, the weather was so nice we stayed on the back of the yacht and enjoyed the evening. Anne went on a ride in their Zodiac, a small dingy with Ron around the harbor and really enjoyed it. We headed back to the hotel, tired and ready for some rest. It was a great day and the weather was perfect.

August 7, 2017- Monday

Up and out of the hotel by 9AM and we were off to the United States Naval Academy. Our usual group attended and this time the Grand Masters wife joined us. The morning was rainy, but we were not going to let it rain on our parade. Our guide, Bob, did an excellent job as we visited many of the buildings and learned so much about its history and what goes on today. We had a nice lunch on the Yard in the Alley Restaurant (was formally the bowling Alley) and Bob joined us for lunch and continued to tell us wonderful stories. After lunch, we visited the Naval Academy Museum. This was very interesting, I particularly enjoyed the part on my friend President Jimmy Carter.

Following our lunch, we visited the Grand Lodge of Maryland. There Grand Master Gus presented me with gifts including a Masonic Shrine Maryland Apron. The apron had "Maryland and 5 Gold Stars" on it, and on the bib was the Symitar and Crescent in gold. It was beautiful. Anne received gifts as well from the Grand Masters Lady. We thanked them, how great to see Masonry and Shrine working together. We then had a tour of the Grand Lodge facility including the offices, ballroom, lodge room and a museum with items from Washington and Lincoln, among many other old items.

Dinner that evening was at a fine restaurant with the Grand Master, Imperial Sir Raoul, Ill. Sir Mark and their ladies and the Boumi Chief Rabban. It was a delightful evening. Here the Grand Master presented yet another gift, a Maryland Masonic Crest pin hanging on a black and red ribbon.

August 8, 2017 A Tuesday

The morning started easy and we prepared for our trip to Fort McHenry, a battle ground of the 1812 war. We drove to the Fort and took the guided tour that lasted about 90 minutes. The history and sights were inspiring and interesting on how our nation, the United States of America fought in its early days. They story of how Francis Scott Key wrote the Star-Spangled Banner watching from a ship not knowing if his country or the enemy would be in possession of the fort in the morning was so historic. As the American Flag rose the following morning in the fog and smoke-filled air, he knew that the Americans held their fort.

An amazing story of bravery and courage, At the conclusion of the tour Anne and I were able to raise a 15-star flag in the same spot the flag was risen many years ago at this fort on that historic night. We were then presented the flag we rose along with a certificate certifying this flag flew at Fort McHenry. We then went to the Fish Market in Baltimore for a fresh seafood lunch, really good food.

After a trip to the hotel to freshen up it was off to Boumi Shriners where we first greeted the Potentate, Divan members and Past Potentates in the Potentates office for a drink. It was then out to the Boumi Pavilion where 200 of Boumi's members and ladies awaited our arrival for a picnic and drinks. The food consisted of hamburgers, hot dogs, sausage, and soft-shell crabs with all the fixings. It was a jovial time with fun and fellowship. A few speeches were given, and I was able to talk about our trip, Anne's Project and the I AM - RU Committed to Membership program. A wonderful evening and then back to the hotel to pack for an early flight out.

August 9, 2017 - Wednesday

Up early and off to the airport. Good flight home followed by a few hours at work to catch up on mail and to pay some bills. A big thanks to all the employees who keep the business running in my absence.

August 10, 2017 - Thursday

A day at J&J Metro to catch up on work. Had to take time out to go to the doctor because of a terrible sore and stiff neck. She gave me anti-inflammatory, muscle relaxers, and pain medicine. I left midafternoon to go home and pack for a couple of days at Shrine Headquarters. By late afternoon I fought the traffic to Tampa, stopping at Outback to eat. Checked into the hotel, took my medicine and went to sleep early.

August 11, 2017 - Friday

One month already since our wonderful pageant in Daytona Beach, can't believe the time has passed so quickly. My neck is feeling much better this morning, thank goodness. At headquarters the Chief of Staff Doctors are meeting, and I attended in the morning for a while. The remainder of the day was scheduled with meeting after meeting with staff regarding planning, travel, answering questions and letters. Jessica assisted me with getting out more thank you notes. Dinner in the evening was with some of the staff and doctors still in town from the meeting.

August 12, 2017 - Saturday

8AM meeting at Shrine Headquarters with some staff and the Medical Advisory Board where the past year was reviewed and the future of SHC was discussed. This was an interesting meeting that provided how we look to people from outside our organization. They expressed our progress in the past two years was tremendous and that we are moving in a good direction. The meeting concluded at 1PM and I was off to Orlando with a stop at the drive through at McDonalds for some lunch. Again, it was a stop at work to catch up on my duties there before going home. Dinner with David and Marie Angie and then home to pack for our trip the following morning to Montreal, Canada.

August 13, 2107 - Sunday

Up early to finish packing, fill the pool, load up on First Lady's items, load the car and out the door by 8AM to the airport. Whoop - we got upgraded to first class for our trip to Montreal, that's a good Sunday surprise. Good trip, Jerry and Lisa picked us up in Montreal. The airport was crazy busy, so many people. We drove to the Chateau Hotel, beautiful place. We had a one-bedroom suite overlooking the lake, very nice. For dinner, we went to a nice restaurant with Jerry and Lisa, and also Shriners Hospital patient Carter Brown and his mother, Jennifer. Nice dinner, good company, and wonderful time. Back to the hotel to crash.

August 14, 2017 - Monday

After breakfast at the hotel, Jerry and Lisa and Anne and I headed to the Shriners Hospitals for Children Golf Tournament. Beautiful Golf Course, with 54 foursomes registered to play. Jerry and I visited with the players while Anne and Lisa spent time with some ladies making the center pieces for the evening banquet. At starting time, the 100 plus golf carts headed off to the golf holes to begin play. Jerry and I had a cart to go around and watch and visit with the players. Later we got an additional cart, so Anne and I could ride around. The free food stands set up around the course were wonderful and Anne really enjoyed the different foods. After a quick trip back to the hotel we all returned back to the Country Club for the evening banquet.

A nice outside cocktail party was held with all of the players and sponsors. We then moved inside to the dining room that was beautifully decorated and each table was full of appetizers and the floral arrangement the ladies made earlier. Carter and his mother again joined us at our table. Carter is an amazing child who represents Shriners Hospitals for children very well. He made a great speech that brought the crowd to their feet as he delivered a good message, not bad for a 10-year-old. As the evening progressed the food just kept coming as they had a silent and live auction going on. Near the conclusion of the evening the total fundraising number was given, $357,000.00 was raised all for Shriners Hospitals. I was honored to give the closing remarks, giving thanks to all of the volunteers, players, sponsors, and servers. I then closed it out with a talk about hope and heroes to a standing ovation. Great day, great night, and a fantastic day of fundraising.

August 15, 2017 - Tuesday

Breakfast at 8AM with Jerry and Lisa prior to checking out and heading to Shriners Hospitals for Children - Montreal. Anne and I were given a quick tour of the hospital; it is so nice. Jerry and I then attended the hospital board meeting. It was very informative. We then headed for the airport for our flights out. Jennifer and her son Carter rode with us to the airport.

We nearly missed our flight as Customs managed to lose one of our suitcases in the five minutes it traveled from the Delta check-in to Customs. After an hour wait for them to find it we raced to our gate only to find out our ticket had the wrong gate number on it. We were then directed to the right gate and just made it. Back to Orlando for a day to do laundry and repack the suitcases for our next trip a day away.

August 16, 2017 - Wednesday

A day to work at J&J Metro. The day also included three Shriners conference calls. Home that evening to get those suitcases packed again. We are never home long enough to put them away.

August 17, 2017 - Thursday

We traveled to Minneapolis on Delta. Arrived midafternoon at the hotel only to be told we do not have a room. The desk clerk then told us we were to check in yesterday and our suite was sold to someone else now. I let her know that was not the case, she explained she had a regular room we could have. That was fine, we checked in and settled in. Jeff Sowder and Jim Smith and their ladies were there with us and we visited the Marketplace and then went to the Association Dinner. It was good, they also had a good band. After the meal, we took a ride with the Zor Funsters to another hotel to visit the Zor Hospitality room. I wore my ZOR five-star Fez and had a great time, we also did pictures with many of the ZOR people. And, of course handed out Imperial Potentate pins. We then headed back to our hotel for the night.

August 18, 2017 - Friday

Woke up to a cloudy rainy day. We headed out to the Zurah Horse Ranch for the horse competition. The only other competing Temple was Naja and they did not show up. We got a tour of the Ranch, Stables, and meeting room; really nice place, owned by the Zurah Horsemen. Great place to be proud of. We headed to the Motor Corp Competition and found out they finished early. They started early because of the rain. So, we headed back to our hotel and watched some of the Clown Competition. Then it was off to grab a quick lunch and to visit the Ladies Luncheon. The Ladies luncheon was well attended and vary nice.

The men then attended a Ceremonial where 3 new candidates became the newest Shriners. Very well-done Ceremonial. At the completion, we had everyone in the room do an I AM - RU Committed to Membership Video. Worked out well.

The skies cleared up and it was time for the Midwest Shrine Association Parade. At 4 PM we headed to the parade route and were dropped off. Sitting in two chairs on the side walk were two elderly ladies, Marian and Sandy, who were wondering what was going on. We explained to them that a Shrine Parade was about to take place, but they were in the wrong place because this was the staging area.

They decided to take their chairs and walk down the street to see the parade. We stopped them and had a Shriner give them a ride down the street, Imperial Sir Jim Smith went with them and took them all the way to the reviewing stand and placed them in the tent with our ladies. We ended up having a lot of fun with them, they really enjoyed the parade; it was neat to have them with us.

We laughed about them leaving their home with strange men and that there soon could be a Silver Alert out for people to help find them. At the conclusion of the parade we had a Noble in a golf cart take the two ladies and their chairs back to the home. Such fun we had. The rest of us walked over to the hospitality tent for food and refreshment. Soon after we headed back to the hotel where we walked to TGIF Friday's to get some real food. Then it was time to crash. It was a great time for the MSA convention, but it went by quick, really only a one-day session.

August 19, 2017 - Saturday

Up at 6AM to pack, shower, and off to the airport by 7:30. We grabbed some breakfast with Jeff and Cheryl and talked about Shriner plans. I was headed to Washington DC for four days for the Scottish Rite Biennial Session and Anne was headed back to Maitland. Jeff, Cheryl and Anne were all on the same plane and I was off by myself. I arrived in Washington DC and caught a cab to the Washington Hilton, checked in and registered for the event. I was headed to get some dinner when I ran into Kel Broome and his wife, they asked me to join them for dinner. We walked down to the Buca Restaurant and had a delightful time. Saw many others I knew there, and the Grand Master of Utah came up, to me to tell me how much he enjoyed my talk on membership at Imperial. This was nice to hear. After dinner, it was back to my room, a Green Bay Packer game was on, so I enjoyed that. They won!

August 20, 2017 - Sunday

Today my start time was later. I enjoyed breakfast with the Grand Master and the Executive Director of DeMolay. We discussed how the Shrine and DeMolay could collaborate more and specifically spoke of how the Shrine might be able to help with the Commemorative Plaza they are planning at their headquarters. We talked as well on how we could help each other with membership and about the annual Frank Land Breakfast. This was some really productive discussions and I hope we can get some traction for the plans we spoke of. After breakfast, I spent some time catching up on the many emails I had.

At 1PM we were bused of to the Saint Regis Hotel near the White House for an afternoon of finger foods and fellowship. The reception was beautiful and enjoyed by all. Following that we walked a block to St. John's Church, directly across from the White House. Built in 1815, this church has been a place of worship for every President since. In the front pews the names of Past US Presidents are embroidered where they sat when attending church. Beautiful place to see and to be able to appreciate the tradition. Upon the completion of the church service it was back on the bus and back to the hotel. Once at the hotel I grabbed a club sandwich and a beer at the bar.

In the evening, it was a trip over to the Scottish Rite House of the Temple by bus. This was the second time I have visited this incredible place, and once again I found it to be amazing. The night was hosted by an individual dressed as Albert Pike who told stories and started the tour of the building. When it was over, back to the hotel for an evening of rest.

August 21, 2017 - Monday

Monday morning, once again emails etc. to catch up on. The morning officially started with the Public Opening of the Scottish Rite Biennial Session at 10AM. The stage was distinctly decorated, the processional of the ranking officers in was impressive. Not impressive was the AV setup where half of the screens were not working. I know it had to be frustrating for them. They did a nice video presentation on the life of Imperial Sir Jack Jones. This touched everyone in the room, everyone knew Jack, and they loved him.

Following the opening was a very nice luncheon. I spent the afternoon working on following up on work I had to complete. One interesting activity I was working on was with a reporter from the Portage, Wisconsin newspaper. Portage is where I grew up at and graduated from High School in 1972. The reporter was working on a story about me and was requesting information and pictures. I interviewed with him and had our Public Relations Dept provide him with additional information and pictures. The evening concluded with a nice dinner with members from Georgia and Alabama including the SGIG's, a total of 18 people. Again, we walked down to the Buca D Bepo restaurant. I was very honored to have been asked to join them, it was an enjoyable time.

August 22, 2017 - Tuesday

Up at 6AM this day, packed and headed off to Reagan International Airport. Heading home for a day. Time to switch out the suitcases and to pick up Anne for our next trip. I got a message from the reporter at the Portage Daily Register that the story was in today's paper. Boy, that was fast. I was able to read it online and found it to be very good. Made me proud to know some of my old friends and classmates would be able to read about what I am doing as a volunteer for Shriners in its top position worldwide.

Upon returning to Orlando it was time to go to J&J Metro for a few hours to catch up there. Lucky to have the committed staff there that allows me to travel this year as the Imperial Potentate.

August 23, 2017 - Wednesday

A day of work at J&J Metro to catch up and pay bills etc. Left early to go home and pack for a 9-day trip to Atlanta for the Imperial Divan and Trustee Workshop, and Retreat. Lots to do at the house, things are a bit behind but will do them as we can, this is a big year and we have to concentrate on that. Packing extra bags for this trip.

August 24, 2017 - Thursday

Up early to do a few things around the house and then load up the car and off to the airport. We are both really looking forward to this trip. It is the first time a joint workshop with both the Directors and the Trustees has been done, I felt it was important we do this. It was something I thought to be important to work together and to build on teamwork. We arrived in Atlanta about 2 PM and Richard Burke picked us up. We traveled to the Marriott Evergreen in Stone Mountain Park. We arrived, and the place is really nice, I know our members will like it. Judy had our room all set up with food, drinks, fresh flowers and fancy little items. She did a great job and the suite was large with a big patio overlooking the lake. We are so lucky to have Richard and Judy as our Marshal's, not only do we really like them they are great to work with and do an excellent job.

For the evening, we headed off along with the Burke's and John Piland to have a nice dinner and then visited a neat ice cream shop where it is all homemade. Mamma GOOD, Great food and next door was the Georgia Grand Lodge building from the 1920s. They had moved and sold the building, but it still had all the Masonic emblems on it. Then off to the hotel for our first night in our fancy suite. This is going to be a nice time.

August 25, 2017 - Friday

We were able to sleep in till 9AM. Guess we were tired, and this was the first day we could sleep in, in who knows when. Sure, felt good. This was a relaxing day for us as we waited for the attendees to arrive. They started coming in after lunch and began checking in to their rooms. By now the hospitality room was ready to go and again the Burke's along with Tommy and Susan had everything under control. Food, drinks and neat decorations. Judy had a real nice framed picture made of the Anne's Tree of Life with all the quotes and signatures of people who were at her luncheon in Daytona Beach.

By 6 o'clock it was happy hour on the deck, dinner followed in the Rotunda Room. We had a delicious Buffett that included several great selections and a fancy desert. Everyone was enjoying our time together and stayed to talk following dinner. After dinner a nightcap was had in the hospitality room.

August 26, 2017 - Saturday

Up early for breakfast with the Joint Boards and then to our 8:30 workshop meeting. Excellent discussion and a few items that will need to be voted on. Good lunch in the hospitality room. The afternoon was followed with more meeting time. The ladies spent the day doing a glass blowing activity and lunch, then returned to the hotel.

Beginning at 3:30 the men and ladies went to Stone Mountain to go up to the top on the Sky Ride and then a tour of the museum. Cocktails were then on the deck at the Stone Mountain Country Club, followed by dinner inside the Country Club dining room. Imperial Sir Jerry was presented with a Georgia Citizen Certificate. After dinner, we all loaded up on the bus and headed back to the park at the base of Stone Mountain for the Laser Show. This show exceeded everyone's expectations, it was fabulous! The laser show, videos, music and fire were so good. None of us expected to enjoy it so much. It was very meaningful and patriotic. At the completion, we were all tired and returned to the hotel. Hurricane Harvey hits Texas, coming in at Corpus Christi bringing a lot of water.

August 27, 2017 - Sunday

The morning started off with a church service by the Imperial Chaplain, Illustrious Sir Bobby Simmons in a private room at the hotel. This was a good half hour service and Bobby provided a good message. Upon completion of the service we all went to the dining room at the hotel for the wonderful Sunday morning breakfast buffet. We had hoped Imperial Sir Gene Bracewell and Catherine would be able to join us, but Gene was not feeling good. After breakfast, the men went to another meeting of the Joint Boards, part of it was a called Colorado meeting so items could be voted on. All of the ladies went to a meeting in the hospitality room to discuss First Lady's project info, protocol, convention planning, etc.

At 2 PM, all men and women boarded a bus to head out for lunch and a show at the Agatha Christie Dinner Theater. This was fun, and it included many of us in the audience to participate. Following the midafternoon lunch, the bus took us to the Skyview Farris wheel ride in downtown Atlanta near the 1996 Olympic Park. We then proceeded by bus to an ice cream shop for dessert and the final food for the day. It was delicious. Back on the bus to the hotel where we all had a night cap in the hospitality room. Another great day of business and fun.

August 28, 2017 - Monday

Monday started off with an early breakfast for men and women and then onto the bus at 9:30 for the ride to the Carter Center. When we arrived at the Carter Center we were greeted by Phil Wise, he shared with us some stories of his relationship with President Carter and of when he worked in the White House with him just outside the Oval Office as the scheduling secretary. He informed us that President Carter had hoped he could be with us but that he was unable to do so as he had a family activity. We proceeded with a wonderful guided tour through the museum by a guide who was a former CNN reporter who did a fantastic job for us. During our tour Larry Leib's lady Debbie fell and had to go to the emergency room. She fractured a bone in her arm. After the Presidential Museum tour, we went to the Carter Center for lunch.

After lunch two representatives from the Carter Center gave a talk to us on some of the missions of the Carter Center. At the end of the program I presented Phil Wise and Dr. Blount each an Imperial Potentates MEDALLION, and then Kelly, the other speaker one of Anne's project necklaces. This was an event that was enjoyed by all, it gave them a much better knowledge of what President and Mrs. Carter have accomplished in their lifetime of public service.

We loaded back up on the bus and went to the Fox Theater, the former home of Yarrab Shriners. Built in the 1920's this place is amazing and beautiful, and so historic. This was defiantly worth the trip and there were many signs and designs that made it clear the Shriners had something to do with this building. Back on the bus, and this time we were headed to the current location of Yarrab Shriners. When we arrived, we were greeted by their Divan and ladies. We made some **I AM - RU Committed to Membership** videos and then had some finger foods and drinks. Thanks, were given to the Yarrab members and ladies for all they do to help our organizations.

We then headed to the Commerce Club for cocktails and dinner in their downtown rooftop dining room. This was the final evening for the directors and trustees to be together as the trustees would be leaving in the morning. Another good evening of fellowship. The dining experience conclude with some magic from a manic man. The final event had everyone standing to watch as he laid on a bed of nails with a cement block sitting on a board on his belly. John Piland then swung a sledge hammer hitting the cement block breaking it into pieces. The magician got up and flipped over what was left of the block and showed the word CAT written on the bottom. This was the same word John Piland gave him earlier in the evening. Everyone was in awe as to how he did all of this. The evening concluded, and the bus took us back to the hotel.

Hurricane Harvey still causing problems in Texas, dropping over 50" of rain in Houston. All areas are flooded. Both Texas Shriners Hospitals did not receive significant damage. Both of our Texas hospitals are still in operation.

August 29, 2017 - Tuesday

After breakfast, the trustees began leaving for the airport. The directors had a full day of meetings on fraternal matters. As a result of my meetings with DeMolay leadership, I made a presentation to the Directors on a plan DeMolay had for their upcoming 100th Anniversary. After the presentation the directors decided to financially assist DeMolay with their Centennial Plaza they were building at their headquarters in Kansas City. In the Plaza will be an "*Editorial Without Words*" statue that will be in memory of Imperial Sir Jack Jones. This was a proud moment for me as I admired Jack so much and this will provide a lasting memory of him. In addition, there were many discussions on the future of Shriners International. It was a full day of open discussion by the board that was very good.

The ladies had a day at the Atlanta Mart where they were able to see many items at wholesale pricing that will come in handy for them in the future. The men and ladies then all met at Pappadeax's for a dinner with portions so large we could not eat everything. It was again a nice evening of fun and fellowship. What an honor to be able to work alongside this tremendously committed group of men and women.

August 30, 2017 - Wednesday

What a treat to wake up each day during the workshop and look out the window at the relaxing effect of the lake and woods. The day started early with breakfast with the directors and then a three-hour meeting to talk about future conventions and the fraternity's strategic plans for the future. Challenging but extremely exciting to see the opportunities we have in front of us. The ladies had a free morning to sleep in.

At noon, we all gathered to get on the bus and head out for lunch. After lunch, we went to the lake for our team building afternoon on a houseboat, men and ladies. Despite the rain we all loaded up on the 90-foot houseboat with plenty of inside dry space. Drinks were had while our dinner was prepared in the kitchen of the boat. The rain did not slow us down as the live one-man band provided plenty of entertainment. The bottom half of the line have developed their own singing group, the Fab Five. What they lack in talent they excel in enthusiasm. What a hoot to watch these guys enjoy themselves and bond together. They represent our future. Hope they lead better than they sing, I'm sure they will. Home cooked dinner and dessert was delicious and enjoyed by all.

What a great way for all of us to spend time together and to get to know each other better. This was truly a good way for all of us to learn more about each other, this should allow all of us to work better together in the future. As we docked, it was off the boat and on the bus then back to the hotel. This was one bunch of tired Shriners and Ladies. No one stayed up very late on this evening.

August 31, 2017 - Thursday

As the last day began to unfold it was the ladies who were up before dawn to get ready for their early departure to CNN for their tour and to be in the audience of the Robin Meade show. They had a super time! The men had their normal breakfast and participated in their last day of meetings. By 3 PM men and ladies alike were beginning the process of packing up for departure the following day.

Dinner for the evening was at the hotel and our group had shrunk from about 44 at the brining down to about 18 for the final evening. Our children who live in the Atlanta area, Jami, Jared, and granddaughter McKenna joined us for dinner. Anne went home with them to spend a couple of days in Atlanta with the kids. After dinner with Anne gone, I finished up the packing for an early trip to the airport in the morning. Reflecting back on the workshop/retreat I could not be happier. We had great meetings, good bonding, fellowship, and everyone appeared to get along well. Richard and Judy as the Marshal's exceeded every expectation with their attention to detail. All goals accomplished for this event!

Chapter Three
September 2017

September 1, 2017 - Friday
Up early, finished up last minute packing and off to the airport with a smile of accomplishment on my face. Had breakfast at the airport and was home by 1 PM. Spent the next 4 hours catching up at J&J Metro. New A/C system was installed at the office while I was gone and the temperature in the office was much better. With Anne still in Atlanta I grabbed a quick sandwich and headed home to unpack and do some laundry. Sleeping in my own bed felt good for a change. Oh, it's the small things you come to enjoy when gone from home so much.

September 2, 2018 - Saturday
Slept in till about 8 today. Then got up and headed into the office at J&J Metro. Was the only one at the office for the day and was able to get a lot done. Spent over an hour booking upcoming air flights and worked on Shrine trip schedules. On the way home stopped at Lowe's and picked up some paint to paint the cook shack at home. Watched TV, worked on catching up these Potentates Notes and headed to bed. So quiet when home alone.

September 3, 2017 - Sunday
Got up and painted part of the cook shack in the backyard. Then I spent some time charging the batteries in the old cars and then took each one for a spin. Love old

cars! Then I worked on cleaning up the garage some. Then it was time to cleanup and shower and to get ready to go pick Anne up at the Airport. After picking her up we grabbed something to eat at Chili's and then headed home. Oh, good to have Anne back at the house.

September 4, 2017 - Monday

LABOR DAY - A day off and a time to relax some. Worked in the yard and did some honey-dos around the house. Spent time on the phone with John Piland working on a way to raise money for the Masonic victims of Hurricane Harvey in Texas. We talked with the Texas Grand Lodge and are planning to work with an implementation process of using all Shriner communication tools to solicit donations to assist Masons and Shriners. This will be a first, we have never done a fraternal wide fundraising event to support storm victims, but I felt committed to answer this call to action. As Shriners, it should be a natural effort we should make, to assist other members in need. I would hope to be able to raise one million dollars for this effort.

Anne and I went to Red Lobster for a good dinner and then returned home and watched two movies. Nice evening at home.

September 5, 2017 - Tuesday

Full day at work, getting things caught up good fashion. I'll be ready to travel again. Continued to work on implementation of fundraising campaign for the victims of Hurricane Harvey. Spoke with the three Potentates of the affected Temples and the Grand Lodge to put this communication together. The Shrine has the biggest reach to do something like this; no other Masonic organization has the communication tools we have to reach Masons worldwide. We have over 140,000 e-mail address we hope will be effective in raising relief money. I have now set my goal to raise one million dollars. Anne and I had dinner with David and Marie Angie. Now, hard to believe, but there is a hurricane headed our way.

September 6, 2017 - Wednesday

This was a partial day at work and then packing and preparing for the possibility of Hurricane Irma hitting our home and office while we are going to be gone. Another hurricane so quick after the last one is unusual. We had mixed thoughts about leaving but figured we had done all we could, and we should go to Canada as planned. We have family in town that will assist in looking out after our properties if needed. Bags, packed and ready to go.

September 7, 2017 - Thursday

Flying Air Canada with no status showed us how valuable having status is. Had to pay for our bags, both ended up in middle seats and had three legs to our trip. The final flight was an adventure, an 18-passenger prop plane, and we almost missed it due to the prior flight running late. We just made it on. Nine seats down each side of the plane, very rough interior, fumes coming up through the floor boards. Interestingly, the pilot's area had no door on it, it was open to the passenger area. First time we had flown on a commercial plane with an open cockpit like this since 911.

When we landed, we exited down some outside steps and walked across the tarmac where we entered the small airport of Charlottetown, Nova Scotia. Several Shriners were in their red Fez and their ladies were there to greet us too. What a treat at eight PM in the evening. One of our bags did not make it and was expected to be in before morning. We checked into the hotel and were taken to a reception in our honor at the hotel where many Shriners and their ladies were waiting from two Shrine Clubs. Drinks and finger foods were plentiful. A short program was held where Anne received a beautiful locally made all wool commemorative blanket celebrating Canada's 150th Anniversary. Her program products were being sold and over three thousand dollars in donations were made. The highlight of the evening was my opportunity to present a Noble with his 50-year pin, what an honor. Our room was all fixed up with flowers snacks, drinks, and goodies. What an incredible evening by people coming out so late to greet us.

September 8, 2017 - Friday

Our morning started early with a 7:30 AM breakfast for the men and ladies. The continued enthusiasm of the people to greet us was so nice. The breakfast included a couple of speakers, one from the Parliament, and another who gave us a history talk on the area. We finished up by nine, packed our bags and loaded up for our trip to the home where the Lt. Governor lives with a caravan of three vehicles. We arrived at this home built in the 1800's with a beautiful view of the water. The Lt. Governor and his wife meet us on the front steps for pictures and to raise a Shriners International flag on the property down near the water. What an honor this was. We then proceeded inside for coffee or tea in this historic building where he lives. He is appointed by the Queen of England for a four-year term. I presented him with an Imperial Potentates MEDALLION.

At the conclusion of our time he instructed one of the ladies to give us a tour of the upstairs. There were several guest bedrooms, this is where the Queen stays when she visits. Other visitors who come to spend the night have included Prince Charles and Camellia, and William and Kate.

Next, we loaded up into a van of a tour company who took us on a tour on our way to Halifax. We went over the 9-mile bridge that got us off of Prince Edward Island. We arrived at Cumberland Shrine Club where they were having a luncheon in our honor. Over a 100 Shriners and their ladies were there for this. They were selling Anne's products; the Mayor and his wife were there as well. We had a nice lunch, did an I AM - RU Committed to Membership video and visited the awesome Masonic Lodge on the main floor. The local newspaper was there to do a story on our visit complete with pictures. Then it was back in the van and we continued on our trip to Halifax.

Our flight home on Sunday was cancelled because of Hurricane Irma coming into Florida. The Orlando airport was going to be closed for most of the weekend. We were rescheduled for Tuesday. This is going to give us two additional days in Nova Scotia.

We arrived at the Weston Hotel and were taken to our suite. It was a large one-bedroom suite with a conference room attached, a bar, 2 bathrooms and two TV's overlooking the harbor and water. The room had flowers, baskets of goodies, liqueur, and wine. In the refrigerator was smoked salmon, fresh fruit and cold drinks. An Imperial Potentate had not visited here in 17 years and we were getting the royal treatment. How nice.

For the evening, they had a BBQ planned on the rooftop of one of the members apartment buildings. Again, a large contingent of people who welcomed us. Masons, Shriners, ladies, and members of DeMolay. Food was cooked on the grill, beer and wine was available and it was a great time.

Near the end, the DeMolay boys did an abbreviated initiation, and I was included along with two new boys. We took the obligation and received the flower talk. I was very touched by the flower Talk. I received a certificate of membership and Anne received a certificate as a DeMolay Sweetheart. We both were also presented DeMolay medals of Appreciation. What an honor they bestowed upon us. Anne was given flowers as well. Another great weekend. After we got back to the hotel, we had drinks with Paul and Linda, our Aides, and Mike and Michelle, the Potentate and First Lady.

September 9, 2017 - Saturday

The morning started early again. For the men a Cabiri breakfast and for the women a luncheon in a private room in the dining room. I enjoyed the Cabiri one and had a question and answer time, and they asked many questions, mostly related to the hospitals. After breakfast, we changed into casual clothes and set out for some sightseeing and to the lighthouse at Peggy's Cove.

About 20 of us then boarded a sightseeing boat and toured out into the harbor, the ocean and back into a cove where we stopped and had lunch on the boat. They set up tables and we were served 3-pound lobsters outside on the boat deck. This was outstanding, and man did the lobster taste good. This is living the good life. After lunch we headed back to the Harbor and disembarked. On the way back to the hotel we stopped at the Flight 111 Memorial recognizing the lives that were lost when a plane crashed into the harbor here.

When we got back to the hotel, we had an hour to rest and to get into our formal wear for the reception and dinner downstairs. Anne looked beautiful and we headed down to the great formal event. Again, there was a wonderful turnout including the Grand Master. We were piped in and received, they pulled out all the stops, great time. Again, they had a table set up to sell Anne's products. There were speeches from another member of Parliament, the DeMolay, the Queen of the Daughters of the Nile, and the Potentate. The Grand Master who was to be made a Shriner by me tonight became ill and had to leave early.

In my remarks, I gave thanks to many individuals for all of the work they did to host us. I also told them the story about Zion and they were touched by it, many with tears in their eyes. I told the group that in our 10 years on the Imperial line this was one of, if not the best trip we have made, mostly because of how welcoming and friendly the people are. As I closed, I asked Ill Sir Mike to come forward and presented him with an Imperial Potentates MEDALLION. He was speechless. After the banquet, many of us talked for a while and then retired to our rooms for the night.

September 10, 2017 - Sunday

This was supposed to be an early day to be up and on our way home. But because of Hurricane Irma in Florida we could not go. We slept in late and had a casual morning in our hotel suite. We then took a nice walk along the waterfront and had a good lunch on the boardwalk. We walked through some of the stores and relaxed. By midafternoon we were back to the hotel suite and watching the hurricane attack Florida.

We walked down to a restaurant on the Boardwalk that was recommended to us by the name of "The Bicycle Thief." It was excellent, we had a nice dinner in a really relaxed atmosphere, even had a good desert. We walked back to the hotel and again watched the hurricane hitting our home state of Florida. By 11PM it became clear the hurricane was going to go up the west side of Florida and the Orlando area should be safe from any damage. Today is also Jason's Birthday, we made a call to him.

September 11, 2017 - Monday

We got up and packed as we had to move to a different room in the hotel. We had to stay longer as a result of Hurricane Irma and the suite we were in was reserved for someone else starting today. Our new room was very nice as well. At 10:30 Paul and Linda Frank picked us up for an eventful day at Lunenburg, Nova Scotia. A beautiful ride out there, we had lunch at a nice restaurant overlooking the water with a couple of local Shriners from the area. After lunch, we visited the Blue Lodge there with a young Noble by the name of Graham. The Lodge was very historic and was a Lodge where many men who fished and built the Bluenose Sailboat attended. I took many pictures here. We did a little shopping and then headed back to Halifax. We attended a corn boil at the Philea Shriners Temple that evening where about 40 Nobles and ladies were in attendance. A great time and we were able to say good bye to the many who were so kind to us over the past few days. They donated and raised money by purchasing Anne's project items in an amount of $14,000.00. This was tremendous!

Upon returning back to our hotel we learned our flight home for the following day was again canceled as the Orlando Airport had still not reopened due to the hurricane. Our original plans to go to the South Atlantic Shrine Association convention were canceled because of the hurricane for the following weekend, and we could not go home. We made changes to our flights for the following day to head to Chicago where we would rent a car and drive to Springfield, IL to attend the Great Lakes Shrine Association Meeting. We would be meeting the Cain's and the Baileys there. We've never had a storm affect our travel so much.

September 12, 2017 - Tuesday

Up and out of the hotel early in a hotel town-car to the airport. We had some difficulty getting our bags checked with Air Canada as they were overweight. They sent us back to repack and rearrange our bags so they would be under weight. We were moving things from bag to bag and finally accomplished the proper weights. Then I had my carry-on bag checked by TSA, the lady agent asked me if everything in the bag was mine. I said of course. She proceeded to open it. Much to my amazement the bag was filled with Anne's purses, make up, and high heels in it as she put them in there while moving things around to get our bags under weight. This turned out to be a little embarrassing and funny as I turned red. How embarrassing! The TSA lady looked at me suspiciously as Anne stood far away and laughed. Man was I glad to get through TSA on this day.

Upon reaching Chicago we rented a car and drove three and a half hours to Springfield. It was around 10PM by the time we had dinner and got to the hotel. We checked into the President Abraham Lincoln Hotel and moved into a large suite that was awesome. The suite was a full one-bedroom apartment with formal dining room, kitchen and two bathrooms. This made the trip all worth going through the TSA check in earlier in the day.

September 13, 2017 - Wednesday

This was more or less a free day as we arrived a day early because of the storm. I caught up on this diary, yes it takes some time and commitment to keep this thing up to date, hope you are enjoying it. Anne wanted to do some shopping and we had lunch. I then left her at the Mall and went and spent 3 hours in the Abraham Lincoln Presidential Museum. Being a U.S. Presidential buff, this was really neat for me and I enjoyed it tremendously.

In the evening, it was a nice dinner with the Imperial Officers, Great Lakes Shrine Officers, Special Guests and our ladies at a local restaurant in the wine cellar basement. Good time and good food was had by all.

September 14, 2017 - Thursday

Thursday morning started the Great Lakes Shrine Association meetings. Good meeting during the morning and a wonderful lunch. On this day, the ladies also had their Ladies Luncheon where Anne presented her program. Her product sales are again going through the roof. During the afternoon meeting I presented an Imperial Potentates MEDALLION to Noble Craig Kent of Ansar Shriners who runs a Shriners Hospitals for Children ad in the Sunday newspaper every week at his own expense. The afternoon meeting concluded at 2:30. At the completion of the meeting, men and women boarded buses for the short trip out to the Abraham Lincoln Tomb. Shriners laid wreaths on the tomb and we all took tours through this amazing tribute and final resting place of our sixteenth President, President Abraham Lincoln. This was definitely a highlight of the trip.

In the evening, we had a wonderful dinner at a Country Club with all of our Great Lakes Shrine counterparts, Potentates and Ladies. Fun, proud evening with this group who have done a great job for the past several years. Anne and I were honored to be their guests for the evening. After dinner we made some hospitality room visits before we headed up to our room for the evening.

September 15, 2017 - Friday

This was Great Lakes Shrine Association Competition day and we made the full rounds with the Imperial Officers present and the GLSA Officers. We attended and spent good times at the competition of the Clowns, Motor Corps, Mounted Patrols, and the Bag Pipers. During this time, we also found time for a full tour of Ansar Temple and to grab a quick lunch. It was a full day. We returned to the hotel after 4PM and it was time to get ready for the evenings banquet.

The Presidents Banquet was a formal affair and had over 200 in attendance. Anne's First Ladies Project items continued to sell throughout the day. We are so pleased by the amount of people who are buying the First Lady's products. Reorders have been placed for all three styles of necklaces and the bow tie. A Free-Style bowtie "tie your own" tie now has been ordered too as there have been many requests. During my opportunity to speak at the banquet I recognized two former Shriners Hospitals for Children patients; Sue Langley, now the wife of a Divan Member and Matt McClure who is now a Shriner. This brought the entire room to their feet in applause. Both were patients at the St. Louis hospital. The evening concluded by visiting hospitality rooms.

September 16, 2017 - Saturday

Up early and out of the hotel for our long drive back to Chicago O'Hare Airport to catch our flight back home, finally. This will be our first time back home since the hurricane passed through a week ago. The flight was good. By the time we got home, got the car and so on it was almost 10PM when we got to the house. Driving through our neighborhood to the house was eye opening, many trees were down, and the road was full of yard trash. It looked like a hurricane went through, well, it did. When we arrived at our home it was as if nothing had happened, all looked good. We were very blessed as the hurricane had not touched our home. We unpacked a few things and went to bed.

September 17, 2017 - Sunday

Home again, in our own bed, we slept in, then got up and made breakfast. The back yard had some branches down, part of the fence had blown over, and the pool was full of trash and had turned a deep green. I spent the day working on the pool as there was no way the pool man was going to have enough time to get it back into shape. A trip was needed to a pool shop to get chemicals to get the water cleaned up. By the end of the day you could see some progress. One of the guys from work was working on getting some new fencing back up for us. All in all, we survived the hurricane well, minor damage and the power never went off. We were Blessed!

September 18, 2017 - Monday

Full day at work after being gone for almost two weeks. Lots to catch up on at work but ended up spending most of the day on Shrine business. The additional business due to the hurricane we are expecting has not kicked in yet as people are having to wait on their insurance adjusters. After work again, I spent time cleaning the pool and picking up branches in the yard.

September 19, 2017 - Tuesday

Another full day at work. Caught up on thank you notes needing to go out and things at J&J Metro. Worked on preparations for a Press Conference at the Daytona Beach City Council meeting tomorrow. Anne and I had a good dinner out, just the two of us, that's different.

September 20, 2017 - Wednesday

Half day at work, then home to pack. By midafternoon we were off to Daytona Beach for a Press conference. Going to have dinner with CVB folks and Mayor Jennings first. The Press Conference at the City Commission office was outstanding. A video of the Imperial Session was played and enjoyed by all. I then spoke to the group and gave many thanks to the Mayor, the Commissioners, and the audience.

At the completion of the presentation I asked permission to invite Chief Capri of the Daytona Beach Police Department and Chief Dawson of the Daytona Beach Fire Deptartment to come forward. I proceeded to present them with the **FIRST EVER** invitation to non-Shriners to participate in an Imperial Parade in the 2018 Imperial Session Parade. A standing applause was given. The Chiefs and about 10 Police Officers who were there followed me out to do some pictures. They were so excited! They expressed planning would begin tomorrow on what they would bring to the parade; they have cool cars, old cars, SWAT vehicles, vehicles that smoke and ones that blow stuff up. This is going to be great to have them as part of the parade.

September 21, 2017 - Thursday

Up and at it early for a trip to the Shriners Hospitals for Children - Greenville. We arrived and had a car rented. They put us into a Dodge Charger HEMI, from the moment I first started it up and heard the roar, I felt like I was 16 for the rest of the trip. By the time we got to the hotel it was time for dinner. Anne and I walked down the river walk area in downtown Greenville and found a nice place to get some food. There was also a band playing outside, it was a nice relaxing time. It was back to the hotel to get some sleep and to get ready for the BIG days coming up.

September 22, 2017 - Friday

This turned out to be a very special day, better than we could have imagined. We arrived at Shriners Hospitals for Children- Greenville about 10:30 and were greeted by patients and staff in the lobby. Additionally, the Queen of the Daughters of the Nile was there, how nice. We proceeded to a luncheon put on by the local Daughters of the Nile local group. At the head table, we were joined by some patients from the hospital. This was a real treat as we got to know them and their parents personally. Each of them had such an amazing story. When we were done eating, comments were made with an opportunity to do pictures. This was outstanding. We then went on a tour of the hospital, what a beautiful, friendly place.

Then Anne met with one of the Doctors and I proceeded to get make-up on for the PGA commercial that was going to be made. This commercial will be used during the Shriners Hospitals for Children Open this coming November in Las Vegas. First, I did some of the lines by myself. Then 11 of the most precious little patients surrounded me on the set for the closing of the commercial. This was so inspiring to be a part of something that included children who have overcome such incredible challenges. All of them did great with big smiles. Can't wait to see the final cut of this on TV. We then did a couple of additional short - quick video recordings. One for the I AM - RU Program and another to congratulate the quarterly Spotlight Shriner recipient.

Once we were done with the commercial and video shoots, we were off to the patient Karate Class in the hospital. Here I was able to watch and participate with the kids. This was a tremendous time, to be surrounded by my Hero's, our patients, in a room filled with inspiration and love. If only every Shriner could experience this, they would be Shriners for life. By the time we left it was time to eat and head back to the hotel to relax.

<u>September 23, 2017 - Saturday</u>

On this day we had some free time. We got up early and jumped into the Dodge Challenger and roared up to Franklin, NC for lunch with Anne's sister-in-law, Judy. It was a beautiful ride up and back. The evening was a planned dinner with the "There's NO Jazz like Hejaz Shriners Divan." Jerry and Lisa joined us, and we had a wonderful time with the Hejaz Divan and their ladies. After the dinner the Hejaz Potentate presented Anne with a check for $5,000. for her project. This was a real surprise and Anne was so appreciative for this wonderful gift to her project.

September 24, 2017 - Sunday
Shriners Hospitals for Children - Greenville - 90th Anniversary Celebration. We knew this was going to be a good day, and a long day, but had no idea how spectacular it was going to be.

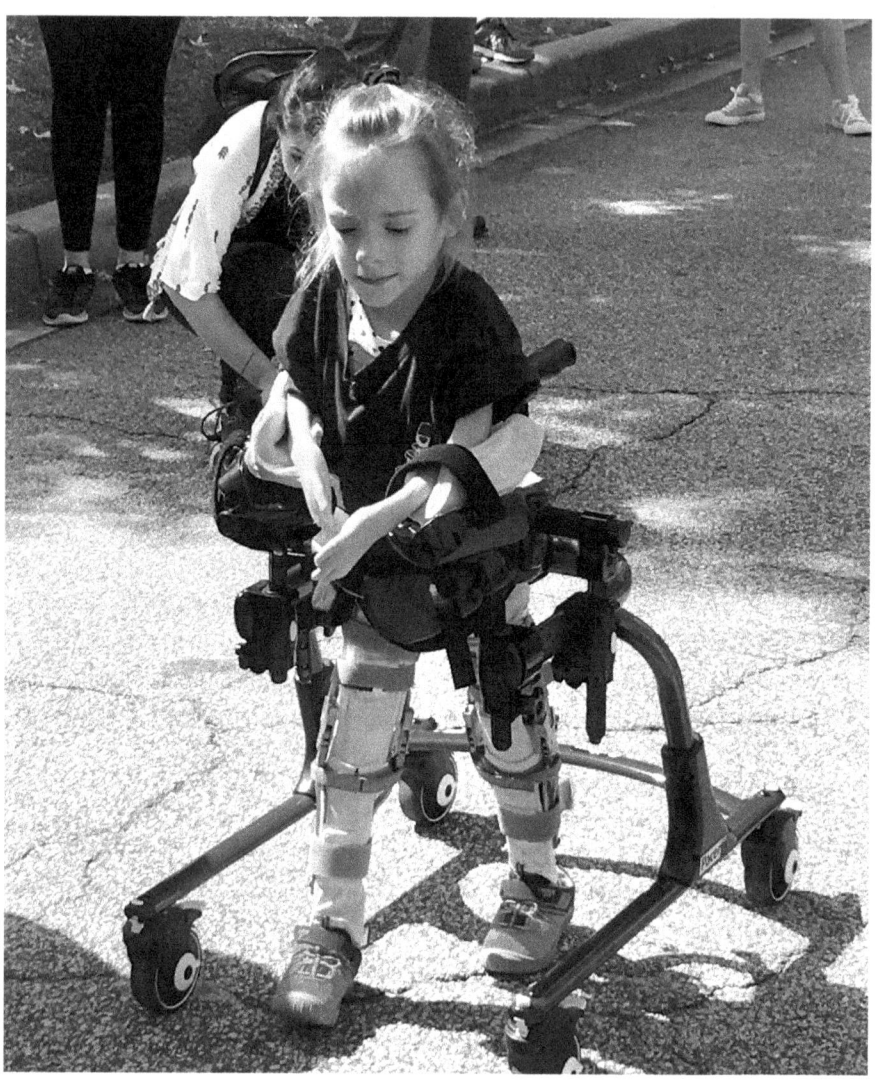

On our arrival, we set up a table for Anne's project items to be sold. ($3,000.00 worth was purchased) they then had several check presentations made by both Shriners and outside donors. Nearly 1000 people were in attendance with many things going on. Emily and her family were there selling her Beads, along with many other patients and a large group of Shriners. At 1:30 a good program was given from a stage in front of the hospital. It was a warm day, but this did not slow down the crowd. At 2PM a "Walk for Love" was held that raised in excess of $36,000.

A highlight of the trip for me was yet to come. Little Brayden took her wheel chair on the Walk for Love. When she got about 10 feet from the finish line she was taken out of her wheel chair and strapped into a walker. She then proceeded to take her first ever steps to the finish line as I waited to welcome her in my arms. This was captured by the local TV Stations as she took these monumental steps. What a thrill to be able to be a part of this, wow! As you can imagine my eyes were full of tears, and my chest was full of pride.

September 25, 2017 - Monday

After flying home, it was off to work at J&J Metro. Had a couple of hours out for a dentist appointment, fun, fun. Spent most of the day working on Shrine travel arrangements and conference calls. The evening was spent with the 2018 Imperial Session Executive Committee and the Daytona CVB. We did a debriefing on the 2017 Session and began planning for the 2018 Session. This is a motivated, high energy group, I'm so proud of them.

I headed home about 9PM to get a few things done and to pack for an early departure the following day.

September 26, 2017 - Tuesday

Early to rise and off to the airport. Anne and I were on our way to the Shrine Guild of America for their annual Imperial Session in Dayton, Ohio. We were picked up at the airport and taken to the (Bob) Hope Hotel. A nice hotel adjacent to the Air Force Base there. We had dinner with several of the ladies at the hotel and visited their hospitality room afterwards. After returning to our hotel room there was a good couple of hours catching up on calls and emails. It was a nice evening with just the two of us for the most part.

September 27, 2017 - Wednesday

We had one of those rare mornings where we did not have to get up early. Once up and showered I headed down to get a coffee at the restaurant. Upon arrival back at our room it was several phone calls to be made. At 10:45 Anne and I met a couple of the ladies in the hotel lobby and then worked our way down to the luncheon location. There were about 100 men and women in attendance. After lunch, a report was given that $31,500.00 was donated to Shriners Hospitals for Children this year. This is an amazing amount to be donated by such a small group of ladies. Outstanding!

I was then asked to make comments. I shared the story of Anne and I having the problem of overweight suitcases, followed by my carry on being checked by TSA. After being asked if everything in the bag was mine, and confirming that it was, how surprised I was when it was full of Anne's purses, make-up, and high heels she had moved into my bag. Of course, she had already made it past TSA and was laughing and laughing. You think she came to help me and explain, nope.

I then gave a report on the condition of our hospitals and headquarters after the Hurricanes and earthquakes. This was followed by patient stories about Zion and Brayden. These stories brought many in the room to tears. I thanked all of them and let them know how appreciative Shriners are for their support.

Then it was time for some recognition, I presented the Shrine Guild of America, as an organization, with an Imperial Potentates MEDALLION for their many years of service and fundraising for Shriners Hospitals for Children. This brought the group to their feet with applause and tears. Following this many picture were taken.

Anne then sold several hundred dollars of her project items. We then attended their necrology meeting and it was then time to head back to the airport for a flight back home. This was a short visit but very well received and appreciated. We had a late-night arrival back at home about midnight. Another long easy day as the Imperial couple, what an honor to serve in this position.

September 28, 2017 - Thursday

Slept in a little and then it was off to J&J Metro to catch up on work there. Been kind of slow there, we are thinking all of the Hurricanes have affected things. In the afternoon, we had a Joint Board called telephone meeting to discuss some important items. All in all, a nice day at home and at work.

September 29, 2017 - Friday

Up early and off to J&J Metro for opening. During the morning, I had a taped radio interview from a Wisconsin station. It was going to be used for a Shrine Football Game that was coming up. Was fun to do as I grew up in Wisconsin. I spent several hours trying to get all of my flights arranged through the end of the year. It was quite a task as there were some international flights involved.

That evening Anne and I had a nice dinner with our friends Jan and David at Sam Sneed's Tavern. It was nice to see them and to spend some time. It was the first time we were with them since the Session and we had lots to catch up on.

September 30, 2017 - Saturday

This was our first and probably one of a few weekends we will be home this year. Anne and I spent the entire day working in the yard and on the pool to get things in order from the hurricane. To be honest there was a lot to be done as well because we have been gone so much. Lots of trimming and getting branches that were down etc. to the road for pick up. We trimmed the palms as best we could too. This was the time to do this as all of the hurricane debris was lined up throughout the neighborhood from the hurricane, eventually they will come pick it all up for free. The pool, although good and blue still needed a good cleaning and we did that too. No rest for the wicked I guess. Was a long hot day and the heat got to me by the end of the day. Anne went over to help David and Marie Angie in the evening at their new home.

Chapter Four
October 2017

October 1, 2017 - Sunday

More yard work to finish up on, things were beginning to look pretty good at home. We had a guy lined up to come pressure wash the driveway too and that came out nice. For dinner, we cooked out on the grill for the first time in 3 months. Funny the things you miss, I've missed cooking out at home. This was like the calm before the storm as our travel was going to really pick up again now. It was nice to have a couple of days at work and at home, but we are ready to get back on the road. Hard to believe two and a half months of our term is already over. Wow- it's gone by fast, but we feel we have accomplished so much, hope others do too. So glad I am keeping this diary, I'm going to love reading it when we are done with this incredible year.

October 2, 2017 - Monday

A half day at work and then it was off to Tampa for a few days. Our home for the next few days is the Tampa Airport Marriott. The first couple of days I was on my own, Anne would be joining me later. She definitely needed and deserved a couple of days all by herself, just to do as she pleased. I got checked into the Presidential Suite at the hotel, really nice. Then had dinner all by myself down the hall at PF Chang's. Shrimp and a Dirty Martini was for dinner and it hit the spot. Sitting at dinner by myself, I was able to reflect back on some of our travels, we have been really on the run and surprisingly, really not all that tired. Guess we are just too busy to be tired. I also thought about our kids and grandchildren, kind of missing them. We have been gone too much to see them, so thankful they are so understanding of what we are doing this year. Having their support makes things much easier. Then, it was an early night to bed.

October 3, 2017 - Tuesday

Up and early start over at Shrine Headquarters. I brought some additional items to display in my office. The Imperial Potentates office is so nice, to bad you're not in town more often to use and enjoy it. It's starting to feel like home as I get more of my own things in it. Today's meetings were with one of the Governance Groups, we worked on hospital regulations and proper ways to do minutes. These will be rolled out eventually for approval by the board, and if approved will be implemented. Different groups are working on a number of projects to make our system better and more streamlined while encouraging all hospitals to be more uniform.

For the evening dinner, I joined the Executive Team of the Membership Committee. They were arriving for the annual Shriners International Membership Seminar. This is going to be a BIG one as we are implementing our "I AM - RU Committed to Membership" Program. The excitement is really building with videos, social media, and more. The excitement is higher than I have ever seen in the nearly 20 years I have worked with Shrine Membership. I hope the excitement and awareness turns into an action of creating new members. It was a great dinner full of great stories. They are all working hard on building membership.

October 4, 2017 - Wednesday

The first half of the day was spent back at headquarters in meetings and following up with different departments on projects. I turned in several more thousands of dollars for Anne's project as well. The afternoon was spent with the Imperial Membership committee, what a great meeting it was due to the excitement and expectations of what's to come with our new programs rolling out. Although we are working with many new nobles and staff members this group is hitting it out of the park. As the Imperial Potentate, I had the last comments. I had a hard time making it through my comments as I cried most of the way with pride of what's being done and in speaking of Imperial Sir Jack. I had originally appointed him as Chairman of this committee, he picked the members, and worked with me on the plan. It is so unfortunate we lost him, he would have been so proud of what was happening. I, as many others, sure miss him. He was a mentor to each of us on this committee, an awesome man.

Several of us had dinner down the hall at the Hard Rock, not to good at all. Then off to bed. Anne is due to join me again tomorrow.

October 5, 2017 - Thursday

This day was filled with meetings for the Membership Regional Directors. I joined them for the start at 8:30 and did my best at giving them a real motivational talk on why we are here and the importance of what we have to do. I sure like what I'm seeing, I have so much faith in what we are doing and am feeling better all the time that we will hit our 12,000 new members by next July. I've publicly taken responsibility for reaching the 12,000 and I know we can do it if we just keep working at it. It would be so cool if we were able to hit the mark in memory of Imperial Sir Jack. Anne arrived midday and began working with the ladies on setup for the conference.

The opening took place beginning at 4:30 and it was a fireball of excitement. "Swinging for the Fences" for Membership was the theme. It included a baseball theme that made it all fun. After my opening remarks, I exited the room and hurried up to our hotel room and changed into my SHRINERS number 17 baseball uniform. The uniform was complete with jersey, pants, socks, shoes, and a five-star baseball hat. It even had I AM - RU on the sleeve. I hurried on back and waited for them to call me back in.

When I was called back in to the cheers of the group it was fun to be wearing the SHRINERS baseball uniform, caught them by surprise. I was then presented an official "Louisville" I AM - RU bat signed by Gary Bergenske. How cool is that. I then proceeded to do my speech on "BELIEVE" that hopefully proved to everyone in the room that reaching 12,000 new members was not only possible, it will happen if we all believe in it and do what we have to do to make it happen. The message was well received. The meeting then concluded.

A group of us went down the hall for dinner at PF Chang's and again it was good. While we were there a number of times people would stop by to give the I AM - RU chant as loud as they could in the restaurant. This also continued in the halls of the airport as we walked back to the hotel. Wow- the excitement and awareness is contagious and building. I firmly BELIEVE we are on our way to 12,000 new members in the July to July time frame. History is being made.

October 6, 2017 - Friday

Up early to meet the nobles as they headed to their 8:30 meetings, moral is good, and everyone is happy. They are ready to get going. Every person here was challenged to add five names into the referral system by the end of the meeting. Since last night after the closing many have already come in, the system is working, we just have to feed it with more and more prospects. The stars are aligned for success, it's up to us to make it happen. Anne was down with the ladies for their opening session of the day. I'm so proud of her, she always makes me look good.

By 10 AM we were on the road, Anne headed home, and I went over to Shrine Headquarters for a couple of hours. I got back to Orlando by 3 PM and spent three hours at work before going home for dinner. After dinner, it was time to unpack and repack for a ten-day trip to the country of Cyprus. There we are to be a part of a Shriners Hospitals for Children Clinic where over 350 patients are scheduled to be seen. In addition, we will be meeting some dignitaries, having an Imperial Potentates Ball, and a

Ceremonial to bring in new members. This is going to be a great all-around trip that touches on many things we do.

October 7, 2017 - Saturday

Up early and into J&J Metro so Jason could have the day off. I got the crews going and spent about two hours there. I then had several errands to run and then it was back to the house. The few things at home I needed to do were done and then we had to finish up our packing for our Cyprus trip. By 3PM we were off to the airport for over a day of flying to reach Cyprus. This country is an island in the Mediterranean Sea, near Greece.

I was stopped going through TSA and they wanted to go through my bag. This happens often with all of the Imperial Potentates pins I have in there. The man, after going through my bag and seeing my Imperial Potentates pins, cleared my bag. As he closed it up, he said, "I can tell you do a lot of humanitarian work and I thank you for what you do." I found his comment to be a rare one from a TSA officer and appreciated it very much, made me feel good. Peter and Vicki were part of our team going and we met them at the airport for our 5:35 departure on British Airways, first stop London. We will arrive there tomorrow morning.

Our first-class tickets were provided by the Paraskevaides Foundation that has been helping children find Shriners Hospitals for the past 36 years. It's an amazing thing they do to help children in need. Sitting here it's amazing to me that some group would think enough of my efforts to buy me a plane ticket to go overseas, yet alone a first class one. They have to be special people.

The Membership Seminar wrapped up today, sorry I had to miss part of it, but I have no doubt the Team there did an outstanding job. I was able to watch parts of the closing on a live feed on Facebook some of the people were streaming. Proud of this TEAM!

October 8, 2017 - Sunday

This day started really early as we landed in London at 2:30 AM. (7:30 London time). Here we caught our next flight to Larnaca, Cyprus. Dr. Ken Guidera and his wife Carol joined us here. On the flight, we did the best we could to get some sleep but were not real successful. I saw an elderly man on this flight playing solitaire, not that unusual to see on flights, but he was doing it with real cards, not on a computer.

When we arrived in Larnaca we were greeted by Costas and Maro from the Foundation. They had large arrangements of flowers for each of the ladies. Anne and I were placed into a Mercedes S600 limousine, the rest were loaded onto a bus. We were whisked off to the Lordos Beach Hotel in Larnaca. Our hotel accommodations were a two-room suite overlooking the Mediterranean Sea and a beautiful pool and beach area. We settled in and unpacked. We then all loaded up on a bus for transportation to a local tavern and restaurant for dinner. About 30 of us including hospital staff, local Shriners, and Foundation people arrived at the restaurant; an old home converted to a Greek restaurant. We ate in the courtyard, where we were served several different samples of local Cyprus foods. It was a delicious treat, and the company was outstanding.

After dinner, I was presented a handmade, one of a kind silver "olive tree." The entire tree was made of silver with blood stones for olives, it is about 8 inches tall with a nice inscription on it welcoming the Imperial Potentate, Gary Bergenske to Cyprus. Anne received a gift as well, a necklace of very large pearls, beautiful. What an honor. The hospitality and people could not have been nicer, very welcoming.

October 9, 2017 - Monday

We were able to sleep in a little. At 10AM we were picked up by our personal driver for our time here, Giannakis Ioannou, in the Mercedes S600. Peter and Vicki rode with us to the Clinic where we visited and watched what was going on. At 11:30 AM we had a private meeting with the Cyprus Minister of Health, the Nicosia General Hospital Director, and the Orthopedic Chairman. Many on our team also attended. The discussions were on how we could expand on and improve on our collaborations in Cyprus to help more kids. The discussions went very well with the Minister of Health committing to participate.

At noon, there was a Press Conference with 6 TV Stations attending at the hospital in a Press Room. It was a panel discussion of the Minister of Health, Dr. Drvavic of SHC - Springfield, Costas of the Foundation, and me. The Press Conference went very well and was shown on the numerous TV stations the following two days to bring awareness of what the Shriners were doing for the Cyprus Children.

Costa then took us sight-seeing and to lunch. We saw some local historical sights and also the point where you can cross to the Turkish side in the Old City. (The part of the island which is occupied by the Turkish Army since 1974) He explained the war of 1974 and the invasion of Turkey into Cyprus. A sad story as many Cyprus people lost their property and were run out. We had a nice lunch in the Old City of Nicosia. Costas is a wonderful host, we all enjoy him and his kindness.

Dinner for the evening was at the home of Thelma Paraskevaides. She and her late husband George are the founders of the George and Thelma Paraskevaides Foundation that has been providing transportation for Cyprus children to the United States for the past 37 year. The home had to be one of, if not the nicest home I've ever been in. The grounds, home, pool area and furnishings are picture perfect and extraordinarily beautiful. Again, everyone here was so nice, no AC was needed, all doors were open as you got your food and moved to a table in the patio area overlooking to the pool to eat. On this evening, I presented Thelma and Maro, on behalf of Anne, one of her project green necklaces. I then presented Thelma and Costas an Imperial Potentates MEDALLION. This was followed by a Shriners Hospital for Children- Springfield glass Donor Award given to all family members there. We are all so proud and thankful for their efforts.

Efty Paraskevaides, the son of Thelma then gave a nice talk on how proud they are of Shriners and how Shriners Hospitals has changed so many lives of children from Cyprus. He went on to say the visit of the Imperial Potentate, Gary Bergenske to Cyprus is one of the best things to ever happen to Cyprus. He also said during the day on television, "Shriners are the single most important thing that has happened to the children of Cyprus, ever." That is a tremendous statement for all the work Shriners have done here. At the conclusion of his talk he then on behalf of the family presented a silver and gold replica of a Cyprus made bowl from 3500 years ago that was found in a grave. The item was historic and beautiful. And then as if magic, the news conference we did earlier in the day come on during the evening news.

During the evening I was given a tour of George Paraaskevaides's office. They have left it as it was the day he died. In his office was a picture of President Carter, come to find out President Carter was a friend of the Paraskevaides family too. We were able to talk about our times together with the Carters. As we all prepared to leave a picture of all attendees for the night was taken standing on the large stair case in the entry way. Truly a night to remember.

Two quotes I came away with this evening from the late George Paraskevaides are; (1) when you arrived at his home, no matter who you were, he would say "Welcome Home." The other one I found to be good was (2) "You die twice in life, first when your body dies, the second time is the last time your name is ever mentioned." He must have been a great man and mentor.

October 10, 2017 - Tuesday

On this morning, we started at 9AM with a tour guide on a bus. It was Peter and Vicki, Carol Guidera, and Anne and me. We visited a community center run by the government on preserving old culture. Here people did wood carvings, pottery, silver smiting, lace work, and hand making of linens to preserve the way things used to be. We then proceeded to the historical Museum that had items dating back to the Stone Age of Cyprus. Very interesting as people have lived on this island and left history from 3-4000 years before Christ. We then had a nice lunch in the Old City and headed back to the hotel for a little rest before the evening's events.

The evening was very special. We attended a Lodge meeting at Adonis Lodge #5 in the Cyprus Grand Lodge Building. The Grand Master was preset with us. The meeting was very formal, everyone in a suit. Many of the members were young. Several of our group who are Masons attended, I wore my colorful Imperial Potentates Shrine apron with pride. The Grand Master and I were escorted in after the Lodge was opened to the stage. The evening was focused on Shriners Hospitals for Children and what we do and what has been done for the children of Cyprus. The Grand Master presented me with a book on the history of Cyprus Masonry and a pin and ribbon from the recent anniversary of Cyprus Masonic independence. I then presented him with an Imperial Potentates

MEDALLION, he was most appreciative. Watching the closing of Lodge was interesting, more formal than ours and all done in Greek.

After lodge about 35 of us all proceeded to a place to have dinner. It was good fellowship and fun as all of the brothers interacted with us. It was a good time but late, by the time we got back to the hotel it was midnight.

October 11, 2017 - Wednesday

This was a spectacular day. We left the hotel at 9AM and headed to our appointment with Mr. Demetris Syllouris, the President of Parliament. (Second in command after the President of the Republic of Cyprus)

In his prestigious office we talked of how Shriners and the Cyprus Government could collaborate more to help the children in Cyprus. It's sounding like all of the financial part of taking care of more children would be covered by the Government, Grants, insurance money and the Foundation. This is very encouraging.

From this meeting, we went to a meeting at the University of Nicosia Medical School and met with Professor Andreas Charalambous, the founder and Executive Dean of the school. Here we again talked of ways to collaborate and additionally on how Shriners Hospitals should work on getting European research grants. This was very interesting, we will be moving forward with this. The Dean will be visiting the US soon and will make a trip to Tampa to our headquarters while there in November. We then all proceeded, including the Dean to lunch at the Hilton.

At our hotel at Lordos Beach it was Cyprus Night in the dining room. Our entire group, including hospital staff, all attended this event. It was a buffet of local foods and entertainment of Cyprus culture. It was defiantly a fun night. At the conclusion of the evening the ladies received a long strand of necklace pearls and the men recovered a set of worry beads. The worry beads are significant to the area and to George Paraskevaides, who was known for always having a set with him.

October 12, 2017 - Thursday

In the morning Peter, Vicki, Anne, Carol, and I loaded up in the Mercedes S600 with Giannakis and headed to Larnaca for some shopping. On the way we stopped to see the Saint Lazaros Church. This church is 1200 plus years old and had a crypt under it where the body of Saint Lazaros was buried. The body was later taken out and part of the bones are displayed in the main part of the church near the alter. Saint Lazaros was a friend of Jesus Christ. This church was ancient but extremely well built and very decorative with lots of gold in it. We then proceeded on to do some shopping and had lunch. Peter and I had meetings at the hospital in the afternoon. Giannakis took Peter and I to our meetings and girls caught a cab back to the hotel when they were done. This was the final day of the Clinic and 285 children were seen by Shrine Doctors during our visit, fantastic. Many were identified to return to one of the Shriners Hospitals back in the States.

As I spent time on the final day of the Cyprus Clinic, I watched many children check in and wait to see a Doctor. It came to my attention a lady called in during the morning hours in a panic, insisting we see her son. She was advised all of the appointments for the day were filled and that this was our last day. I was told she became very upset, she was coming from another country, she had purchased a plane ticket for her and her son, and desperately pleaded that we see him. She was told if they arrived prior to our closing time we would work him in.

As I stood in the entryway to the clinic, I saw a small woman carrying a 5-6-year boy in her arms. I don't know how she was able to carry him, he appeared to be nearly as big as she was. I walked to her and she handed her son off to me. This young boy allowed me to hold him, in fact he acted like he knew me as he cuddled up to me. As I held this young boy it became apparent to me, he was unable to walk on his own, he was glad to be in some strong arms.

As I stood there, his Mother stood before me sobbing and crying, she said to me; "If you can help my boy, you can take my life." I was speechless, choked up, and filled with tears! I didn't know what to say. The health of her son was so important she was willing to give her own life for help. I expressed to her we would do everything we could and took both of them inside. This was so powerful to me, that we, the Shriners have a such a reputation around the world of helping children. It was an emotional moment I will never forget, this mother who was beside herself pleading for help for her child. I was so sad, yet so proud of what we as an organization bring to the world, that of helping and changing the lives of children.

The Ambassador of the United States of America
Kathleen A. Doherty
requests the pleasure of the company of

Mr. Gary Bergenske and Mrs. Anne Bergenske

at a reception in honor of Shriners Hospital Doctors and Nurses

on Thursday, October 12, 2017
from seven to nine o'clock p.m.

Attire: Business
R.S.V.P. by October 9, 2017
Tel: 22-393337 / rsvpnicosia@state.gov

Davies House
7 Ploutarchou Street
Engomi, Nicosia

Please present this invitation at the entrance

The evening was a special event, it took place at the American Embassy in Cyprus. The cocktail reception hosted by Ambassador Kathleen Doherty in honor of Shriners Hospitals for Children included all of our hospital staff, some local medical students, and local dignitaries, including the Cyprus Minister of Health. The Ambassador gave a nice talk on the great work Shriners do, followed my myself about the work Shriners do and what we represent. This was followed up by a few words by the Minister of Health. The evening was delightful, held outside with cocktails and finger foods. The Embassy had a photographer taking pictures that were put up on their Facebook page. The Embassy, called the Davis House, after Ambassador Davis, a former American Ambassador there who was assassinated in 1974.

We left there in the Mercedes S600, stopped to get something to eat and proceeded back to the hotel. Another long late day, but so worth it. It was a great day, one we will remember.

October 13, 2017 - Friday - Anne's Birthday

The morning started at 9AM as we were all picked by a Tour Bus for our day off to enjoy some relaxation and be able to visit some of the sights of Cyprus. Also joining us were some Shriners from Germany and Denmark as they arrived for the Shrine Ceremonial the following day. We traveled about an hour and forty-five minutes to the Curium Ancient Theater where we toured the mosaics of a bathhouse from an archaeology dig that has been taking place for years. This dates back thousands of years and overlooks the Mediterranean Sea. It was a public bath house and also has a large outdoor amphitheater that will hold 2500 people. The bath house is to view only but the amphitheater is used for outside concerts and plays. Amazing place, the history is incredible.

We then went to another ancient dig in Pafos where an entire home has been discovered. The only thing remaining is the floors, the floors in every room are done in tiny mosaic tiles. It's unbelievable how it has lasted so long and looks so good. They have built a structure over the dig to preserve what has been found. From here we headed to a local restaurant for lunch. Again, delicious native food of Cyprus.

As were sitting there for lunch, a message popped up on my phone, "Happy Birthday Mom." Oh my, I had forgotten today was Anne's Birthday. To tell you the truth, with the 7-hour time change and as busy as we have been, I stayed confused on what day and date it was. We knew we were going to be in Cyprus for Anne's Birthday, but it had slipped past me. How embarrassing. Boy was I in trouble, she had been waiting all morning for me to say, "Happy Birthday" and now she knew I had totally forgotten. Now it was so embarrassing she did not want me to tell anyone.

After lunch, we walked around and did some shopping. I purchased a nice gold crucifix for her to have something from Cyprus. I also mentioned to Peter I had messed up and forgotten Anne's Birthday. We climbed back on the bus and headed back towards the hotel, a two-hour trip. About half way we stopped for dinner at a beautiful hotel and restaurant on the sea for dinner. The hotel, The Londa Beach Hotel in Limasol was owned by the Paraskevaides family. George Paraskevaides designed and built it, it was a place he loved. The hotel is recognized as one of the best small hotels in the world, they had the awards displayed in the lobby to prove it. During dinner Peter and Costas set up a Birthday cake and the singing of Happy Birthday to Anne. One of the hotel workers shared with Anne how much Shriners meant to him as one of his children were treated by Shriners Hospitals for Children. He presented Anne with a gift from the hotel of two candles.

As Anne and I made the rounds from table to table I admitted to all I had forgotten her Birthday, turned out to be some interesting conversations. Soon we loaded up on the bus to finish the trip back to our hotel and to hit the bed for some rest.

This was a wonderful day. Our hosts, Costas and Moro Paraskevaides of the Foundation work so hard to be sure patients are taken care of and also that the group that comes over from the United States enjoy their time while tending to the children.

October 14, 2017 - Saturday

This was primed to be yet another great day. Breakfast at the hotel overlooking the Mediterranean Sea and a relaxing morning, a great way to start. It was then time to load up into the Mercedes S600 and head to the Emirat Shrine Ceremonial in Nicosia at the Hilton Hotel. Ten new candidates were waiting to become Shriners. They performed the ritual portion and I did the Shriners Creed. I then proceeded to give each of them an Imperial Potentates Pin and a coin from the 143 Imperial Session in Daytona Beach. They had four stunts they put all of them through individually. They were good ones. The best was presenting them with a plate of whipped cream on a plate and instructed them to find a piece of candy in the cream, and to then chew it. They all found the candy and began to chew it, but the candy was really a piece of garlic. Some interesting faces were made and they all spit it out being left with bad breath. They were all presented their dues card, certificate and Fez to be worn at the Imperial Potentates Ball that evening. It was exciting that Nobles from 9 different countries attended the Ceremonial. They traveled from Cyprus, Turkey, Germany, Romania, Moldavia, Greece, Denmark, Lebanon, and the United States. Very impressive.

It was then back to the hotel for a quick change into a Tux and to pick up the ladies. We then headed back to the Hilton for the Imperial Potentates Ball. Anne and I were escorted in to a beautifully decorated room of 150 people waiting for the evening to start. They all came through a receiving line, so we could meet each and every person. First thing on the agenda was for the new Nobles to be Fezzed by their Ladies. Anne was selected to help as one new Noble did not have his lady with him. Introductions were then made, and a wonderful buffet line was opened.

After dinner I made some presentations, one to the Alasia Shrine Club for their efforts and good work. Then the Doctors, Nurses, and Hospital staff were introduced. This was followed by introducing two Shriners Patients in the room. I called the beautiful 25-year-old girl who had been to the United States seven times for surgery to come to the stage at the request of the audience for comments. She got out a few words of thanks and then broke down in tears and wept in thanks for how her life had been changed because of so many generous people and the Shriners. She touched every heart in the room and brought a clear reason as to why we do this to every individual. Although she was crying so hard she could not verbalize her thanks, her actions were so much more powerful than her words could ever be. The crowd gave her a standing ovation. Another gentleman who was a Shriners kid was also a Shriner now. He was treated for Polio and his life was changed because of the Paraskevaides Foundation and Shriners. Today he leads a very successful life.

It was now time for my final presentation and a heartfelt thank you to the "George and Thelma Paraskevaides Foundation." It was their vision that made this Cyprus and Shriners Hospitals for Children partnership possible to treat over 3500 children. In my mind, proper recognition had never been given, and it had been bothering me for a few years. They had been providing transportation to and from Springfield, Massachusetts for 37 years and no one had recognized them with a Shriners Donor Award. I was the first ever, in 37 years, Imperial Potentate or for that matter, an Imperial Officer to visit.

I called to the stage Costa Paraskevaides and his wife Moro, the Executive Director of the George and Thelma Paraskevaides Foundation, and the nephew of the late George Paraskevaides. I did my best to give thanks to them and their entire family for the generous contributions they have given to the children of Cyprus and to humanity in general. They were presented with a plaque of appreciation that included medallions of their contributions to Shriners Hospitals for Children of over fifteen million dollars to hang in their Foundation office. Additionally, they were shown the donor recognition plaque that would return back to Springfield to be displayed on the hospital's donor wall. It was a proud moment for me to be able to give proper thanks to such outstanding people. Costas and Moro gave their thanks to a standing ovation.

At this time Shriners from three different countries presented Anne and me gifts and made donations to Anne's First Ladies Project. Anne then sold First Ladies items while the dancing continued into the evening. What a wonderful day it was, one that makes a man so PROUD to be a Shriner.

October 15, 2017 - Sunday

Our travel day began as usual with breakfast on the patio overlooking the sea. There was a lot of packing to do to get ready. We were taken to the airport midafternoon for our flight to London where we would spend the night for or flight on Monday back to Orlando. Traveling with us was the Diaz's and Guidera's.

This day found me reflecting on the past several days of this International trip; the importance of what we do both Fraternally and for our Philanthropy is so precious to so many. Making men better, improving the lives of children and their families is our mission and we are doing it well, but it is clear we can do even more, and we should.

Today marks the first quarter of this tremendous honor of having the privilege to serve as the Imperial Potentate and First Lady of Shriners International. It is really hard for me to even think that we have been given this great honor but can assure everyone we take it seriously and give it our best effort every day. Anne does an in incredible job, she is so supportive, generous, and attentive to our duties, and is always a lady who represents our organizations in a professional and first-class way. I'm so proud of her for being at my side as I chased this dream of mine.

Our flight into London arrived about 8PM. We checked into the airport Hilton, grabbed something to eat and called it a day. Yes, we spent a partial day in England during this year.

October 16, 2017 - Monday

Another International travel day as we work our way back to the United States. Our morning started in the dining room of the Hilton for breakfast. Our travels would continue to Orlando with the Diaz's, the Guidera's were headed separately to Tampa. Another day with British Airlines, very nice too.

We arrived in Orlando about 3:30 PM, a five-hour gain of time from London. I dropped Anne off at the house and I headed to work at J&J Metro for a few hours. I needed to do a quick catch up there as I needed to be in Tampa the following morning for meetings. Not much time for sleep during this whirl wind of activity. Thank goodness, our son Jason is looking out after and running our business while we are moving around the globe doing our Shriner work.

October 17, 2017 - Tuesday

Up real early today and on my way to Tampa for participation in interviews for a new Director of Communications and Public Relations. Great candidates, this is very reassuring that we will be taking our efforts to the next level. During the time at Headquarters I was able to also catch up on things with many of the other departments. Jessica helped me work on getting a Visa for Bolivia. Good dinner and an early turn in at the hotel.

October 18, 2017 - Wednesday

Today the interview process continued and wrapped up at noon. We all agreed on who the best candidate was and we're ready to move forward. I rushed to an appointment in Tampa to get the Yellow Fever shot required to get my Bolivia Visa. Then drove directly to my dentist in Orlando for a dental appointment. By now it was 3:30 and I headed to work at J&J Metro. First order of business was to get my Visa info completed, uploaded, and then sent off by FedEx. What a mess to do all this. Needed help from Jason and finally got it to the FedEx office at 7PM. I grabbed something to eat and headed back to Work until 9:30 PM. Then it was off to the house to begin packing for our flight out the next day.

October 19, 2017 - Thursday

Up early to finish off the packing of our bags. Then loaded them up and headed to the airport. Our normal airport parking place was full, so we were turned away. The Terminal Airport was full too, so we had to find alternative parking. Got to the airport and we're going thru the line to find out Anne's driver's license had expired. Good thing we had her Passport with us. We arrived in Sacramento that evening and got checked into our hotel. We then went immediately to the hospital where Imperial Sir Jeff had arranged for a Membership Meeting. This turned out to be a great deal, they got 8 petitions that evening and are doing an excellent job. Afterwards we grabbed something to eat at the hotel and then went to bed.

October 20, 2017 - Friday

The morning started off with an Shriners Hospitals for Children - Sacramento Meeting at the hospital with a few key people and board members to discuss how things are going and what the future holds. Imperial Sirs Jerry and Jeff were also there. We had lunch at the hospital and continued our discussions afterwards.

The evening was the 20th Anniversary Gala where many donors were invited. Anne and I had the pleasure of sitting by "Rose" who was in her 90's and was a large donor. A few years ago, she sent in a hand-written personal check for one million dollars to Shriners - Sacramento. We enjoyed our time with her, amazing lady. Anne did a nice talk on her project and they showed her project video.

I told a couple of stories about some patients that touched me. One in particular was about a patient from one of our hospitals. A few months earlier when Anne and I recorded her video for her project, ***"Love Grows Miracles"*** we met a young seven-year-old girl. Anne and I were sitting at a small child's table playing a game with this young girl when I asked her if she knew what she wanted to be when she grew up. She instantly answered, "I'm going to be a policewoman, I'm going to get the bad guys, I'm going to chase them, up and down the stairs if I need to, I'll catch them to make the world safer." She was focused, she knew exactly what she was planning to do when she grew up. I was so impressed.

When the three of us had finished our game and discussions, the young girl stood up, grabbed her walker and scooted on to something else. With that I walked over to her Mother, I told her how beautiful and loving her daughter was and added how impressed I was with her. I then asked her Mother, "Do you know what your daughter is going to be when she grows up?" She answers, "Yes, she is going to be a policewoman." With that she began to cry and told me her daughter had for the first time in her life, at the age of seven, walked down a set of stairs this week, all due to the surgery she had at the Shriners Hospital. With that my eyes quickly filled with tears too and I hugged her. I hear stories like this over and over again, on how Shriners change the lives of children. I am so honored and fortunate to serve in this position where I get to hear wonderful stories like this daily. It was a wonderful evening enjoyed by all.

<u>October 21, 2017 - Saturday</u>

Today is a BIG day, the 20th Anniversary of the Shriners Hospitals for Children - Sacramento location. In total, it is the 94th as they were at the San Francisco location for 74 years previously. The morning started off with a full Board of Governors meeting. We then moved to the large tent in front of the building for a Patient Alumni Lunch. This was a great event as they had a number of patients there to tell about their story, including a couple of ladies from back in the 1930's. They talked about the months they spent together in the hospital and how they all became family. Also, about how their parents could only come once a week for about an hour to visit, and then only through a window at the hospital. Many more stores were told as well.

The afternoon activities consisted of a carnival on the back lot of the hospital where a stage was set up for music, face painting, old cars, venders, etc. A table was setup to sell First Ladies products and a bunch was sold. Food was served, and it was just a jolly old good time. For dinner, we went to a very nice restaurant in downtown Sacramento, good food and good company.

October 22, 2017 - Sunday

Another full travel day across the country back to Orlando. After landing and dropping Anne off at the house I proceeded to J&J Metro to work for a while on caching up at work. One thing about working at night with no one else there you can get things done faster. Still, it was a long day.

October 23, 2017 - Monday

Up early and out of the house to Tampa for a week of committee meetings. I arrived at headquarters mid-morning and joined in on the Building and Equipment meeting. There was a lot to cover and the meeting concluded late afternoon. It is amazing how much Shriners do to change the world and take care of kids. I had a quick meeting down in Public Relations as well and worked on ideas for the Imperial Potentates and First Ladies Holiday Card. This sounds easy, but a lot of thought goes into it. Dinner at Mitchell's Fish House with the committee.

October 24, 2017 - Tuesday

Woke up at the Doubletree Hotel and headed back over to headquarters. Today was The Salary and Personnel Committee meeting and again it was an all-day meeting. I was able to spend some time down in the Membership office working on our "I AM - RU Committed to Membership" Program. I am so pleased with the way the awareness of this program is spreading and the excitement it is generating. I only hope the implementation phase will go as well. Our Fraternity desperately needs his program to be a success, our future depends on building our membership.

Dinner was at the Rusty Pelican with the committee members and some of the staff. We really have a great team from every area, what a pleasure it is to work with everyone this year.

October 25, 2017 - Wednesday

Up again and back to headquarters. Today consisted of a few smaller committee meetings and of course for the entire week many meetings have been by conference call in an effort to save money. Some still are best held face to face to be able to accomplish the most. I was able to go to some of the different departments in Headquarters today to work on a variety of different projects. A quick dinner tonight and then watched the World Series in my hotel room.

October 26, 2017 - Thursday

Wake up again at the Doubletree and head over for an all-day meeting with the Budget Committee today. Working on the budget can be a frustrating thing. Even with all of the money the Shrine has it is still restricting as to what we can do. We could help so many more kids if we had more money. We are at a point in history, with the changes in the way medicine is delivered, that we will be forced to make some substantial changes in how we do business.

Change is never easy but change we must do it if we hope to be relevant in years to come. Failure to change will result in not being efficient, not keeping up with the times, and finding ourselves approaching a point of no return of keeping up with our values and our commitment to children. Hard decisions will need to be made, ones that will be hard to accept but necessary. The committee meeting lasted till 6:30 PM. Again a quick dinner and back to the hotel. Man, I'm ready to go home, Missing Anne, one more day left.

October 27, 2017 - Friday

Up today and checked out of the hotel. Today's meeting over at Headquarters was with a group from South Carolina. They wanted more information on building a Shriners Burn Unit. They are considering and looking at the possibility of including one in their plans of building a new medical complex. It was great discussion and next steps and action items were identified. Everyone agreed further discussions were needed.

I drove back to Orlando to my office at J&J Metro to catch up things there. Had a lot to catch up on and stayed till about 6 PM. Anne, David, Marie Angie and I all got something to eat out. We then headed over to their new home where they were working to get it ready to move into on Sunday. We helped them for a while and then headed home and hit the bed.

October 28, 2017 - Saturday

Up early and off to J&J Metro to get the crews out for a day's work. Jason took the day off. Once I got them off I worked on some office stuff there. In the afternoon, I worked on Shrine business, mostly on setting up flights for the next 3 months. It's a lot to set up all these flights, get rental cars where needed, and to advise people of our plans. Of all the planning and setting up of activities I think I least like making flight reservations. It can be aggravating, maybe because I do a bunch of them at once.

In the evening, it was back over to help David and Marie Angie get ready for the movers the following day. They have done a great job redoing and painting the house, looks really good.

October 29, 2017 - Sunday

Early to rise and over to the moving company to get the crew off who were going to help David and Marie Angie. I worked at the office till about noon. I then ran some errands to get ready for our next trip. Had laundry to pick up, clothes to buy, etc. for our trip to Las Vegas. By midafternoon I was home to pack for the Las Vegas trip for the Shriners Hospitals for Children PGA Golf Tournament and our trip to Washington DC to lay a wreath at the Tomb of the Unknown Soldier.

Once most of the packing was done it was time to head back over to David's to see how the move was going. Things were coming along nicely there. Anne and I then went to get I bite to eat and then headed home to finish packing. I ended up watching the best World Series game ever until 1 AM. The Astros beat the Dodgers 13 to 12 in the tenth inning. What a game.

October 30, 2017 - Monday

Today started off good, we got to sleep in until 9AM. Then it was time to jump up and get ready to head to the airport, we are heading to Las Vegas for a week of fun at the golf course. We also have a trip within a trip as we also go to Washington DC during the week. We didn't arrive in Vegas until the evening, but we had a rental car waiting on us and we headed to the Red Rock Hotel. We checked in and were in a nice suite overlooking the pools and mountains, how beautiful.

October 31, 2017 - Tuesday

HALLOWEEN- On this day it was up early and on our way to the golf course. The few Board members present took a tour of the course and viewed the setup that included many signage changes that will be much better when the TV cameras are running. We then attended a meeting of all of the departments of the golf course and tournament offices. The men had lunch in the clubhouse.

The ladies had an amazing lunch attended by about 400. Also, in attendance were our awesome two national patient ambassadors, Isabella and Emily. The special guest of the day was **Kechi**, the Shriners burn patient who had just completed her unbelievable competition on **"Americas Got Talent."** She did an awesome job speaking and singing, the audience was in awe of her. Kechi is an inspiration to everyone who has the pleasure of meeting her.

In the evening, there was a patient experience event at "The Hill" where several patients gave lessons to those attending on how life goes when you are physically challenged. This was a fun and educational event. The week of the tournament is off to a great start.

Chapter Five
November 2017

November 1, 2017 - Wednesday

Another day to rise early and have breakfast with other Board members. Things started off with Kenny and I doing a video with Sam Saunders at the driving range, a PGA golfer and the grandson of Arnold Palmer. This went really well and should turn out as a great video.

All Board members present then attended the Board of Governors meetings of Pasadena, Salt Lake City, and Galveston. This was very nice that we could all attend 3 different meetings in one day. We made a I AM - RU video with each one of them. Our ladies attended a Goodie 2 Shoes event where they participated in giving away 400 pairs of shoes to needy children this is always a memorable event. That evening we all had dinner together at a restaurant back at the Red Rock Hotel.

November 2, 2017 - Thursday

This is the Opening Day of the Shriners Hospitals for Children Open. We had breakfast at 5:30 AM and were on our way to the golf course at 6:10. I presided over the Ceremonial Opening Ceremony at 7 AM. A welcome was given at hole number one, mention was made of this hole being the Wayne Lachut Memorial hole. I sure miss Wayne and his contagious laughter. Alec was at my side as we did this. I then presented two Shriners patients to make the ceremonial opening tee shot. The two of them, one girl and one boy teed off at the same time. This was an exciting time. Soon after this we discovered Alec had a flat tire on his wheel chair. Jerry Gantt took the wheel to find a place to get it fixed. In the mean time we got a golf cart for Alec and his father to use, boy did Alec like this, he lit up like a light bulb. About three hours later Jerry returned with the repaired wheel.

As this was Opening Day, all of the Board Members and their ladies were working around the golf course. That evening was the Imperial Potentates BBQ that included SHC patients, volunteers, and Shriners. This was a good event and the food was excellent. During the evening, we did an I AM – RU Committed to Membership video LIVE on Facebook with about 400 people, this was awesome too. The night was full of fun and fellowship. Many video interviews were being made during the evening for future events and use.

November 3, 2017 - Friday

This is an interesting day. It is an Imperial Potentates trip within a trip. Anne and I are leaving our trip in Las Vegas for a day to go to Washington DC to lay a wreath on the Tomb of the Unknown Soldier. The following day we will return back to our original trip and hotel in Las Vegas to finish out the golf tournament event. We are so excited to have the opportunity and honor to lay a wreath at the Tomb.

Our arrival into Washington Reagan airport was at 9 PM. We were picked up and taken to our hotel. As we walked in the front door many Legion of Honor members were lined up to greet us. We visited their hospitality room for a drink and then went to the rooftop restaurant for something to eat. We were joined by two Bahia couples (Kennedy and Coughlin) for dinner. Our thoughts were on our following day and the honor it will hold.

November 4, 2017 - Saturday

Up at 6AM to get ready for a 7AM breakfast. Immediately following breakfast, we moved to the Ballroom for a meeting that included a memorial service, recognition of leaders, and a flag folding presentation where the flag was presented to me. From there we loaded up on several buses and headed to Arlington National Cemetery. The buses took us right up to the location of the Tomb for the Unknown Soldier.

Upon reaching the Tomb we were met by a man who gave us instructions on how it would unfold to lay the wreath at the Tomb. We then proceeded to the top of the steps where we would proceed upon command. As we approached the Tomb we were met by a Soldier who had the wreath we were going to lay. After we laid it, we stepped back and taps was played. We then carefully and together stepped back to the top of the stairs. This was one of the most awesome experiences ever, so touching and such an honor just to have the chance to do it. We proceeded across the street where all Shriners put a Poppy at the foot of a Memorial for Canadian Veterans. This as well was very touching.

As we rode the bus back to the hotel many thoughts and memories went through my mind of how honorable this event was. We had lunch with over 400 Shriners and ladies. During this time, I also had this large group do an awesome I AM - RU video. It rocked! Additionally, I thought about my father, an Army veteran who passed away 37 years ago. He would have been so proud of me on this day.

A Year as the Imperial Potentate of Shriners International

I posted a video taken at the Tomb on Facebook and also Tweeted out the following;

I cannot express the humble honor of representing every former and current Mason and Shriner as I laid a Wreath today at the Tomb of the Unknown Soldier. To be a member of this great fraternity where every member respects and honors God, County, and Family while giving to those in need just puffs me up with pride. Thank you for your trust and the privilege to serve you.

Gary Bergenske
Imperial Potentate

By 3 PM we were back off to the airport to head back for the conclusion of the Shriners Hospitals for Children Open in Las Vegas. We were in Washington DC for a total of 19 hours, but did we have a good time and had the opportunity to participate in something big, yes, we did. We will remember this forever. Wow - what an honor this day was. By the time we got back to Las Vegas and back to the hotel it was midnight again. Where does the time go? The video of laying the Wreath at the Tomb of the Unknown on Facebook became the most viewed video I posted all year with 174,000 views.

November 5, 2017 - Sunday

Up early at 6AM again for the final day of the golf tournament. It was good to be back and to catch up on the past two days. They had some windy weather while we were gone. The tournament seemed to be a great event with everything going as planned or better. During the afternoon, I did an interview with the Golf Channel on who Shriners are and what we do along with what the tournament means to us. This is televised in many countries internationally. Anne and I did some pictures with some of the patients to potentially be used on our Christmas card depending on how they turn out.

As the final golfers were coming in it soon became apparent, we were going to extra holes as there were three tied for first. So, the 18th hole was played again. I rode back to the 18th tee box to watch the three men who were tied, and I thought, "what pressure, one of these guys is going to win 1.2 million dollars." They concluded the hole and again it was a three-way tie, so back to the 18th tee we went again.

This time we had a winner, Patrick Cantlay. It was a good thing because the sun had set. Had we still had a tie, we would be coming back the following morning to finish up. We lined up on the 18th green, Shriners, patients, staff, and the winner for the presentation of the first "Howard Hughes Cup" trophy. What an experience. Turned into another late night by the time we had dinner and got back to the hotel.

November 6, 2017 - Monday

Up early to pack for our trip home. We had a lot to get packed up, had to turn in a rental car and then get a bite to eat. Our flight was at about noon and we got home about 11 PM. Makes for a long day of travel. Anne gets to stay home for four days but I'm off to Washington DC first thing in the morning again for meetings on the Hill. I will only have a few hours tonight to sleep, unpack and repack. I love what I'm doing having the opportunity to represent so many on such important items.

November 7, 2017 - Tuesday

Another day of travel, this time to Washington DC. This will prove to be a good couple of days as we meet with several Senators and Congressmen to bring awareness to Shriners Hospitals for Children. After landing at Reagan National Airport I caught a cab over to the Capital Hilton. Nice hotel and located in the area close to where we were going to visit. Cold and rainy out, not very nice.

Jerry and I had diner at the Trump Hotel along with Bob and Susan, two locally connected people 1st Degree set us up with to arrange for all of our meetings. It quickly became clear they knew what they were doing and had a great plan set up for us. We were set to meet with 10 to 12 Senators and Congressmen or their staffers over the next two days. They had a complete bio on each one of them and also what committees they sat on. Very interesting and surely would prove to be helpful. John McCabe ran late and was unable to join us. After our wonderful diner we headed back to the hotel and turned in. A cool thing for the night at the TRUMPH Hotel was the Maple Bacon, they bring it to your table on a mini clothesline and cook it with a torch in front of you, a bit different. Delicious!

November 8, 2017 - Wednesday

Eight AM start, we met our driver for two days that had been set up for us. Bob really knows his way around town and with our own driver we made good time getting from appointment to appointment. We had a Fezzy Bear that we left behind at each meeting, he was a hit. We focused on meeting with people on the Hill who had one of our hospitals in their state, was a Shriner, or was or had a connection to a Shriners patient. I have to say we were welcomed everywhere we went. On every occasion Bob had it set up and they were expecting us. There were big meetings going on in both the Senate and Congress related to Trumps Tax Bill, this caused some of our meetings to have to be with staffers. Staffer meetings were defiantly not as good.

Our best meeting of the day was with the father of one of our patients who served as the Secretary of Health and Human Services. He was really ready for us and even had others in the meeting with us. He loves what we have done for his daughter and it really showed. Once he found out we were needing help transporting patients from foreign countries who were burned, and how time was of the essence he quickly brought in another Deputy Secretary. After he heard our story, of the care we provide to children, he raised up his hands and said, "You are like a gift from Heaven." He gave us his commitment to help find a way to expedite patient travel provided by the Government. This was great news for us. In the past, President Jimmy Carter has also been trying to help in this area. The more we have working on the Government helping us with International patient transportation, the more children we will be able to help and save.

We had a great meeting in Richie Neal's office with his Chief Staffer. Senator Neal of Massachusetts was caught up in the Tax Reform meetings. Senator Neal has been helpful to us in the past with our two, hospitals in his state, Massachusetts. They remembered Imperial Sir Gene Bracewell who had been by often. They are going to send Gene a card as he is not feeling well. We were taken out on the balcony of his private office that looked out over the Capital. We also talked about former Senator Teddy Kennedy, also from Massachusetts and about where his office was located.

Fortunately, it did not rain much during the day and we wrapped up our calls about dusk. During the day, I made several calls to Yana as we worked on our plan for the Imperial Potentates Holiday Card. The ideas are churning but are narrowing down. For dinner, Jerry, John, Susan, and I walked a few blocks to a steakhouse called Joe's. The food was fantastic, what a treat. Little cool walking back to the hotel. We all agreed it was a very successful day, we even think we may have a second visit tomorrow with Health and Human Services.

November 9, 2017 - Thursday

Another 8 AM start with our driver as we hit the Hill. We dove right back into our appointments and soon also found out we were invited back to Health and Human Services. We were excited about this. Our meeting there was very touching. We met with a man who had just got back from Puerto Rico after the hurricane did tremendous damage. He expressed medical care there was not good, only 20 % of the island has power and most hospitals were not fully operational. A hospital ship, the Comfort was docked there and was the main place for medical care. We talked about our need for help with transportation and he talked about the Governments need for Pediatric Doctors. A real synergy was developing. He committed to help us and we committed to provide services when needed. He was going back to Puerto Rico in two days to evaluate where they were and expected he would be calling for our help. We expressed we were ready to go. When leaving he gave me a nice challenge coin. This connection all started from a conversation with one of our patient's parents who worked on the Hill, Wow.

Another good meeting that afternoon was with Senator Orin Hatch. He was from Utah and a Senator for nearly 40 years. When we sat down with him, with a big smile on his face he expressed, "The Shriners, I love the Shriners, and this is the first time they have ever come to visit me." That was music to our ears. Jerry then said, "Well, we wanted to wait till you got settled in." That brought on a lot of laughter. We had a good discussion, we have his full support. We presented him his Fezzy Bear, got some pictures and headed out.

Our last call of the day was Great too. It was with a former patient who we treated for cleft lip and palate many years ago. His Staffer told us we were running late and would have to reschedule. He heard this and came out of his office and said, "No, these are my Shriners, you all come in, I have 15 minutes." When we got in there we could not hardly say a word, he kept on and on how we changed his life and are responsible for who he is today. When his Staffer came in again to tell him time was up, he said "Nope, 10 more minutes." We knew he had to go so we got up, handed him his Fezzy Bear and got some pictures. We had a hard time getting out of the building as it was all locked up. Once we got out and were waiting on our car, here came our Congressman patient, literally running as he was late for the Gala he was to attend. As he went by he again said, "Thank you all."

By now it was dark, and the Capital looked beautiful all lite up on this crisp evening. When we got back to the hotel, Jerry, John, and I walked down the street to get a bite to eat. During dinner, I advised them we had received a Demand letter from an attorney with regards to our new Recorder, regarding his duties and pay. This Demand letter will probably lead to litigation, very disappointing. And to top it off, diner was not to good either.

November 10, 2017 - Friday

I had a late morning flight, so I didn't have to rush. As I sat there and thought about the past two days and what we accomplished it was pretty amazing. For me especially, a kid that was always interested in our national government, the buildings and history of Washington DC, and in particular our Presidents, this was like a dream come true. To have been able to run through the halls of the Senate and Congress was pretty cool, even for an Imperial Potentate. I wore my Fez during these visits and received many positive comments about Shriners as we roamed the halls.

When I arrived back in Orlando, I went by my office for a few hours to catch up there. I was only home for a few hours, I had to drive to Tampa in the morning for meetings. Anne got my suitcases unpacked, clothes washed, and ready to go. I would be in Tampa for the next several days. Where is "Home Sweet Home?" I miss it.

November 11, 2017 - Saturday

I drove to Tampa late morning. The Investment meeting was going on. The entire Imperial Divan was coming in this day for our first Futures meeting the following day. I re-implemented this committee to strategically plan our fraternity's future. The committee has had some meetings and now it was time to involve the entire Divan.

By dinner time most of us were in and we all ate together at the Westin. It was a short night as we had an early start time the following morning. That was fine with me as I was ready to hit the hay. This is daughter Carries Birthday, I talked with her on the phone for a while, she is working hard and raising two wonderful boys along with Bronson. Family birthdays is something you are rarely able to attend as the Imperial Potentate.

November 12, 2017 - Sunday

This TEAM, the Imperial Divan, is working so hard, even on Sunday, 8 AM start. Our fraternity needs so much work and help to successfully move into the future that we planned a day to talk about nothing but this. It is essential we take care of our future as to what Shriners do in the world. This is so important.

We first looked over the past. Imperial Sir Ed as the Chairman led the discussions. It became more and more clear we have a lot of work to do. The committee had the day well planned and we left with some action plans and a planned meeting to take place with all of us again in about six weeks. The I AM - RU Program fits into this but it's going to take much more than just membership planning to get this ship headed in the right direction again.

By the afternoon the Trustees had now arrived for the Board meeting starting tomorrow and we had dinner at the Rusty Pelican. It is such a pleasure to be leading the Joint Boards when everyone respects one another and gets along. It's amazing how much you can accomplish when everyone works as a team. Good night.

November 13, 2017 - Monday

The Fall Joint Board meeting starts today in Tampa, Florida at Shriners International Headquarters. Start time 8:30 AM. The meeting was opened and most of the day was spent on hospital business. We seemed to really get bogged down over discussing things at times, but everyone was polite, how nice. We had lunch in the room and continued on till 5 PM. By the end of the day it was clear we were running behind. Solution; start thirty minutes earlier tomorrow.

We had a nice evening, a few drinks, dinner, and off to bed early. Most were worn out.

November 14, 2017 - Tuesday

On this day our Board Meeting knocked out some Fraternal business in the morning. We had a special guest for lunch, a Shriner and his wife, Jeff and Heidi Jackson who had donated one million dollars to Shriners Hospitals for Children. We had a special ceremony in the memorabilia room to recognize them and to place a plaque on the Wall of Fame. Imperial Sir Jerry and I did the presentation and it went very well. Jeff and Heidi both spoke as well on what it meant to them.

Our meeting in the afternoon continued to run long. We had a lot of business at hand, so we worked late, till about 6:30. NASCAR Driver and Shriner David Ragan joined us for dinner at the Bahama Breeze. We all made an I AM - RU video with David and he addressed the Board. He is scheduled to be at our meeting in the morning too. It was really a good night of fellowship, having David Ragan there with us made it even better.

November 15, 2017 - Wednesday

The morning started out at 7:30 in the Memorabilia room with David Ragan. He was donating the NASCAR Shriners Hospitals for Children helmet he wore in three races this year to our museum. Pictures were made of him giving me the helmet for social media postings, this was really neat.

Our meeting then started at 8AM with the Sports Committee reports. NASCAR was the final one and David did part of it. He then signed the helmet he had just donated to us earlier. Everyone was really engaged in this. Jeff then let everyone know David had set up an insurance policy for Shriners Hospitals for one million dollars. I then presented David with a Shriners Daytona belt buckle and an Imperial Potentates MEDALLION for his outstanding work as a Shriner, an Ambassador, and as a donor. He was given a standing ovation.

Just before lunch we recognized to valuable longtime employees, Dr. Ray Novak and Attorney Charlene Haynes. I also presented them both with an Imperial Potentates MEDALLION. In their speeches Charlene brought me to tears. Jerry then had a dozen red roses for Charlene. This was a special time to give thanks to two great employees.

Our meetings continued through the afternoon, but we continued to run behind. We had a SHC - Tampa patient, Riley, give us an inspiring speech that lifted all of us up and reminded each of us why we donate our time to this cause. So, still running behind. Solution- tomorrow we start at 7:30. Another nice dinner and early to bed, who said Shriners party all night?

November 16, 2017 - Thursday

Up early for a 7:30 AM start that started with a two-and-a-half-hour Executive Session. And, we continue to run behind. As time became shorter so did the reports and we finished up by about 2:30. It was a good meeting, one I was proud to have had the privilege to run. Peace and harmony prevailed through the entire meeting and many good decisions were made and we had a ton of action items to implement. I continued to work at headquarters for the rest of the afternoon on planning of upcoming trips and meetings with staff.

One item of interest was setting up a Go Fund Me account to raise money for our Puerto Rico Shriners who are in desperate need of help from the hurricane. We are planning for me as the Imperial Potentate to visit them soon for a day to show support and to help in raising money. It will need to be a day trip in and out as conditions are so bad there are not even any hotel rooms available. This is a time where brother love, and support needs to be shown and exemplified. It was after 5PM before I left for home and my normal hour and a half trip took 3 hours. Got home after 8 PM.

November 17, 2017 - Friday

Arrived at work at 7:30 for a full day of catching up. A highlight was our new 2018 high cube moving van showing up. Now that's a nice truck. It was a busy trucking day and I had a bunch of mail and correspondence to do. Of course, the never-ending duty to send thank you cards to all the kind people who welcome, and support Anne and I continues. We need more hours in the day. We approved the final design of the Holiday card today, it will now go to production, it turned out very nice, we are both proud of it. It follows our theme of Shriners Globally, and it fits in just right. It is complete with us in a picture with our International Patient Ambassadors.

This was also the day to put up all the Christmas decorations at the house, really the only day available for us to do so. All of the decorations were moved from storage to the house, Anne put them up, and the empty boxes were returned back to the warehouse. This was a busy day for both of us. Anne stayed up half the night working on it and was exhausted.

November 18, 2017 - Saturday

Back to work at 7:30 to get the crews out. Jason had the day off. Anne spent the day still finishing up decorating the house. By noon I was home and began my "honey do" list that will probably never be completed. Hard to keep up with this when you're home so few days. Anne and I tried to work in some shopping time with the holidays coming up, again, not enough hours in the day.

November 19, 2017 - Sunday

Finally, a day to get an extra hour sleep in the morning. Washed Anne's car and checked it out for her upcoming trip to Atlanta. Jason and Avery came over for lunch and Jason helped me with a couple of things around the house. David and Marie Angie came over in the evening for a while. We have to squeeze in some family time every chance we get, it was nice.

November 20, 2017 - Monday

Again, a full day at work, but had several errands to run just to catch up on many things. Spent at least half the day running around in the car. Worked on my visit to

Puerto Rico again and now looks like it will not be possible until December. I did the hard pack job for Bolivia that needed to be done in carry-on bags only for 5 days, this was a challenge for sure. Had to schedule my flights separately to save money, that means checked bags will not follow you, oh well. International travel to support our growing global membership is so important. I'm glad Imperial Sir Ed and I are making this historic trip to help Bolivia reach its 300 members needed to become a Temple. We as an organization need to concentrate on this more.

November 21, 2017 - Tuesday

After spending a couple hours in the office, I headed to the airport for my flight to Atlanta, then to Sao Pablo, Brazil and then on to Santa Cruz, Bolivia. Had to fly north to Atlanta first to go south, yep that's Delta. The flight to Sao Paulo was good, slept about 5 hours, not bad.

November 22, 2017 - Wednesday

Arrived at 6 AM in São Paulo and then needed to work my way through security again to get on my next non-connected flight. This proved to be harder than expected with the language barrier.

Fortunately, a Delta representative came by and was able to confirm with TSA that I had a ticket even though I did not have a paper one and it did not show as confirmed on my phone. I proceeded to my gate and confirmed I was at the right place and showed the gate agent my unconfirmed ticket on my phone. I was told no problem.

Well, when I went to board there was a problem and I was not allowed on the plane. I was told I needed to go to the Brazilian Federal Police office in the airport to confirm I could board. Now I was afraid I would miss my flight. At the Federal Police office, I found the one man who spoke a little English. He felt like everything would be ok and escorted me back to the gate. At the gate they checked my Passport, Brazil Visa, Bolivia Visa, and reservation, but there was still a hold up from the airline supervisor. The Federal Policeman, who was very nice, said, "I am going to TRY and help you." He left with one of the gate agents. As the doors were about to close the gate agent returned to inform me I could board without a boarding pass and she told me to just go find a good seat. Wow, this was a confused mess, but I was so happy to get on the plane. They had to pull some strings to make it happen I believe. I was feeling thankful, in a Foreign country. One thing I thought about though, had I got stranded here, I had good Shriner friends in Brazil nearby who would help me. Great to be a Shriner! The reason I purchased a non-connecting flight was it saved over a thousand dollars, glad it worked out in the end.

I landed in Bolivia and was greeted by two Shriners as I approached the baggage area, the Potentado and an Aide, along with an airport security man. We were taken to the front of the customs line, and then to the front of the baggage X-ray line and we were out the door in five minutes. Now that's service. They drove me to the hotel, Los Tajibos, a five-star hotel, my room was waiting. Ed had already arrived and came down to greet us. They gave us a couple of hours to rest and then picked us up. They took us for a tour of the area and out to Tommy's brothers retreat out in the middle of nowhere. Wow what a place in the middle of this hard to get to, rugged dirt road area. What we found was this paradise he built. Red brick road leading up to it, beautiful building with sleeping rooms and an enormous outdoor area overlooking this incredible pool that overlooking the hills, mountains, and a small lake.

We then returned back to town where we met up with others for a lovely dinner of great food and wine. They were truly happy Ed and I had made the trip and we were so excited to be here on the occasion of the Ceremonial that should put them over the 300 needed to become a Shrine Temple. History in the making. Time for bed, haven't seen one in two days.

November 23, 2017 - Thursday

Ed and I had breakfast at the hotel and then were picked up at 9:30 by Tommy and taken to a small airport for our flight to San Jose'. We were flying in a small six passenger, twin engine turbo prop plane about 300 miles away. It took one hour, we landed in a small grassy field of an old airport that was closed. We were greeted by several enthusiastic Shriners and ladies! This is building membership at the grass roots level. The Mayor of the town was also there to greet us. We were then transferred to cars and headed an hour away where we visited a church and monument in the mountains that was spectacular; built next to tremendous rock formations. In the 90's there was a flood that washed out the railway bridge causing a train wreck that killed 15 people. The monument and church were built by hand in honor of the Virgin Mary for saving all of the lives that made it through the flood and accident. This was very beautiful.

We returned back to town and met several Shriners and the Mayor for lunch at a local outside diner. Here we had homemade food and great discussions pertaining to this small poor town and how it had a vision to grow and to become a tourism destination. At the conclusion of lunch, we were taken to a Music School for children the town had just built.

The town was investing in its children by creating the music school for children where they practice for three hours per day in addition to their regular schooling. Upon entering this small theater, the children, ages 9 to 17 began playing. It was incredible, I could not believe what I was hearing it was so good. A local man, now 24 years old went to college, he received his master's in music and then returned to his village to teach children how to play string instruments. One man has made such a difference, these kids' lives are forever changed. I would imagine all of them could now get a scholarship for college, they are just that good. This visit to the Music School was unexpected and considered to be a top highlight of this trip. Truly amazing.

We then proceed to the old church in town that was built in 1748. This old structure was built well and is still used to this day. It is a large facility also including school rooms and a museum. An interesting item is a sun dial clock dated 1748 in the middle of the courtyard that still keeps time just fine.

It was now time for our group to head back to the grassy field runway to board our small plane and to head back to Santa Cruz. With the engines running, we had dogs jumping at the plane. The pilot had to get out and chase the dogs off, waving his hat at them they ran off, so we could go. Once we started down the grass runway, the dogs chased us until we took flight, we laughed and laughed.

Imperial Sir Ed and I had a quite dinner at the hotel talking about the Shrines future with International Development. We have a lot of work to do but the opportunity is huge, and all of the people are so excited and friendly.

November 24, 2017 - Friday

Friday morning was free, it was nice to rest. Illustrious Sir Michael Gordon of Almas Shriners joined us on this day. We were picked up at 11AM, did a little touring and then went to a steak house for lunch that included some other Shriners. The food was really good. We also stopped by a couple of local stores to see some of the locally made tourist items. We were then taken back to the hotel. Later we were picked up for a 5PM meeting with the President of the Community Civic organization of Santa Cruz. This was a nice event for about 30 people where we had coffee and pastries and information about the area was presented. The President is a Shriner.

Our next stop was the Grand Lodge of Bolivia. Beautiful building that included 12 Lodge rooms within this large building in downtown Santa Cruz. This is the location of the Shrine Ceremonial tomorrow. After our tour, Ed, Michael, and I returned to the hotel where we had dessert only for dinner, we were still full from the big lunch we had.

November 25, 2017 - Saturday

This is the big day, the Bolivia Shriner Ceremonial. They have enough paid and voted on petitions to put them over the top of the 300 to get their Charter, just need them all to show up. We arrived at the Bolivian Grand Lodge about 10AM and things were really rolling already. They had a Grand Entrance for me into the Lodge Room and then they brought in the candidates. A few were no shows but over 80 showed up. They will have to catch the rest later, they have already paid. They did an excellent job on the Ceremonial, so neat to see a bunch going through all at once. At the conclusion, we took many pictures and did a I AM - RU video to post on the web.

We then moved to the dining room where the ladies of the new Nobles and some of their children were waiting. A few speeches were given, a representative from the Mayor's office presented some Proclamations and extra nice label pin. Then we had the Fezzing Ceremony where the wives Fezzed the new Nobles. This was followed by a great lunch. After lunch, we were all excused until the Gala that evening at a nice hotel.

At the Gala, everyone was dressed up for this special occasion. A professional interpreter, McGill, was provided to me for the evening, he shadowed me everywhere I went, it certainly helped with the language challenge. He shared with me that his favorite interpreting job was with Patch Adams. (Robin Williams) He worked with Patch, as he called him during the filming of the Patch Adams movie. He shared with me that Robin Williams never used a computer or a cell phone, and that he was always wired up and very brilliant. He says he always remembers the scene with Patch Adams in the hospital with the sick kids wearing a red clown nose. Patch had told him, "If you always have a red nose in your pocket you can make anyone smile." McGill told me he had four with him if I need to use one at any time. I then told him I love that scene in the Patch Adams movie as well and have used that clip many times in my presentations.

A violin band played at the beginning and it was so good, we were given a CD of their music. A presentation by the Grand Master was made of Medallions to certain individuals in recognition of the 300th Anniversary of Bolivian Masonry. I was so honored to have received one. It was soon time for dinner to be served and it was really good. Pictures were taken at each of the tables with the new members and their ladies, it was a special night for the ladies. We even used the red clown noses a few times to get the people smiling.

The night closed out with more presentations of Honorary Memberships, Bolivian made cutting boards, and some trophies. What a spectacular evening it was, we wrapped up about midnight. Going to have to sleep fast, have to get up early and head back to Orlando for a few hours before heading out again.

November 26, 2017 - Sunday

Had to get up at 6 AM for breakfast and then off to the airport. I will not arrive back home till 6AM the next morning, going to be a long day. Good byes were made with Tomi and Odean, they have done a great job putting this event on and taking care of us as visitors. So, PROUD of what they are doing, they really get it and I know they will be successful building Bolivia Shriners.

At the airport, it was arranged for us to meet one of our patients, Joel, who was returning from Shriners Hospitals for Children - Cincinnati where he had some ear reconstruction done.

Joel, about eleven years old, was born missing both arms. So, he was also a patient at our Tampa Hospital. I was anxious to meet him as we stood in the hallway of the airport. Then he appeared, walking towards us, a big smile on his face. His mother walking beside him, and he was wearing a prosthetic arm on his right side. As he approached me he extended his bright neon green plastic hand to me to shake my hand. I was in disbelief; his confidence and maturity was tremendous. As he shook my hand he thanked me for changing his life. The eyes of his Mother and me filled with tears as she too thanked all of us Shriners in attendance. I gave both Joel and his Mother an Imperial Potentates pin. His Mother through a translator expressed how honored they were to meet the top Shriner in the world as Shriners have made Joel's life complete and functional. Joel then put on a set of arms, one on each side and showed us how they worked together. As we were leaving I gave the Mother three more Imperial Potentates Pins. She nearly began to cry as she said, "that is the perfect number," now each person in our family can have one.

Ed and Mike were on the same flight back to America, my flight was a few hours later going back thru São Paulo and then on to Orlando. My experience in São Paulo was better this time, I stopped by to see my buddies in the Brazilian Federal Police Office and my connections worked out fine, although I was nervous till I got on the plane.

November 27, 2017 - Monday

The plane arrived right on time into Orlando International Airport at 6AM. I got my bags, headed home, unpacked, repacked, took a shower and headed to work. Who has time to sleep, just too much to do. I caught up on things at work. I'm so fortunate to have staff to cover things as I am on this Imperial Potentates journey.

That evening beginning a 5PM we had a 2018 Convention meeting that lasted until 7:30. We reviewed and expanded on our plans for the upcoming convention in Daytona Beach. At this meeting, we decided to have a Holiday Thank You party for all of the Chairman and Vice Chairmen of the convention corp. It was decided to have it at the home of Anne and me on Dec 20. We will be expecting about 100 people. Whew, we got some extra work to do quick. At the completion of the meeting, I jumped in the car and drove to Tampa for an important meeting the following morning at 8AM. When I arrived at the Doubletree and checked in, that bed sure looked good. It had been 41 hours since I saw a bed and I was ready for some sleep.

November 28, 2017 - Tuesday

Our meeting started at 8AM for the purpose of discussions with Andreas, the Dean of the Medical School in Nicosia, Cyprus that I had met a few months ago. Dr. Diaz along with several SHC staff members were present for discussions that primarily revolved around funding and how we could possibly get some European Grants. The meeting went very well.

During the afternoon, I caught up on other tasks around headquarters that need attention. By 4PM I was on my way back to Orlando to meet Anne for dinner. Seems like I have been running a Marathon, well, actually maybe I have, an International Marathon.

November 29, 2017 - Wednesday

This day was spent at J&J Metro Moving, catching up on things and spending some time with the employees there. A couple of SHC conference calls split the day up. That evening Anne spent some time with the kids and I went to the 2018 kickoff meeting for Bahia Shriners held downtown Orlando. They went over plans of the remodeling of the new building, upcoming events and the clothing for 2018. And, of course, we had to do an I AM - RU Committed to Membership video. At the conclusion of the meeting, a few of my buddies and I had a couple of drinks and a cigar out on a patio. It was really nice to spend some time with some of my Bahia friends.

November 30, 2017 - Thursday

This was another partial day at J&J Metro and Shrine conference calls. Jason and I went to tour the remodeling of the new Bahia Shriners location. Much smaller but going to be very nice and at a great location. They have already done a lot of work and the hope is to have it up and running in about 60 days. When we left there, we visited the graves of my Mom and Dad. We need to get back with some new flowers for them.

That evening we ate at home and packed. For Anne it's a three-day trip to ZOR Shriners in Wisconsin for a Ceremonial, for me it's a ten-day trip, the Wisconsin one plus seven more days going to the Philippines. Packing for ten days takes a little extra. Ahhh, get to sleep in my own bed again, two nights in a row. Whoopee!

"It is by example that we help others grow in character."
GARY BERGENSKE

Chapter Six
December 2017

December 1, 2017 - Friday

Both of us, up early and ready to go to the airport. Off to Appleton, Wisconsin where we are renting a car and driving to Plover, WI. I have my ZOR Fez with me along with my ZOR Cheese Head Fez and cheese tie they presented me in Daytona Beach, this will be fun. All of the people here are always so supportive of us, it will be great to be with them. I have been an Associate Member at Zor for ten years. For December, the weather even looks mild for our trip.

We had a really good conference call at the airport in Orlando before we left with John, Jessica, and the Exec Team of DeMolay International regarding our involvement with the implementation of their Centennial Plaza in Kansas City. In August, the Imperial Divan voted to participate in this DeMolay Plaza by purchasing the "Editorial Without Words" statue that is incorporated into it. The agreements have now been signed and it is time to start an awareness campaign on this project and to also create even more awareness to encourage people to purchase bricks there. For me it's an honor to be in this position when this is all taking place.

I am impressed what DeMolay does for young men and am very supportive of their efforts. But most importantly, our Board decided to dedicate this statue in the DeMolay Plaza to Imperial Sir Jack Jones. Jack was a mentor and support person for me long before I was an Imperial Officer, as I served with him on the Imperial Membership Committee. Furthermore, Jack and I were both from Florida and spent a lot of time together, I encouraged him at a private dinner with Anne to consider taking on the role of Imperial Potentate when Imperial Sir Terry McGuire passed away. After our discussions he decided to do it and he was ever so successfully. He often mentioned to me that he would never forget that dinner and my request for him to consider being the Imperial Potentate.

I served as his Marshal when he was Imperial Potentate and had the pleasure of appointing him as the Chairman of the Imperial Membership Committee for the 2017-2018 year. This position was a challenge we were both so excited about with our plans to roll out the new I AM - RU Committed to Membership Program. His unexpected, untimely, tragic death took away his ability to be with us, but his leadership and inspiration to so many has kept him alive in our hearts and in our push for success with the I AM - RU Program. It is going to be so special for me personally to carry the torch to complete the DeMolay Centennial Plaza in Jacks name and in the name of Past Imperial Potentate, Dad Frank Land, the founder of DeMolay. This project will truly be one of my favorites this year, in honor of Jack.

We arrived in Appleton's small airport and proceeded to get our rental car. Get this, a brand-new Dodge Charger for $13.41 per day. What a deal! They are over stocked on cars in the area. We arrived at the hotel after about an hour drive and checked in. We then went to one of those nice small-town restaurants for a good dinner with the ZOR Divan, Grand Master, and their ladies. After dinner and a short stop at the hospitality room it was time for bed.

December 2, 2017 - Saturday

This is going to be a full, busy day as we have a Ceremonial to bring in 24 new Shriners. It started out by setting up Anne's First Lady's Project items for sale. (They sold nearly $1400.00 worth) Then it was time for the beginning of the Ceremonial in a public forum. The Ritual Divan did a great job with their work and it was enjoyed by all. The combined men's and ladies' luncheon was excellent as about 170 were in attendance.

The afternoon included the Arch Degree, a Parade of Glory where the Clubs and Units donated money. Announcements were made, and it was here that I sported my Cheese Head Fez and tie to everyone's pleasure. Wearing this Custom Cheese-ware I announced that Green Bay Packer Brett Favre would be inducted into the EWSG Hall of Fame. This brought a round of applause. The afternoon concluded with a touching story from a 78-year-old former Shriners Hospitals for Children patient.

The banquet that evening highlighted all of the new Nobles and their Ladies. In my closing remarks, I thanked all of the ladies for what they do to help our Fraternity and Philanthropy. I then told a patient story about Shelby, a young girl Anne and I met in our Sacramento Hospital.

The highlight for me and the entire group was presenting an Imperial Potentates MEDALLION to a member of this Temple of which I have been a member for 10 years. After I explained the high significant of this award, I called upon Past Grand Master and Noble Joe Harker to receive it. The audience went into a standing ovation for Joe who very humbly received it.

The rest of the evening was spent with a drink in the hospitality room, and then packing and preparing for our 2 AM wake up call.

December 3, 2017 - Sunday

Yes, short night, the alarm went off at 2 AM and we were on the road by three for our hour ride back to the airport to turn in the rental car. As we walked out through the hotel lobby there was a group of Shriners who got up to tell us goodbye. Truth be known, I don't think they had been to bed yet, but who's asking? Our flight at five was on time and we were off.

Anne was heading back to Orlando and I was off to Manilla, Philippines. I had twenty-three hours of actual air time ahead of me with the flight time and time changes I will arrive in Manilla tomorrow evening (Monday) at 10 PM. Going to be a long ride. At the Atlanta airport, I said good bye to Anne for a week again. She was glad she was not going with me as there was lots to do at home getting ready for Christmas and a party at our house for 100 people coming up soon.

December 4, 2017- Monday

The flight from Atlanta to Seoul, South Korea was long, a fourteen-hour non-stop flight that landed at 3AM eastern time, or 4PM local Korean time. I was now half way around the world. I had a two-hour layover, and the airport had to be one of the biggest and nicest I've ever been in. By flight time at 6:30 PM, it was already dark on a Monday evening. This flight was on a Boeing 747-400, the biggest plane I have ever been on. This plane actually had two floors of seating and was extremely nice, it was on a Delta partner, Korean Airlines. I arrived into Manila at 10 PM local time, a full half day ahead of the time back home.

Several Shriners met me inside the security area of the airport with a large sign that said, "Welcome Imperial Potentate, Gary Bergenske." They presented me with a Lei of flowers. We got through security and immigration very quickly as they got me right to the front of the line. Outside a Jaguar Sedan Limousine waited for me along with two motorcycle police to escort us to the hotel. The wild ride through the city full of traffic was an adventure with the police escort. We arrived at the Diamond Hotel where they had a large suite reserved for me overlooking the Manila Bay. The bed looked good as again it had been over forty hours since I had seen one.

December 5, 2017 - Tuesday

Our delegation of six from the United States were up for an 8AM breakfast in the hotel restaurant. We had Jerry Gantt, Peter Diaz, John McCabe, Ed Slavish and Dr. Ono, and me here for these meetings of future Shriners healthcare in the Philippines. During the morning, we visited a public hospital with 600 beds, however they had 1105 inpatients registered. People were lined up on beds everywhere in the hallways. The Shriners here had made arrangements to pay for the remodeling of an area designated for burns, and their Temple name was the on the wall as the sponsor of this area. It was done very nicely in this old hospital.

After lunch, we visited the General Hospital where the Shriners were being offered a similar opportunity to remodel an area for pediatric orthopedics and be able to get their name on this project as well. This looked to be a good opportunity and offered a way for Shriner referrals to have priority in getting into a bed.

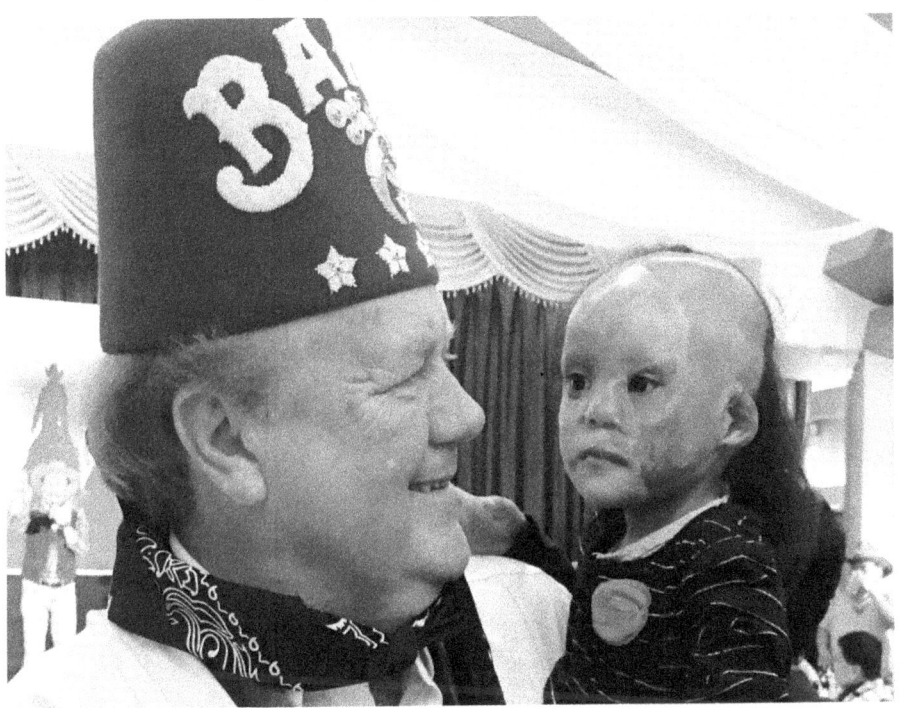

On this evening, they had the Chief Rabbans party and it was a hit full of fun. With about 500 Shriners and ladies present for dinner, bull riding, singing, and fellowship everyone had a good time. They had three patients in attendance, and I became very attached to Clowe, a young female burn survivor. At three years old, she buddied right up to me and let me hold her as much as I wanted. We did an I AM - RU video with this large crowd and also a video of all of them singing the song "Blowing Bubbles," a song they all learn before becoming a Shriner. It was exciting to watch!

December 6, 2017 - Wednesday

After breakfast, it was time to load up our bags for a flight to Davao, Philippines to meet with members of Agila Shriners. We had a police escort to the airport and then again once we arrived in Davao from the airport to the hotel. When we arrived at the hotel, we had lunch with the local Divan while we waited for our room to get ready. During lunch, we were measured for Barongs that were going to be custom made for us. We would wear these on the formal evening coming up.

After lunch, we were taken to see a piece of property the Agila Shriners had purchased to build a hospital on. The sight was not good and was not in a good location or close to another hospital. More importantly, we were not here to talk about spending money to build a hospital, but rather to look at ways we could help children more efficiently. We then proceeded to a restaurant, the Vikings, for dinner. At their spectacular buffet they had so many options. It was then back to the hotel for some rest.

December 7, 2017 - Thursday

Our three-hour morning meeting with Temple members and Doctors got very intense as there were some who thought we were there to talk about building a hospital. This was not the case, we were there to talk about taking care of more kids in more places in the world, efficiently, and that did not include spending money on a structure. By the end of the meeting most understood. We had lunch at one of the Doctors homes where they were celebrating his Mothers 88th Birthday.

After lunch, we proceeded to the hospital that had a pediatric orthopedic ward where the local Shriners were paying $100.00 towards each club foot child's surgery. Over 100 were treated this year due to the Shrine Temples support. This was a very crowded hospital too; however, they were expanding, and the Shriners were to get a new larger area. Here in this crowded, busy hospital half way around the world hung the Imperial Potentates picture, I was proud to be a part of these efforts to help children and so surprised to see my picture.

After our tour, we attended a hospital Christmas party for the club foot patients sponsored by the local Shriners. We all attended and enjoyed the kids and the entertainment. Following the party, we loaded up and headed to the cleft lip and pallet clinic the Shriners had associated with. It was a small office with a "Smile Train" sign out front. We spoke of ways the Shriners could help more and also take over the signage and sponsorship of the clinic. It appeared it would be very reasonable to do so.

We then headed back to the hotel to change into our new Barong shirts and to go to the Agila Shriners party at another hotel. The event was good with plenty of entertainment, food, and drink. Of course, we did another I AM - RU Committed to Membership video and one of them singing "Blowing Bubbles." By the time the party was over we were all whipped. With the busy schedule, we were keeping and the 13-hour time change, it was catching up with us.

December 8, 2017 - Friday

Right after breakfast we had an extra half hour, so we all took a Jeep-nee ride around the local area. It was a fun ride but soon to warm out. After arriving back at the hotel, we loaded up for a ride to the Tim Tebow CURE Hospital. It was the nicest hospital we had been at in the Philippines and they were doing great work. After discussions, we found out this was yet another place to send Shrine pediatric orthopedic patients for a reasonable cost. Many doors seemed to be opening up to reasonably take care of more kids without building a hospital. This was a special visit for me as I have met Tim Tebow a few times when he played for the Gators and have been to his foundation office in Jacksonville, Florida for discussions. Shriners has a relationship with Tim as his foundation and has provided "Timmy's Playrooms" in some of our Shriners Hospitals.

We went to lunch at the Waterfront Hotel, a beautiful hotel on the water with a great view. The food was excellent here. After lunch, it was back to the hotel for a quick one-hour meeting on our thoughts from our visit. All positive information and very doable. All except building a hospital and all in the room understood.

We then changed into coat and tie and headed to a Lodge public installation at Madayaw Lodge No. 403, where the son-in-law of the President of the Philippines would be installed as the Worshipful Master. The daughter of the President was in attendance and she is the current Mayor of Davao City. The installation although long, four hours, was good. From here we proceeded to the Convention Center for a large banquet in honor of the new Worshipful Master with a few hundred in attendance. The food and Scotch flowed smoothly while a five-piece band entertained us. Again, it was a long day, the bed in the hotel was good to see.

December 9, 2017 - Saturday

Again, we were up early, had breakfast, and were off to the airport to return to Manila. With our Police escort, back entrance into the airport security, and help with baggage and tickets, it was a breeze. We were soon in an airport lounge waiting on our flight. We said good-bye to the local Shriners and boarded our plane.

When we arrived in Manila everyone with the exception of me continued on to their next flight out of the country. The Mabuhay Shriners were waiting on me and we had a police escort back to the hotel. That evening I had dinner with their newly formed Jester Court and this was enjoyable listening to them talk about building their new Court. Soon it was time to go to bed.

Today a short six-minute version on the I AM - RU Committed to Membership Presentation I did at the Imperial Session came out from Headquarters on Social Media. This is yet another attempt to raise the awareness and to inspire nobles to turn in petitions. Our goal of 12,000 new members this Shrine year needs a boost, hopefully this will help.

December 10, 2017 - Sunday

The last day of this trip had arrived. I had breakfast with three of the local Shriners and then they took me to the airport. Yes, we had a police escort all the way to the airport, awesome. They know how to take care of an Imperial Potentate for sure. As we went through the airport we saw Miss Universe who was also flying out this day. Security again was a breeze as they just whisked me right through.

This is going to be another 40-hour day returning home. I'll get to sleep in my own bed next, whoopee! I lose all the hours I gained going back home

December 11, 2017 - Monday

Was a day to work at J&J Metro, a lot to catch up on after being out of the country for over a week. Adjusting to the 13-hour time Change was also taking a toll on sleeping. Christmas is just around the corner, but it sure didn't seem like it as being on the road so much defiantly keeps you occupied. This was almost a normal day at home.

December 12, 2017 - Tuesday

Another day at home, wow, two in a row. The day was filled with Shrine conference calls though. So many good things are happening, I'm so proud of the people working around me in every area. In the evening, I got my bags packed for an early trip to Tampa for meetings.

December 13, 2017 – Wednesday

Up at 5AM and out the door by six, headed to Tampa. At ten we meet with the President of Henry Repeating Arms, they make the Henry Rifles. He was there to present me with a new Shriners International rifle, serial number 1, to be placed in the Shriners Memorabilia room at Shrine Headquarters. This is a beautiful 22 rifle that actually goes on sale this same day to the public. We did several pictures and videos, both in the memorabilia room and the Imperial Potentates office. We then went to lunch along with John Piland to celebrate this great new partnership. During the afternoon, there was plenty of work to catch up on with numerous departments at headquarters.

December 14, 2017 - Thursday

Into the Shrine office early today. Our Imperial Potentate and First Lady Christmas Cards have arrived. The bulk of them were in the mail, but a 150 were delivered to me for use by Anne and me for ones we wanted to personally send out.

Headquarters closed at 11AM today for the annual Shriners Headquarters Holiday and Awards Party. It was held in downtown Tampa at the Hilton Hotel. Anne drove over from Orlando to join me for this occasion. With over 400 guests it was a great event. During my talk I presented Laurie Spieler with an Imperial Potentates MEDALLION for living her life in a way that represents my personal quote of "People will forget what you say, and forget what you do, but will forever remember how you make them feel." Laurie was really surprised, and she received a standing ovation as she accepts the award. This was a fun party as many were presented awards for their years of service and they all enjoyed attending.

After the party Anne and I each drove our cars back to Orlando. I went first to J&J Metro and spent a couple of hours addressing Imperial Potentates Christmas cards. Anne and I then met for dinner with a couple of the kids before going home to unpack and repack for our flight out early the next morning.

December 15, 2017 - Friday

The alarm went off at 4:30 AM, we jumped up to get ready for our early flight to South Carolina for the Shrine football game there. The weather is to be cold there, so we loaded up on warm clothes. We arrived in South Carolina, were picked up by Shriners and made our way to the Marriott Hotel in Spartanburg. Anne and I had a nice lunch there at the hotel. After lunch was a quick meeting with the game committee.

The evening was the players banquet with nearly 500 people in attendance. It was a wonderful evening of fellowship, recognition of the players, and a good program. I was awarded the "Walt Disney Award" by the Football Committee, this caught me by surprise, I'm very grateful to have received it. After the banquet, Imperial Sir Kenny Craven along with our wives, Anne and Jennifer visited three hospitality rooms. It was obvious this was a well-run game and the nobility was engaged in making it the best they could. It was a pleasure to be here.

December 16, 2017 - Saturday

The morning began with a men's and ladies' breakfast with several of the Shrine couples in attendance. At the men's there were 10 of us, most of them were near or over 50 years as a Shriner. There was a lot of laughter as we talked about the good ole times they had in the past. There was further discussion on what the future of the Shrine holds, it was interesting to hear their take on where our beloved fraternity was headed, they were concerned.

By 10 AM we were on our way to the football field where we felt so fortunate as the sky was blue and sunny with a temperature in the mid 50's. A "Play 60" event was set up and had many kids in attendance. Also, there were several NFL Legends who spent time with the kids and did autographs, including 1980 Heisman Trophy winner, George Rodgers. A few of them even had Super Bowl rings they let the kids hold. We did a Facebook Live video that was viewed by a bunch of people. We then had lunch at the stadium.

The pre-game time included mid field activities including presenting the Game Junior King and Queen, two adorable patients of Shriners Hospitals and the introduction of the players. The game was good with some great players. I was able to participate in a couple of TV interviews.

The evening was spent at Hejaz Shriners Temple as we attended the Director Staffs Christmas Party. They have a nice Temple, a former Country Club they can be proud of. The party was nice, but by 10 PM we were ready to head back to the hotel to pack and get some sleep for an early departure back to Orlando in the morning. This proved to be a great day of awareness and fundraising for Shriners Hospitals.

December 17, 2017 - Sunday

Another early morning as we got up to finish packing and to get ready for our 7:30 AM ride to the airport. We arrive back in Orlando by midafternoon. I need to get Anne to the house, unpack, repack, and drive to Tampa for a 6:30 PM dinner. Although all travel related this was a long busy Sunday.

By the time I arrived in Tampa I had several calls from Board members who were stranded at the Atlanta airport. There was a fire and the entire airport was without electricity. Some of them had been stuck on their plane for hours on the runway with no way to unload. All stores, restaurants, etc. were closed as there was no electric. Hundreds of flights were being canceled. By 8PM all seven of them had made it out of the airport and were on the way to a hotel. Flights for the following day were already being canceled as well and it soon became clear they were not going to make it to Tampa for our important meeting on strategic planning for the hospital system. We decided we would try doing a conference call meeting starting in the morning.

As I reflected back on the day and our travel, I started to do a timeline of the day. Looks like Anne and I made it through the Atlanta airport today about 30 minutes prior to the closing down of the airport. Feeling Blessed right now.

December 18, 2017 - Monday

The Atlanta group had made plans to get to Yaarab Shriners in the morning. They were start our conference call with the rest of the Board in Tampa starting at 8:30 AM. We were doubtful this was going to work based on the importance of this meeting and the need for good discussion, but we had to try. By afternoon we were convinced this was working much better than expected. We were making good progress and were running ahead of schedule as far as time was concerned.

We completed the meeting, had dinner and head for the hotel. Turned out to be a good day and we felt we accomplished a good amount of business despite the challenges.

December 19, 2017 - Tuesday

We again started at 8:30 with a conference call. Our strategic planning was going well as we focused on how we would restructure our hospital system to; 1) see more kids, 2) in more places, 3) more efficiently. We found a need to repurpose 4 of our hospitals, and to find a way to have more locations in the form of clinics, rehab, tele-health, etc. At 11:30 we had a called meeting to present ideas on legislation that would be needed to coincide with our thoughts to make this all possible. It passed. Now would begin the work on how to present it to the nobility for passage at the Imperial Session.

After lunch, I worked with several people on different projects I had going on at Headquarters. By midafternoon I was back in the car and headed down I-4 to Orlando.

I am a member at Eola Lodge 207 in Orlando and attended Lodge this evening for a special event. On this evening, a dedication was made. My Lodge brothers dedicated a picture of me wearing my Imperial Potentates Fez and my Masonic Shrine Apron. (The apron was one I purchased as part of the Imperial Potentates Project for the year.) This picture was then hung in the lobby of our lodge in honor of me achieving the high position of "Imperial Potentate." I was overwhelmed with appreciation and am forever grateful of being recognized by my peers. Outstanding night, thank you Eola Lodge #207.

December 20, 2017 - Wednesday

The first half of the day I spent at J&J Metro catching up on things. After lunch, I headed home as Anne and I had a lot to do to prepare for 60 people coming to the house for dinner. We had invited the Chairman and Vice Chairmen plus their spouses of the Convention Corporation to say thank you and to update them on the 2018 Convention. Anne had the house well decorated for the holiday and everything looked beautiful. I had several things to do in the yard and around the house too. Soon the caterer arrived along with the bartender, and before you knew it the house was full of guests.

It was a nice evening, everyone had a good time. Most importantly, I hope our guests knew how much we appreciate their help. This Team of men and women have done so much with regards to putting on two consecutive Imperial Sessions. They have gone above and beyond for Anne and me. A Temple has not done two Imperial Sessions in a row for 70 years and Bahia Shriners were doing it high fashion. The night was a great success with wonderful friends.

December 21, 2017 - Thursday

The entire day was spent at J&J Metro working on catching up on business there. There was a lot to do based on being away so much. At 6PM the office staff of J&J Metro arrived at our home for cocktails and food we ordered in. It was a fun time enjoyed by all. This night provided to be a nice chance for Anne and me to thank them all for working extra hard while we have been gone so much with our Shriner duties. As the night ended, we were ready for a good night's sleep.

December 22, 2017 - Friday

Another day at J&J, I was beginning to feel good about catching up on my work there. We closed up at 3PM for the Christmas weekend. David and Marie Angie joined us for dinner at Palma Maria Restaurant for some good food and fantastic dessert. We finished up some Christmas shopping and headed home to turn in early for a good night's sleep. Santa will be coming soon.

December 23, 2017 - Saturday

A day at home to get ready for Christmas. We had family arriving from out of town, but they were in and out as they visited other family too. Jami, Jason, and family moved in for the holiday, great to have them with us. We spent the evening together planning out our next few days. Time to enjoy these grandchildren.

December 24, 2017 - Sunday

Christmas Eve - there was cooking and baking going on all day as preparations were made for our 35 guests who were to arrive for Christmas Day dinner. The yard was spruced up and the pool was vacuumed an extra time in preparation of our guests arriving. It was like a free night, imagine that. Anne and I went to see the movie "Wonder" and then went out to eat, Jared joined us. Our Christmas Season has arrived.

December 25, 2017 – Monday

Christmas Day - A beautiful day out, warm and sunny. There were plenty of presents to open in the morning, Santa was good to all of us. After a nice breakfast, everyone left but Anne and me to visit other family members. Anne and I continued to set things up for the arrival of our dinner guests.

At 5PM they all began to arrive, all 35 of them. Anne had a wonderful Christmas dinner and desserts to die for. Great night with family and friends, the house was full, and it was decorated so nice. We all counted our Blessings on this special day. We give thanks to God for our family, and for keeping us safe in all of our travels. Great day with the grandkids. Got to bed about midnight.

December 26, 2017 - Tuesday

Up early and out of the house to work at J&J Metro. Things are going well there and feel like I'm getting caught up on things after being in town a few days. A group of us all went out to dinner for a family outing, and then back to the house. Still lots of family at the house.

December 27, 2017 - Wednesday

Another day at J&J Metro. Today spent working on Shrine planning for upcoming trips and projects. Had a meeting with personal CPA on planning. That evening Anne and I had dinner out. We came home and began packing for our trip to Pasadena for the Rose Bowl Parade.

December 28, 2017 - Thursday

Very busy day at J&J Metro and my last day there for a while. Planned things out for me being gone most of January. All of the family still in town for the holidays got together for a taco dinner out. After dinner, we had everyone back to the house, Jason and Avery joined us and Avery opened her Christmas presents. It was fun watching our two-year-old granddaughter open things up, so much excitement. Anne and I then got all of our packing done as we had to leave for the airport at 6 AM. A short night of sleep and back on the road again.

December 29, 2017 - Friday

Up at 4:30 and out the door by six for the airport. We were excited to be leaving for Pasadena for the Tournament of Rose's Parade. We had a direct flight to Los Angeles where we were picked up and taken to a hotel in Pasadena. For dinner, we were taken out with all of the float riders including Emily and family, Isabella and family, Kechi and family, (Alec and his Mom went to a Lakers game) And Peter and Vicki. We were joined by several local Al Malaikah Shriners who had worked extra hard planning and implementing our experience to come.

After dinner, we were given a run down on what was going to happen the next three days and it was a busy schedule. Prior to leaving each family was given a gift bag that included information and a blanket. We could not have asked for a better group of people to participate in this parade with us. We are so blessed to have assembled this "Rock Star" group. It was a long day and we were ready for bed.

December 30, 2017 - Saturday

This morning started with breakfast at the hotel with our group and then it was off to Phoenix Decorating where our float was being assembled. This was an experience in itself. What we saw was so impressive, as this facility is building 17 different floats all under one roof, one of those being the Shriners Hospitals for Children one. We were all in awe as we watched each of these floats in its final stages, that of putting on hundreds of thousands of flowers on them.

For our own float seats had to be assigned, flowers were being put on, (over 300,000) and final adjustments were being made. The Tournament of Rose Parade Judges were making their rounds to each float to examine its current state and to interview its top participants. Peter and I had been prepped on what the questions might be and on key statements we wanted to make. The entire amount of time with the Judges was 5 minutes, the time was started with the ringing of a bell and concluded with the bell. I felt like we did a great job with our interview and that the float was looking good. Our float was one of the smaller ones but the theme of our float of *"Caring for Kids Around the World"* coincided well with the parades overall theme of "Making A Difference." Actually, they could not fit better together in my mind. One of the floats had the famous band "Earth, Wind, and Fire" who practiced playing on the "Forum" float. Afterword's they did pictures with Bella and Kechi and her Mom. Yes, they were so excited.

By midafternoon it was time to head back to the hotel to prepare for our evening event, a reception at the Shriners Hospital Medical Center in Pasadena. The reception was well attended by Shriners and their families, patients, and Donors. It started with drinks and finger foods and plenty of conversation.

When the program started each of the patients who were riding on the float, Emily, Alec, Isabella, and Kechi, gave a short speech on what it meant to be a Shriners Hospitals patient and to have the opportunity to ride on the float. When I say each of them did outstanding, that doesn't even begin to say how good they did, each of them did it unscripted from the heart, their talks hit it out of the park! I could not have been prouder of the patients we selected to participate in this Tournament of Roses Parade, each of them represents us so well and they all complement each other.

I closed the evening out with a short motivational talk and an I AM - RU Committed to Membership video. This was a very inspiring evening and the LA Shriners are working so hard on our membership program, super proud of them. We received our clothing to wear on the float and it was really nice, we are going to look awesome. First time for the Shriners float to have all of its participants in matching outfits. An extra little touch. Then it was back to the hotel and to bed early, as we all had to get up early.

December 31, 2017 - Sunday

Up and out of the hotel by 7AM as we headed back down to where the float was being built. This was the Judging day so all of us were dressed up in our space outfits to match Fezzy on the float. When we arrived, the float had transformed into this beautiful flower covered extravaganza. Final touches were being made and a few flowers were being added. It was beautiful.

Soon we all took our places on the float and were strapped in. The animations were started up and the music began to play, it was our turn to be judged. The judges seemed to be really impressed with what we had, they only spend five minutes with each float, so we had to look our best. The competition was tough; we hoped we had a chance for a trophy, but we knew it was not going to be easy. They announce the winners just before the parade starts in the morning, we all said a little prayer that we might have a chance at one.

We headed back to the hotel for lunch and then had a free afternoon. My cousin Matt who I rarely get to see drove an hour to come by and spend some time with me. That was really nice, we had about an hour together before he had to leave.

Our group all had dinner together at 6:30. It was a good meal and we celebrated the New Year early complete with hats and horns. This had to be a night of - early to bed- as we had to get up at 3AM so we could head out for our big day of riding the float. I could not be prouder of the group we assembled for this event or those who were helping us from the local Al Malaikah Shrine. Everything was going along perfectly, what a great feeling.

Gary Bergenske's Shriners Diary - Our Mission – Our Members – and Me

2018

Chapter Seven

January 2018

January 1, 2018 - Monday

NEW YEARS DAY - Talk about an early day, we got up at 3AM and left at 4:30 for our big adventure of participating in the Tournament of Roses Parade. We had a box breakfast and then all of us headed to the parade site. Our float was lined up with all of the other floats waiting for the parade to start. We did numerous family pictures, allowing each rider to have their family all on the float for pictures. They were all so excited! By 7AM those not participating as a rider left and made their way to their seats in the grand stands.

Soon all of us riding on the float took our places and were strapped in for the big event on his beautiful sunny day. A Stealth Bomber flew over escorted by two additional military planes and the parade promptly started at 8AM. The excitement and anticipation was high as our float began to roll down the street. We even got more excited when we found out our float won the prestigious *"Tournament Volunteer Trophy"* for most outstanding floral presentation of the Rose Parade Theme among floats 35 feet and under in length. When this happened, our float was escorted by two people carrying a banner in front of our float for the entire parade.

A Year as the Imperial Potentate of Shriners International

As we passed through the television corner there were thousands of people and hundreds of cameras as we were all waving with smiles from ear to ear. The six and half mile route took us over three hours, Alec and Kechi were recognized by fans all the way as people yelled out their names. By the time we reached the end of the parade it was reported we had been seen by one million people on the parade route and by over fifty-one million people worldwide on TV. How incredible is that.

When the parade concluded we grabbed a quick lunch back at the hotel. We then proceeded to the Rose Bowl for the football game between the Georgia Bulldogs and the Oklahoma Sooners. What a tremendous adventure this was, just being in the Rose Bowl was something special. Many people recognized Alec as we worked our way through the crowds. The game was awesome, the Bulldogs won after double overtime. It was outstanding! Following the game, we all had dinner back at the hotel, packed our bags for an early morning departure, and went to bed. This had to be right up there with one of the best days of our life, we all agreed on this, so awesome. This whole trip was a pleasure as we all got along great and the local Shriners did a fantastic job taking care of us and making sure we were always where we were supposed to be.

January 2, 2018 - Tuesday

Another travel day, we were up early again and handed back to the airport along with Peter and Vicki. After getting through TSA we had breakfast and then boarded our non-stop flight back to Orlando. By the time we got to the house it was after 7PM. Anne was sick with a cold by the time we got home and went straight to bed. It was cold in Florida compared to California. I unpacked and repacked for my trip the following day to Tampa.

January 3, 2018 - Wednesday

After stopping by my office for a couple of hours I headed to Tampa for three days of meetings. Cold and rainy today, not the usual Florida weather.

January 4, 2018 – Thursday

Today was a full day of meetings with a selected group of Shriners, HQ staff, Board of Governor members from different hospitals, and some individuals from some of the different Shriners Hospitals. This was the review of tasks 4 different groups did related to Governess of our Hospitals over the past seven months. Although the day started out slow we eventually began to move along faster and ended the day on schedule. At least half of the participants called in and worked with us by phone.

This was also a big day as our new Corporate Director of Communication and Marketing, Mel Bower arrived for, his first day of work. Although we had a strategic way for him to start, we basically threw that all away and started him on some fast track projects of importance. I believe he is going to fit in well and be a great addition to our Team.

The weather in the Northeast was bad and over 5000 flights were canceled including Anne's to New York City with Jami and McKenna. They rescheduled for February.

January 5, 2018 - Friday

We continued with our group going through the governess items until noon. This proved to be a very good project and we all felt great about what we accomplished. Now, next would be the implementation phase which would be much harder. Much of this will require change and we all now at times change is hard. The group had lunch together and then departed.

My afternoon was spent catching up with many of the different departments at headquarters, following up on different projects I had going. When visiting the staff in the Membership Dept. I learned that Shriners International as an organization ended up the entire year as a "Bronze" winner. This was great news as this had not been accomplished in a number of years. We are crediting in part this success to the "I AM - RU Committed to Membership" Program I rolled out in Daytona Beach. It was great to see some positive results. The awareness for this program has taken us to an all-time high, however it still takes time to implement it around the world. Over all, I couldn't be happier.

Jessica, who I have come to really admire assisted me with my upcoming schedule and planning. She does a great job of assisting the Imperial Potentates Office in a delightful way.

January 6, 2018 - Saturday

Our third day in a row for meetings at Shrine Headquarters started promptly at 8AM. Today's meetings were spent on discussing how the Shriners Hospitals for Children Strategic Planning that was ongoing could be delivered in the upcoming Leadership Seminar along with the many other topics that needed to be discussed. Again, this was done with over half of the participants calling in. By midafternoon we had laid out a proposed agenda for staff to tweak and finalize.

By midafternoon I was driving home, Anne and I had a nice dinner with our friends David and Jan. After dinner it was back to the house where I unpacked my suitcase and repacked it for a 7AM departure to the airport for a flight to Kansas City for a meeting at DeMolay International Headquarters. I spent a total of 10 hours at the house before departing again. Not spending much time at home this year, however it is so rewarding to be in a position to represent such wonderful organizations. What an honor!

January 7, 2018 - Sunday

Up at 5:45 and out the door before 7AM for my flight to Kansas City. I'm actually really excited about this trip to DeMolay Headquarters. We will be signing an agreement between Shriners International and DeMolay International with regards to a Centennial Courtyard they are building in celebration of their upcoming 100th Anniversary in 2019. Shriners will be purchasing the "Silent Messenger" that will be a part of this courtyard and it is being done in honor and in memory of my good friend Imperial Sir Jack Jones. I'm am so honored to be serving as Imperial Potentate right now and to have the honor to represent all Shriners in this meeting. Jack had been a dear friend and mentor to Anne and me for over 20 years prior to his untimely, unexpected death last year. I know that Jack would be so surprised yet honored that this was being done in his name.

I was picked up by Christian, the Executive Director of DeMolay at the Kansas City airport and taken to the hotel to check in. Ron, the Grand Master of DeMolay then joined us and we went for a tour of the DeMolay building. During this tour I took on even more respect for what DeMolay represents and does for young men. I learned much more about Frank S. Land, the founder of DeMolay and later the 1954-55 Imperial Potentate. Much of the memorabilia in the building is personal effects of Imperial Sir Land's and the presence of Shrine items were everywhere. Frank Land and Harry Truman were good friends, both being active in Masonry in the Kansas City area. There are numerous reflections of their friendship in the building including many references to their admiration for each other even when Truman was serving as the President of the United States. They were both members of Ararat Shriners in Kansas City as well.

In the building is a replica of Dad Land's office as it was at the DeMolay headquarter offices when he served as Imperial Potentate. This incredible reflection of what the office of a successful man looked like in the 1950's was amazing, especially one who had served as an Imperial Potentate. In the office is his Imperial Five Star Fez, his Imperial Potentates Flag, his Imperial Potentates Jewel, and several items he received as gifts while serving as Imperial Potentate. In the office as well are numerous autographed pictures that were sent to Imperial Sir Land including Presidents, Generals, actors and more. Being a history buff, I could have spent hours in there.

We spoke of the many ways Shriners and DeMolay complement each other at dinner and how collaboration on this project is so good. We had further conversations on other projects we should be able to work on together, especially in the area of membership. It turned out to be a very productive evening.

January 8, 2018 - Monday

After a quick breakfast at the hotel we were off to the Headquarters of DeMolay. I've been looking forward to this day for a while. The signing of the agreements was on auto pilot, this was just a formality now. The real task for the day was to kick off this collaborative project in a big way to promote the sale of bricks in the courtyard. The production of doing this was going to take place in the iconic office of the Founder of DeMolay, Frank S. Land with myself and the Grand Master of DeMolay being live streamed on Facebook. We both sat behind his desk with pictures and the Imperial Fez of both Imperial Sirs Land and Jones. This was so incredibly done in a historic way to honor two great men. The live feed went great, we delivered a wonderful message of unity, and the agreements were signed, all live of Facebook.

Ron, the Grand Master and myself then did a fireside chat in front of the fireplace in this historic office, it was recorded for future use. We spent an hour talking about many related subjects that involved both of our organizations. These video clips will be used for future projects and promotions after edited. After lunch we did some additional video focusing in on some of the historic and interesting displays within their building. This raw footage of video will be used as well in the future, primarily to show DeMolay members the neat items that are in the building.

My 24 hours of time in Kansas City was up and it was off to the airport again. So much was accomplished in a short 24-hour period, and I believe we met or exceeded all of the tasks on our list. This was truly an honor for me that I enjoyed so much as we recognized two outstanding Past Imperial Potentates who had such an impact on everyone they knew. After my flights, I arrived back home at midnight.

January 9, 2018 - Tuesday

Home in Orlando for the day. Up early and off to work to catch up on things there. Business there going good, staff doing a great job in my absence. They kid me by saying, "What are you coming here for, we got this." Anne and I worked, mostly Anne on getting all of the Christmas decorations down and back into storage.

January 10, 2018 - Wednesday

In Orlando and spent nearly this entire day on planning upcoming Shrine activities, making reservations for airline flights, working on speeches and confirming activities with Shriners Headquarters staff. The day became all-consuming in planning.

January 11, 2018 - Thursday

Last day in Orlando for a couple of weeks. This day was committed to my business, J&J Metro Moving and Storage. Planning and confirming of upcoming activities. Also, the task of pulling together end of year 2017 numbers and info.

I also worked on getting the numbers from the efforts of Mason's and Shriners with regards to raising money for the areas affected by hurricanes this year. It was my mission to help in these areas, by way of an Imperial Potentates pushed to request people to donate money to help our members. With the money being accounted for through a partnership with the Masonic Service Association, things were looking good. The areas we were raising money for were, Texas, Florida, and Puerto Rico. As I was going to San Juan, Puerto Rico in the morning, I wanted to give them a report.

When I got the numbers, I was astonished on how our members had stepped up to the plate. The totals thus far were as follows, Texas - $1,000,000, Florida - $600,000, and Puerto Rico - $400,000, a total of over $2,000,000. This was more than the Masonic Service Association had ever raised before and it was because of the Shriners data base being used as well. I was so proud of our Fraternity when I heard this, to hear how they were helping each other. I was proud to be the first to initiate this program with Shriners.

Then, early in the evening Anne and I attended a cocktail party at one of our company's key accounts, Alegro. Following this we had dinner with all family members living in town at a BBQ restaurant.

January 12, 2018 - Friday

Up at 3:30 AM to begin a long and exciting day. Had a 6AM flight to San Juan, Puerto Rico to visit the Al Rai'e Saleh Shriners there regarding reporting to them on our efforts of raising money to help them. I was also going to talk with them about helping to raise additional relief money because of Hurricane Marie's damage to help them with their members' dues. Many of their members could not even contact them as phone service was down, and mail was undeliverable.

I was picked up by the Potentate and another Shriner who drove us to their Shrine Temple. I was greeted by about 25 enthusiastic Shriners who were happy the Imperial Potentate had come to see them. We first did an I AM - RU video outside their building where they had an I AM - RU banner up, and every single one of them had on an I AM - RU Committed to Membership lapel pin. They were committed and let it be known.

We then proceeded inside the building where introductions were made, stories were told, and gifts were given. Some of the stories were heart breaking, hearing of what they have been through because of the hurricane and of the damage some of them had. They assured me they were resilient and would come back stronger than they were before the hurricane. It was rewarding to hear of their courage, compassion, and commitment to rebuild. I was extremely touched by what I saw and heard here. This was a time of really connecting with members who needed so much help, not only monetarily, but also in inspiration. They needed to know how much we all cared about them.

We all went to a nice lunch together an continued our great discussions. By 3 PM it was time to head back to the airport, my 5 hours of time with them was up. We crammed a lot into those five hours and we all felt better for having done so. It was truly five hours of brotherly love for ones who had experienced tragedy. I was so glad I took the time to come and visit them even if it was only for a few hours. I would have planned to stay longer if hotel rooms were available, but nearly six months after the storm there were none, FEMA workers occupied them working to get this part of the world back together again.

Upon getting back to the Orlando airport I jumped into my car and drove to St Petersburg, FL where for the next 10 days I'd be for meetings and activities related to the East West Shrine Game (and a quick trip to Texas in the middle of all that.) By the time I arrived at my hotel in St Petersburg and settled in it was nearly midnight, a 21-hour day. It was worth every minute to be able to talk with some of our Nobles in Puerto Rico and share with them our concerns for them and their families. The job of the Imperial Potentate is not always easy, but it is so rewarding.

January 13, 2018 - Saturday

Waking up in St. Petersburg Beach at the Tradewinds Resort was nice. We had a meeting that started at 8:30 for Strategic Planning and to finalize the agenda for the Leadership Conference that was to start in a couple of days. The meetings went well. This Board has courage and commitment and is passionate about making change to move our hospital system forward. We want to "serve more kids in more places and preserve the endowment fund." Not an easy task but we have a plan that could do exactly that if properly implemented, but change will be needed. A plan to do more with less, it can be done.

Anne arrived in the afternoon, glad of that. We all went to dinner down the street where we had a private room in the back. Again, a nice evening to kick off our several days of activities. Richard and Judy, our Marshals do such a great job! They look out after every little detail to make things so nice for everyone. We are extremely fortunate to have a couple we like so well to be working beside us.

January 14, 2018 - Sunday

Anne and I were up early and headed up to Shrine Headquarters. We spent some time in my office and then greeted Jon and Kathy who were there to do the Joint Board photos for the Annual Report. We did the Imperial Divan in the Memorabilia Room in front of the wall of Fez's. It looked great and I don't think it has been done before. We then did the Board of Trustees outside in front of the Silent Messenger. It was a cold morning out.

All of us then proceeded to the Shriners Hospitals for Children - Tampa for the annual East West Shrine Game Players visit. This is one of the best events of the year, where Shriners, players, patients and guests gather for fun, fellowship, and lunch. The players were greeted, speeches were made and then the real fun set in. Players and patients then interacted with each other, and both groups left with a memorable day in the now warm weather. I have found over time, that years down the road, the players remember the visit to the hospital much more than they remember the actual football game itself.

We all headed back to the hotel, changed, and went to dinner. We had a nice dinner together in a private room at the hotel that was thoroughly enjoyed. I feel as though we have the most unified Joint Boards since I've been a member, sure hope I'm reading it correctly.

January 15, 2018 - Monday

Another early start as we had hospital strategic planning in the morning, followed by fraternal strategic planning in the afternoon.

We were at a restaurant on this night where we were setup with many tables. Anne and I had at our table, Alec, our national television star along with his mother and two sisters. We also had Jon and Bob, two attorneys who work closely with our Board. It was a wonderful evening as the eight of us enjoyed each other and our good discussions. Alec is such a neat young man. He does a great job on our commercials and is recognized everywhere he goes.

January 16, 2018 - Tuesday

We started a Joint Board meeting at 8AM at the Tradewinds Resort. We moved through a lot of business and made good progress, all in a professional polite manner. It has been a complete pleasure leading the meetings and having everyone getting along so well. You can accomplish so much when everyone is pulling together.

Anne and I had dinner with Peter and Vicki and the leadership of our Springfield and Galveston Hospitals. In addition, our patient superstar from Americas Got Talent, Kechi and her friend joined us. This was another fine night of fellowship where a good time was had, and relationships were built.

January 17, 2018 - Wednesday

Our Leadership Conference began today, we had leadership from every one of our Hospitals in attendance. This was an important meeting as more accountability and responsibility is needed as we work on building a system of Healthcare as opposed to a system of Hospitals. Change is in the air and it's all about, "Treating more Children in more Places with less draw on the endowment." Of course, change can be hard to deal with, we have to work as a team.

After lunch we had had a presentation by Kechi and then she sang for us. A remarkable story filled with miracles by a beautiful young lady. Kechi is so genuine and humble. Personally, I'm so proud of her for all she has accomplished, what an inspiration. And he voice, she knocks it out of the park every time. She has also just done a commercial for us that turned out fantastic.

Following Kechi's presentation Anne and I headed straight to the Tampa airport to head to Waco, Texas. Our flight was ok, but when we got to the airport we were unable to pick up our rental car. Enterprise had already closed. We caught an Uber to our hotel, checked in and went to bed about 11PM. Sometimes you just have to make the best of it.

January 18, 2018 - Thursday

The morning started by catching an Uber back to the airport to pick up our rental car. We then hit a few stores and visited the tourist area of Waco, Magnolia. Then a quick bite to eat and back to the hotel to change so we could attend the Texas Grand Lodge opening session at 1PM. There was some confusion as to what we were to do when we arrived, but it seemed to be sorted out. When the visiting dignitaries were introduced I was not on the list but was invited to introduce myself. Later I was asked to give some remarks; I spoke about how the Shrine helped with the recent hurricane relief for Texas, Florida, and Puerto Rico; to help and assist Mason's and Shriners. The donations were impressive, and the best ever raised with the Shrines help; one million for Texas, $600,000 for Florida, and $400,000 for Puerto Rico. The applause was loud.

We arrived at their Awards Banquet on time and checked in, however our name was not on the list again. Eventually we were told to go on in and just find a table. After we were settled in at a table, we were asked by the Grand Master to sit at the head table, so we did. This was not organized, we felt a little uncomfortable.

One of the awards given was a humanitarian award for our Dr. Barnes from our Houston Hospital. This was an impressive award and Dr. Barnes gave a wonderful acceptance speech. I was then asked to speak too, I congratulated Dr. Barnes and spoke on the greatness of our hospital system and how we have had patients from 176 countries. That's 90% of the countries in the world. Simply amazing, and its all because of the expert medical care we give. After the banquet we went back to the hotel and went to bed early. We had a long day coming up.

January 19, 2018 - Friday

Talk about an early morning, Anne and I were up at 2:30 AM to catch a flight out of Waco to make our way back to Tampa. After we landed in Tampa we went by Shrine Headquarters to catch up on some things there. We then headed back to the Tradewinds Island Resort for a busy afternoon and evening. Once back at the hotel it was a quick change of clothes and back out.

The Joint Boards along with another 50 or so Shriners plus ladies assembled in the silent auction room to initiate a new noble. Mathew MaCrane was a player in the East West Shrine Game and was already a Mason and had petitioned to become a Shriner. Mathew along with his father and grandfather who were already Shriners along with the rest of his family participate and watched Mathew take the obligation of a Shriner. This was such an exciting and unique event; a loud round of applause followed the announcement that he was now a Shriner.

The next event of the day for me was meeting the Hall of Fame inductees in a private room at the Tropicana Stadium to present each of them with a Shriners Tribute Henry Rifle. The President of Henry Rifle was there to assist as his company was donating the rifles. The Hall of Famers; Brett Favre, Willie Roaf, and Gary Huff were all excited to receive them. They also autographed some items and we were able to spend a private half hour talking with them. This is where I also had Brett sign the Cheese Head Fez I was given by Zor Shriners from Madison, Wisconsin. Brett chuckled as he signed it ans said, "I've never signed one of these before." Brett is a fan of Shriners Hospitals, he recently did a TV commercial for us and has visited some of our hospitals. A special experience for me as a lifelong Green Bay Packer fan who grew up in Wisconsin.

Next up was the evenings East West Shrine Banquet. With over 900 in attendance it was the largest banquet in recent memory. It was my honor and privilege to be able to stand on stage to announce and present the three Hall of Famers. This was no doubt one of the highlights of the year for me. I then presented the "Pat Tillman Award" to J. T. Barrett. This award - celebrates a player's achievements and conduct both on and off the field; given to the player who best demonstrates sportsmanship, intelligence, and service. Following this I brought Mathew MaCrane up on stage along with his father and grandfather, so I could introduce the newest Shriner in the world to the audience. Mathew then presented me an East West Shrine Game jersey with my name on it and the number "1".

I closed the banquet out with a motivational talk about Vince Lombardi and the Green Bay Packers; challenging all of the players to use their God given talents along with passion and commitment to find greatness so they could reach an NFL roster. I also talked to them about being good citizens as now everyone was watching their every move. These young players had great opportunity in front of them, I wish them all the best. By the time we got back to the hotel and settled in it was midnight. Wow - this was an exciting 22-hour day, and we were both feeling it, a bit tired. So proud of Anne, she works at this just as hard as I do.

January 20, 2018 - Saturday

By 10 AM we were ready to head to the stadium, it was game day! When we arrived, we spent a couple of hours in the tailgate area greeting people and doing pictures. The weather had warmed up and it was beautiful. The food prepared by Imperial Sir Chris, his son Allen, and their team was fantastic as usual. By 2PM we arrived inside the stadium and were preparing for the pre-game events and introductions. The 93rd East West Shrine Game started at 3PM and was nationally televised on the NFL Network. It was a good game that come down to the final minutes.

After the game we headed back to the hotel and had something to eat. Then the silent auction ended, and it was time to get items picked up and paid for. This conclude over a week of intense days; a lot was accomplished but our team was ready for a day off.

January 21 - Sunday

Anne and I got up, packed our bags, loaded the cars, and headed for Maitland. We grabbed something to eat at Chili's and were back home by midafternoon. Bags were unpacked, laundry done, and the house checked out. We have a couple of days at home before we head out again. Boy did this feel nice.

In the mail, waiting on me was a letter from a dear friend and mentor of mine, Ill. Sir Howard McHenry from Kansas City. It was a wonderful letter touching on our recent Shrine successes, Howard has always been a positive influence. He went on to say, "Your enthusiasm and positive attitude has got me fired up!" and offered to help me in any way he could. A special letter from a special Shriner. I was touched and inspired by this letter from a man of high integrity.

January 22, 2018 - Monday

A day at J&J Metro to catch up on tasks there. We are in the middle of having one of our busiest January's in our history and I've been gone the majority of the time. This is a real tribute to the Team I have working there, especially my son Jason. I'm very proud of all of them.

January 23, 2018 - Tuesday

Today I spent most of the day at J&J Metro but really spent my day on Shrine work. Several calls, conference calls, planning, and paperwork. By late afternoon I was on my way to a 2018 Convention meeting at Stumpy's for planning and implementation of our second Imperial Session in Daytona Beach. We wrapped up at 8:30 and then stopped to get a bite to eat on the way home. Upon reaching the house, Anne and I packed for our early trip to the airport in the morning.

January 24, 2018 - Wednesday

Up at 5AM and out the door at 6:30, headed to the airport for a trip to Fort Worth, Texas. We met Richard and Judy in Atlanta and they continued on with us to Texas. We checked into "The Fort Worth Club" hotel and it is a really neat old hotel. It is also the home to the "Davey O'Brien Award" that is given to the best college quarterback each year. There is a great museum and bar area that has lots of memorabilia related to this.

The evenings event was held in the hotel to present the C. Victor Thornton Humanitarian Award, he was a Past Imperial Potentate. The evening was well prepared and was spectacular. With over 300 people in attendance, Moslah Shriners did a fantastic job with the decorating, agenda, and silent auction. The winner of the award was the head coach of the TCU Baseball Team, Jim Schlossnagle.

I was the keynote speaker for the night. My talk tonight was on the relevance of our Shiners Hospital system and how we change lives. This was followed up by talking about Hero's and how everyone in this room was a Hero to children or they wouldn't be here. I expressed God was watching us and was very proud. This event was very well done, Richard and Judy attended with us and we enjoyed our time there. Great event!

January 25, 2018 - Thursday

Our morning started out by returning to the airport with Richard and Judy. We are on our way to Mexico City for a couple of pre-con planning days for the upcoming Spring

Board Meeting that will be held there. Woot - woot, all four of us got upgraded to first class for this trip.

When we arrived in Mexico City Anthony and Maria were waiting to pick us up and take us to our hotel. We arrived at the hotel and it was very nice. Anne and I were placed in a large elegant 2-bedroom suite by the hotel. Our dinner for the night was a tasting along with the Executive Chef and his staff. It was excellent. We picked the menu for the upcoming event and enjoyed some fine wine.

January 26, 2018 - Friday

Up for an early breakfast and then to Shriners Hospitals for Children - Mexico for a tour. For Anne, Richard, and Judy it was their first visit. We were welcomed from the time we stepped out of the van until we returned to it by patients, parents, and staff. It is an amazing place. Each of us were overwhelmed with tears of joy during our visit from the gratitude and thanks from patients and parents.

One young boy who I visited in his hospital bed along with his Mother seemed to be distressed. He had surgery the day before and was not feeling well. He did not speak English, so an interpreter assisted me. When I asked how he was doing his eyes filled with tears. With that mine did too and his Mother began to hug me. Soon all three of us had tears running down our cheeks. Nearly every child in a hospital bed had a family member right there with them. The love shown by these people was extraordinary. Never before had I seen such appreciation and heard thank you so often as when in the presence of the walls of this hospital. I could not be prouder to be a Shriner, "Having Fun and Helping Kids."

Another little guy, because we were wearing our Fez, called us the Kings (Shriners) and asked his Mother if we would be back the next day. We spent 3 hours there and it was so touching, as we walked through the hospital with our Fez's on, people would applaud and cheer for us, ask for pictures, and embrace us with tears in their eyes. If every Shriner could experience this, they would be so proud and pay their dues until the day they die with pride.

When leaving the hospital, and it was not easy, as the patients and parents followed us to the van wanting pictures. We returned back to the hotel for a meeting regarding food and meeting rooms for the upcoming Joint Board Spring meeting. The staff was great to work with. We then went to visit a restaurant we were going to plan to have one of the off-site dinners at. It was a festive Mexican place complete with a bull ring. We sampled foods for our lunch and made the appropriate plans for dinner and entertainment for when we returned for the board meeting.

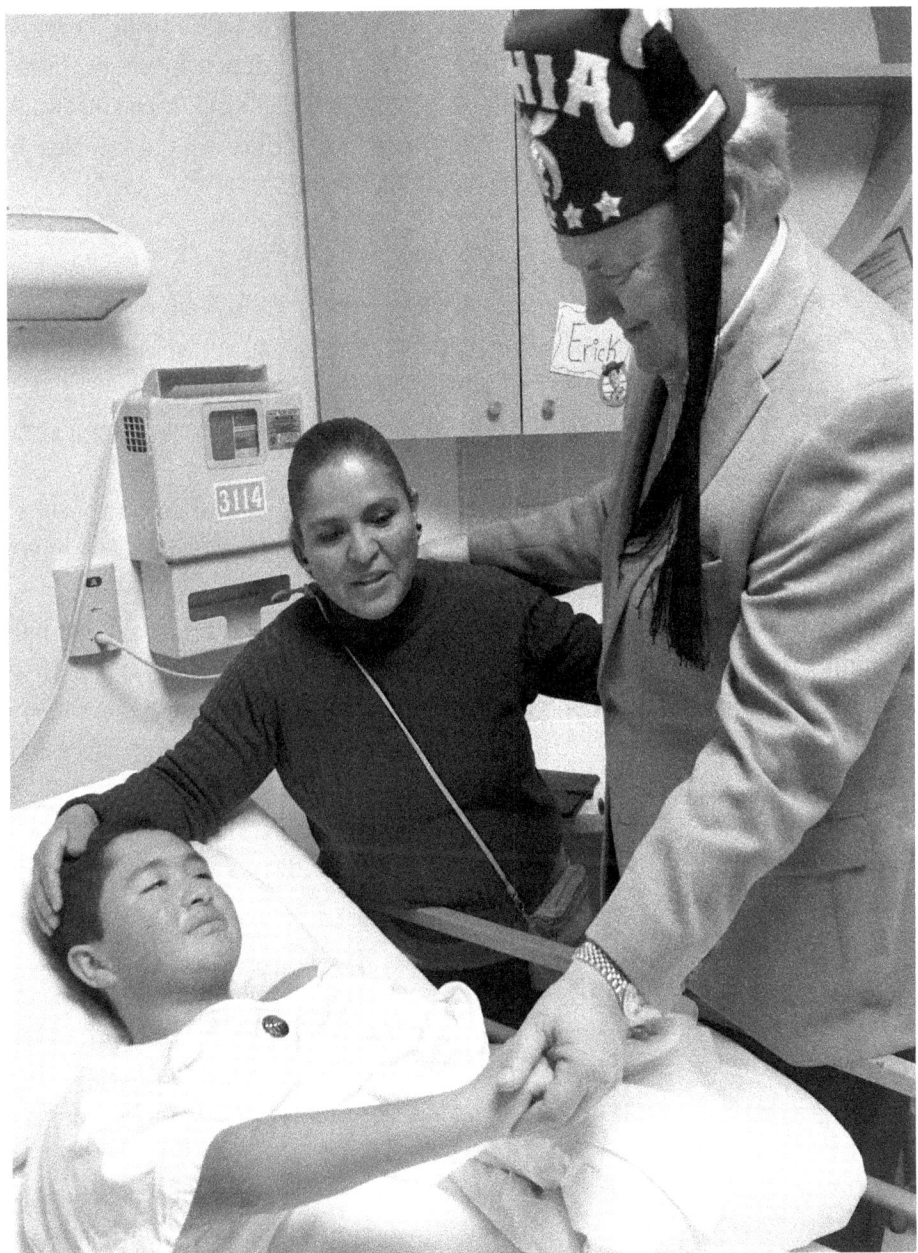

We then visited another restaurant for an additional offsite dinner. It was a beautiful setting complete with peacocks roaming around the grounds. We picked the areas for both cocktails and dinner, this will be a real treat for everyone. We made dinner reservations for the following night to return for a food sampling and to select the menu.

Then it was off to visit yet another restaurant to plan for another offsite dinner for the Board meeting in April. This one did not go as well unfortunately because it was a really nice setting. They would not be able to serve us until after 8 o'clock and that would not work for our large group. We did decide to have dinner there and it was very nice. By now it was time to head back to the hotel to get some sleep.

January 27, 2018 - Saturday

After breakfast we headed out to look at some places for the ladies to visit during the April Board Meeting. We went to downtown Mexico City and visited some of the old ruins, the Presidential Palace, and the Catholic Cathedral that dated back to the 1500's. Anne picked these places for one of the lady's trips. We then had a light lunch at the Grand Hotel.

In the afternoon we visited a Silver Shop and also a large Market filled with hundreds of individual booths with people selling Mexican related and handmade items. It was fascinating seeing all of the stuff and the prices were all so reasonable. Anne selected the Market as another place to take the ladies for a shopping day. The third day trip would be a visit to the hospital and lunch there. The fourth day for the ladies would be a trip to the Pyramids along with the men, and their fifth day would be a free day at the hotel for spa or pool relaxation. So, we had the ladies schedule about all figured out for the Board Meeting.

We all then proceeded to the tasting we set up the previous day at one of the restaurants. We enjoyed dinner as we selected the menu. By now we were all ready to head back to the hotel to get some rest, we have an early morning flight the next day.

January 28, 2018 - Sunday

The alarm went off at 4:30 AM to finish packing and to get to the airport for our early morning flight. Richard, Judy, Anne, and I got through TSA early enough to catch a quick breakfast. We said our goodbyes and headed to our gates. We were on Areo Mexico today with our Delta ticket.

After arriving home, it was time to quickly change my bags out and repack as I had meetings in Tampa the following morning. However, first Anne and I were to attend a Daughters of the Nile Supreme Queen visit in Orlando. The Nile dinner was a 6:30 and then the drive to Tampa was awaiting me. I arrived in Tampa at 11PM at the Doubletree

Hotel. Another long day, 19 hours as the Imperial Potentate. I can tell you, I'm enjoying every minute too. My battery is charged up for a long time now after visiting our hospital in Mexico City this week.

January 29, 2018 - Monday

Today the meetings start at 8 AM for the purpose of a Burn Summit with leadership of our four Burn Hospitals. Leadership from our Galveston, Boston, Cincinnati, and Northern California hospitals were present. The numbers of the past, present, and an outlook for the future were reviewed. It was then delivered to them, that based on the total number of patients, they all could be taken care of in one facility. This is due in a large part because of the advancements in medicine and prevention, much of these advancements were because of Shriners. The Joint Boards, based on patient volume and costs, presented that the same level of care could be delivered by consolidating the four hospitals into two, Northern California and Galveston. This created a lot of conversation and displeasure. The theme has been "Taking care of more children in more places and preserving the endowment fund. Change is needed, but as we all know change is not easy."

The meeting was over by two, hospital leadership headed to the airport to return home. At Headquarters, the Joint Boards along with Executive Staff worked on messaging that would be going out over the next few days. This was a difficult day, but the discussions have to be had to preserve the future of Shriners Hospitals for Children. Of course, for any change of this magnitude, the voting representatives will need to approve it at the upcoming Imperial Session in Daytona Beach this July.

January 30, 2018 - Tuesday

Another 8 AM start at Headquarters. This time to work on the message that will be emailed out to the Nobility, a Press Release, and a PowerPoint to be used at Association Meetings regarding the idea of consolidating hospitals to better serve more children in more places in the future. This was done with the Boards and Executive Staff. After lunch there was a town hall meeting to inform all of the Headquarters Staff of what was going on in the event they had calls about this. They were instructed to send all calls regarding this subject to our Public Relations Dept.

I was on my way back to Orlando by 3 PM and got to my office about 5PM. There I worked for a couple of hours. Anne and I then had dinner with Jason and Avery, it was nice, Avery is really growing.

Then back to the house, to unpack, repack, get some sleep, and get ready to fly out the next morning.

January 31, 2018 - Wednesday

After getting up it was time to head to the airport for my trip to Rapid City for the Midwest Shrine Association Meeting. Projected temperatures there tonight, ten degrees. Ouch, going to be cold for a Florida boy.

We were picked up at the airport and proceeded to Deadwood Lodge in Deadwood, deep in the Black Hills. We experience heavy snow and slippery roads on our way. Upon arriving we got our rooms and settled in. We had dinner with several Shriners in the hotel. This was a men's only Association meeting and started out with great fun.

"The future of humanity will depend on our ability to instill excellence in our children."
GARY BERGENSKE

Chapter Eight
February 2018

February 1, 2018 - Thursday

This morning I was able to do some site seeing for a couple of hours. Pat, a Past Potentate from the local area took me to see Mount Rushmore and Crazy Horse. The last time I saw them was fifty years ago. Mount Rushmore looked as great as ever on this morning of three degrees. Crazy Horse, still not completed, had come a long way in fifty years. We also rode through the towns of Deadwood, Lead, and Sturges. He provided a great tour for me.

We were back to the hotel in time for lunch with the other Imperial Officers and the Midwest Shrine Association Officers. After lunch we all participated in a meeting preparing for the following days of meetings. They are a very organized group.

In the evening we traveled into Deadwood for dinner at the Grand Hotel, built in 1902. It was a nostalgic historic hotel and the meal was terrific. Just down the block was where Wild Bill was shoot in the back while playing cards about 100 years ago. He is still famous here along with Calamity Jane.

February 2, 2018 - Friday

The day started early with a 7 AM breakfast. I ate with all of the Potentates. This was followed by their mid-winter meeting with over 300 Nobles in attendance. The meeting was for men only, so I set up a table of First Ladies items and displayed the beautiful Shrine Masonic Apron that is the Imperial Potentates Project for the year.

A good lunch was had by all, and then it was back to the meeting room where reports were given. The main report given was the Hospital Report where facts were given and talk of consolidation was discussed. The evening brought a good dinner and program. Following dinner was the big event of the night, the World Famous, Boat Races. This always proves to be fun.

February 3, 2018 - Saturday

Another 7 AM breakfast and then a fast start to the meeting. All of us Imperial Officers left by mid-morning for the airport back in Rapid City. It was another long day of travel, arriving back in Orlando at 8:30 PM. Anne was gone to New York City with Anne, so I was home all alone for a night.

February 4, 2018 - Sunday

Wow, I was able to sleep in for a while, can't remember doing that for a long time. I spent most of the day catching up on things at J&J Metro. It worked out well as I was the only one there and could accomplish a lot without interruptions.

Anne arrived back home around six, so we went out for a nice dinner. We had a couple of days coming up just being at home and we're looking forward to doing some things around the house.

February 5, 2018 - Monday

Anne and I spent the day in Daytona Beach with the ladies from the Convention Bureau planning for the upcoming Imperial Session. We can't believe we are doing this again already, where is the time going. We looked at restaurants and places for activities for the pre-week functions. We also discussed the parade and sponsorships. We had a nice lunch with them and were on our way home by 4 PM. Everyone in Daytona Beach is so nice to us, everywhere we go. Such a nice feeling, so glad we came here.

February 6, 2018 - Tuesday

A full day at work, boy did that feel weird. They are doing good running our little business while we have been gone. Business has been good, imagine that, and I have not been there to help. What's that tell you, the employees have been kidding me that they do better without me. Anne spent the day at home as we had a new A/C system put into the back part of the house. We had dinner with some of the kids and Avery.

February 7, 2018 - Wednesday

Back to work in the morning with the team at J&J Metro along with several reports to be worked on for Shriners and conference calls. In the. Afternoon I had a meeting with Stumpy, then another meeting with the Executive Team for the 2018 Convention Corp. Anne and I ended the day with having dinner with some of our friends.

February 8, 2018 - Thursday

Up early and off to the airport for our trip to Corpus Christi, Texas for the Texas Shrine Association winter meeting. We flew on United and it was a disaster, so glad we fly Delta most of the time and have status with them. We landed in Corpus Christi and were picked up and taken to our hotel. The weather was cool, Imperial Sir Jim and Alice met us at the hotel. We relaxed for an hour and then headed on down to the banquet room in the hotel for the counterparts evening. Anne and I sat with the 2018 Potentates and had a very enjoyable evening mingling in the crowd and doing pictures. The Texas folks are always great to be around.

February 9, 2019 - Friday

Early morning start with the beginning of the Texas Shrine Association meeting. The morning was spent on Texas business with all of the Divans. They pick on the Oriental Guides and get them to donate funds to the First Ladies Project.

Others donated too, the final number was close to $5,000.00 that will be presented to Anne at the Imperial Session during the Texas Breakfast. During lunch the ladies had a very nice Ladies Luncheon, and a good amount of Anne's products were sold.

The men continued on with their meeting after lunch. First was a good program on Membership including info on the I AM - RU Committed to Membership Program. Following that the Shriners Hospitals for Children Strategic Plan was given. This took a couple of hours, it covers the need for "Change" so that we can treat more kids in more locations and sustain the endowment fund.

Anne and I joined a group for a nice seafood diner at the invitation of the TSA President. It was great food and pleasant conversation. While seated in the dining room we were also able to watch the Opening Events of the Olympics in Seoul, Korea. After dinner we head back to our room.

February 10, 2018 - Saturday

Again, the meeting started early. First the candidates for International offices spoke. Then each of the Imperial Officers spoke and made presentations. It was a good morning and I believe all of the information was good. We wrapped up by 11AM as most of the attendees now had to drive home, some of them a long distance. The Imperial Officers still present had lunch at the hotel along with our ladies.

So, we had a free afternoon. Anne and I headed out to do some shopping. We also visited the burial site of Salena, a young girl who was shot 23 years earlier. She was a local girl who had reached worldwide fame for her singing ability. She had received a Grammy at the age of 23 just prior to being shot and killed by one of her friends. We also visited a memorial for her that happened to be right across from our hotel on the bay. For dying so young she sure made an impact on the world.

Anne and I had a nice dinner with Imperial Sir Larry. We then head back to our room to pack for our flight the following day.

February 11, 2018 - Sunday

We were picked up at the hotel at 9AM for our ride to the airport. We had breakfast there prior to boarding our plane. We flew through Houston; again, it was a full day of travel. We arrived home about 8PM. Good to sleep in our own bed again.

February 12, 2018 - Monday

The day started off for a couple of hours at Jcall as well.

In the afternoon we attended the 3rd annual "Back to the Roots" event and auction on Main Street in Daytona Beach with NASCAR driver and Shriner, David Ragan for the benefit of Shriners Hospitals for Children. David does a great job getting items donated from NASCAR drivers and teams for this event. The event was well attended by Shriners from several Temples to help and assist with the auction.

During the event David and I addressed the crowd and thanked them for coming. It was during this time on stage that David presented me with a wonderful gift. He presented me with the Shriners Hospitals for Children gloves he wore when he drove the Shriners car at the Daytona 500 the preceding year. He had them autographed and framed; what a neat presentation. I really liked this, it was a special gift from a special friend and made my day. David and I then had lunch and talked about the upcoming Imperial Session to be held in Daytona Beach, in particular the parade. David confirmed he would be there for the parade and drive a race car in it. He also said he would work to recruit some other drivers who have some antique race cars for the parade. This is fantastic!

February 13, 2018 - Tuesday

Another day at home and at work. I have had on my Google alerts, Corvette C5's for sale the past year that are for sale in our area. Today one came up, convertible, low mileage, red, and like new. I gave them a call and went to check it out. It was everything they said it was and more, so I bought it. Spent a few hours with them and took it home. Anne was not happy with me, she is not crazy about me having multiple (7) cars, but this was a beautiful fun car. Now to sell a car to make room for it. Jason and Avery came over for dinner and to see the Vette.

February 14, 2018 - Wednesday

Valentine's Day! Spent the first couple of hours at work. I broke a tooth a couple of days ago, so today I spent two hours in the dental chair getting it fixed. Will need to return in a couple of weeks to have the new crown cemented on. The afternoon was spent on Move It Pro software and doing some on-site moving estimates.

Anne and I had dinner at home, and I packed for a ten-day, three-location trip. On the agenda was Pacific Northwest Shrine Association, Conference of Grand Masters, and a Shriners Clinic in Panama. Anne will join me for the Clinic in Panama along with Bill and Debbie Bailey. It was early to bed as I had the alarm set for 4AM.

February 15, 2018 - Thursday

Yep, the alarm went off at 4AM. I was up and out the door for my early flight to the west coast for PNSA. I arrived in Spokane and was picked up by Past Imperial Potentate Bob Turnipseed and the local Potentate. We made the 45-minute drive to Coeur d' Alene and checked into the Coeur d' Alene hotel. What a great hotel, my suite was one of the nicest I have ever stayed in. Looking out from the 18th floor at the lake and hills full of pine trees, all covered in snow was spectacular. This was an amazing place, it even had a working gas fireplace.

There were four Imperial Officers here and we were joined by Trustee, Dr. Brant Bede as this is his local Association. The five us walked down the road a block, it was so cold, and had a nice dinner together and discussed the bright future of Shriners Hospitals for Children. The fresh snow everywhere was beautiful. We don't see much snow in Florida.

February 16, 2018 - Friday

Was up early, had a 7:30 radio interview, an 8AM conference call, and the PNSA meeting began at 9AM. The meeting went well, in the morning we spent the time talking about the future of Shriners Hospitals and the changes needed to keep us relevant. I felt like it was well received. During lunch the Board Members and I all joined in my suite for a conference call with the entire Joint Boards and home office executive staff. The call was related to our Burns Hospitals.

In the afternoon session Public Relations and Membership was discussed. We of course did an I AM - RU Committed to Membership video. I had a lovely dinner at a fine restaurant in the hotel with all of the PNSA Potentates. It was excellent and very enjoyable. After dinner, a stop at the hospitality room for a night cap, and soon it was time to turn in for the night.

February 17, 2018 - Saturday

This day was full of good presentations and information during the PNSA association meeting. A number of different subjects were covered. Tommy Rousseau, a former Imperial Photography Chairman who recently passed away was honored. A display of the many Shrine memorabilia items he collected were available to look at and his son and daughter were there and were recognized. It was very touching, and it was interesting to hear of the amazing life he led. I always enjoyed my time with him.

A snow storm moved in and it was beautiful to see it fall and collect in this picturesque resort. The evening banquet was a nice event. The Oriental Guides entertained us and raised money for Anne's First Lady's project. The total raised for Anne's project for the weekend was announced, it was $4500.00. This was truly incredible and so appreciated.

I gave a good talk on my travels during the time I have been Imperial Potentate that was well received. During my talk I presented Larry Tipton, PP and the current Executive Director of PNSA an Imperial Potentates MEDALLION. He was so surprised he broke down in tears and was unable to talk. He stayed choked up for a while, more so than anyone I have presented one to. He was most appreciative. After the banquet, a couple of drinks in the hospitality room and then off to bed.

February 18, 2018 - Sunday

Another travel day. Somehow these travel days seem like a waste of time, but there is not an alternative. My flight was a midday one, so I had a relaxed morning in this beautiful suite, sitting by the fireplace and watching it snow. The 45-minute trip to the airport was in a heavy snow storm and we saw several accidents on the way because of the icy roads. We were able to ride by the Spokane Temple, El Katif Shriners as it was right next to the airport. My flight today was to Salt Lake City and then on to Indianapolis for the Conference of Grand Masters. The weather was cold, and the flights were bumpy and bouncy, however I was upgraded on both flights. It's nice when that happens once in a while.

The plane landed in Indianapolis at 10:30 and I got to the hotel about midnight. Going to have to sleep fast as we have an 8 AM breakfast. Couple more days and Anne will be joining me for the rest of this trip. That will be good!

February 19, 2018 - Monday

The top half of the Imperial Line along with John Piland and Jody McGuire all met for breakfast at 8 AM prior to the Conference of Grand Masters starting. The conference began at nine and I, as Imperial Potentate was called to the podium to bring greetings from Shriners International. I spoke on our partnership with DeMolay and on the building of their Centennial Courtyard and encouraged others to buy bricks too. I also spoke of Shriners assistance in raising money for Mason's in Texas, Florida, and Puerto Rico from the recent hurricanes. The collaboration of those three Grand Lodge jurisdictions combined with the Masonic Service Association and the Shriners raised over two million dollars for brothers in need. A big part of that came from the email list belonging to Shriners of 140,000 names. The applause was loud supporting this effort.

I then presented Simon LaPlace, Past Grand Master of Connecticut and current Executive Secretary of the Masonic Service Association an Imperial Potentates MEDALLION. This was for all of his help in coordinating the raising of money for

Mason's in Texas, Florida, and Puerto Rico. It was then expressed that the Shriners email list is available for future need if they arise.

Later in the morning we all spent two hours meeting with the team that was going to begin the search for the position(s) open in our Membership Development office. There is a lot of thought being put into this. After lunch we again attended the conference.

In the evening we traveled to Murat Shriners where we had dinner and attended their Stated Meeting. This is a large beautiful Temple from yesteryear. We were welcomed in and found their meeting to be good.

I met Frank, a Noble who has brought in 141 new Shriners, incredible! I brought him to the front, recognized his efforts and asked him how he was able to bring in so many, he replied, "You just have to ask them." After the meeting two Nobles approached me. The first told me he had been a Shriner for four years and this was his first Stated Meeting. The second one told me he had been a Shriner for 41 years and that this was his first Stated meeting and that he drove 110 miles to come so he could meet me. Really made me feel good that we are creating interest and enthusiasm. Following the meeting, we ate again and then headed back to the hotel. This was a great day!

February 20, 2018 - Tuesday

Up at 5AM and down to the convention room where we will have the Frank S. Land Breakfast to promote DeMolay, with 300 Grand Lodge Officers attending. The event has been sponsored by Shriners International for many years. This turned out to be excellent as we had the opportunity to present and promote the DeMolay's Centennial Courtyard that will be erected in front of their headquarters building in celebration of their one hundredth anniversary. After the breakfast many mentioned they would be purchasing a brick.

Shriners International has always sponsored this event and allowed people to come at NO charge. This year, after I met with Shrine and DeMolay leadership, we decided to start charging $20.00 per person with 100% of the funds going to DeMolay, Shriners paid the entire cost of the event. This was well received and $6000.00 was raised from this breakfast to support this boy's youth organization.

At the conclusion of the breakfast it was a hurry up to change, pack, and head to the airport. I met Anne in Atlanta and we continued on to Panama. We arrived at the airport at 10:30 PM and we were greeted by about 30 Nobles and Ladies. This was so nice, especially considering the time of day. By the time we arrived at our beautiful 17th floor suite overlooking the bay, we had a drink on the patio and got to bed about 1 AM. Another spectacular 20-hour day.

February 21, 2018 – Wednesday

We were up early to attend the Shriners Hospitals for Children Clinic. Here we found a large crowd of patients and parents who had arrived to see Doctors from the SHC

Shreveport Hospital. This was amazing, the number of volunteers from the local Shrine Temple along with their wives was incredible.

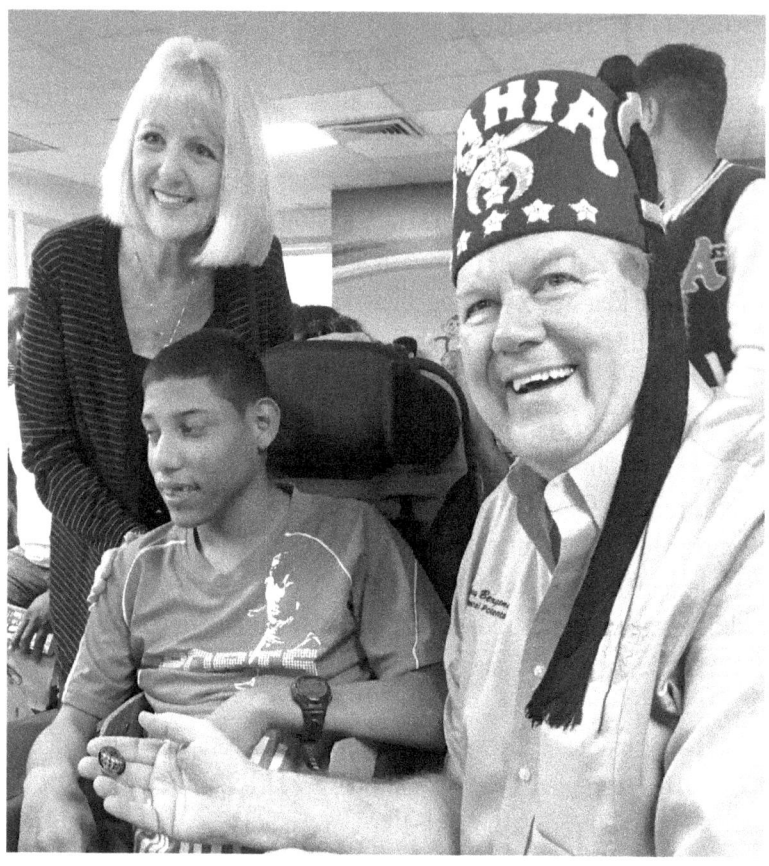

During the weeks visit, 598 patients will be seen, of which, 130 or so will be going back to the United States for surgeries and treatments. A perfect example of how we can see more kids in more places and make a big impact on children and their families future.

We then went to see their Temple, Abou Saad Shriner's home. This is a really neat place, they occupy half of it and rent the other half out, mostly to other Masonic Bodies. It was formally a hotel for the United States Military officers when the US controlled the Panama Canal. The Shriners purchased the building several years ago and have done many improvements. Anne and I were very impressed with the Nobles, their ladies, and the Temple. From here we went to the Panama Canal, where we first had a good lunch at the Miraflores Restaurant overlooking the Miraflores Locks. After lunch we toured the locks and the VIP historical area on the upper level of the control tour. This was so fascinating. Of particular interest was seeing the plaque that was placed by Osman Shriners in 1913 when they came to Panama and had a Shrine Ceremonial at the bottom of the Canal before it was filled with water. This is great Shrine history at a world known location, how fascinating. During the entire time I was here I thought of my friend, President Jimmy Carter, and what it must have been like when he visited here.

The evening dinner was delightful and included all of the Divan and Past Potentates and their wives at a waterside restaurant. During the day Imperial Sir Bill Bailey and his wife Debbie arrived and were also able to join us for dinner. By the time we got back to the hotel we had another full day with great Shriners and ladies.

February 22, 2018 - Thursday

This morning started out back at the Abou Saad Temple where we met up with the Divan. Imperial Sir Bill and I then joined them on a bus ride to go and meet the Panamanian Minister of Health. This was a good meeting as the government is willing to work alongside the Shriners in helping the children in need in their country. They will be purchasing and installing an X-ray machine that should be ready for use by the next Shriners Clinic. It is very exciting to see the government helping.

We then proceed to a Press Conference promoting the upcoming Shriners Golf Tournament to raise funds to allow the Shriners to help children from Panama. This was held at a restaurant owned by Shriners. After the Press conference we had a nice lunch where fun and fellowship prevailed.

After lunch we went to the Institute of Physical and Rehabilitation Medicine. This was a nice facility and is being considered for future use by the Shriners Clinic. It has a lot more room and the exam rooms are much larger. This is also the location the new X-ray machine will be located at. In front of this building is a bronze "Silent Messenger, an Editorial Without Words" statue. This is the most detailed one of these statues I have ever seen, it is very nice. We all took pictures around it, this was a proud moment for all of the Nobles. From here it was back to the hotel to freshen up for a big night.

We were picked up at 8PM and proceed to Abou Saad Shriners for a dinner party. When we arrived, Anne and I rode in on wooded stick horses from their Horse

Patrol Unit to the theme music of the old TV show Bonanza. We were greeted by the cheers and cameras of the Nobles and ladies. This was so much fun with nearly 100 people in attendance. We had a nice dinner and then were entertained by a Panamanian band and dancers who were outstanding.

Great music and colorful costumes. We then watched a video about the Shriners Clinics in Panama. Following this a few speeches were given, and Anne was presented $1000.00 for her project. She was also given a beautiful piece of Panamanian jewelry, a certain type of gold and pearl pin the ladies wear. I was then thanked for attending and presented a beautiful gold belt buckle with my initials on it. It is extremely nice, and I will always cherish it. They kept a supply of Anne's Project items and will sell them for her there. Now, it was time to head back to the hotel for some rest as it was after midnight again.

February 23, 2018 - Friday

Anne and I had breakfast at the hotel. We were picked up mid-morning and headed to the marina for a boat ride to the remote island of Taboga. We went on a 46' yacht who one of the Shriners owned with a group of about 30 nobles and ladies out through the channel of the Panama Canal to the ocean. We saw many large ocean-liner ships that were waiting their turn to go through the locks of the canal. When we arrived at the island of Taboga, it is beautiful but there is no marina, so we were taken in three at a time in a small dinghy. The water was clear and beautiful. One of the Shriners family owned a large condo, first floor and right on the water. We spent several hours here relaxing, eating freshly prepared food, and many went swimming. It was a wonderful afternoon in a paradise. When we got ready to leave everyone had to be taken back to the yacht in the dinghy, three at a time. We cruised back in the dark, all of the ships anchored out were awaiting their turn to go through the locks and were all lite up. There was a city of lights on the water it seemed.

Again, it was a long day, but a fun day. It's days like this that we are really able to connect with Shriners and ladies and express to them the importance of what we are doing in a casual relaxed way. We got back to our room about 9:30, ordered some room service food and went to bed early. Tomorrow is an early travel day.

February 24, 2018 - Saturday

Oh boy, another day with a 5 AM alarm going off. We jumped up, showered, packed and were heading to the airport by 6:30. Anibal who had been our driver during our time in Panama did a fantastic job and we really enjoyed him and his wife. Once at the airport we had breakfast with him and Past Potentate Ricky. Ricky was assisting Anne in finding a gift for her to give at the upcoming Ladies Luncheon in July at Daytona Beach. Anne decided on an item and Ricky was going to order her a sample, so she could see one. He was very helpful.

By 9AM we were on our plane and headed to Atlanta on our way home. We arrived in the Orlando airport by 6 PM and headed home to unpack and wash clothes. Anne did some cooking as the next day we are to have about 30 people over for a "Reveal" party with David and Marie Angie where we will learn the sex of the baby.

February 25, 2018 - Sunday
Up early to get ready for the party, cleaned the pool and picked things up. We had a good time seeing many we have not seen in a while as we have been gone so much. The party was for a couple of hours in the afternoon and we learned that the baby was going to be a little girl. Everyone had a great time.

February 26, 2018 - Monday
A day at J&J Metro after not being there in nearly two weeks. Lots to catch up on that's for sure. Mixed into the day was a couple of Shrine conference calls and a trip to the dentist to have a crown put on. Fortunately, everything is going along good at work even with me gone. This sure is nice as it allows me to be able to enjoy being the Imperial Potentate.

I worked late, until about 7PM catching up on things. David and Marie Angie came over to tell Anne and I they had been to the Doctor that afternoon and they were unable to find the baby's heartbeat. After further testing they learned the baby had died. This was devastating to all of us and tears were flowing. I'm glad we were home when they found this out, hopefully we were able to bring them some kind of comfort.

February 27, 2018 - Tuesday
Two days in a row at J&J Metro, time to get some work done, although the day was filled with doing Shrine business. Again, I stayed there until about 7AM. Anne and I then met for a quick dinner. We then headed home to pack for our trip to Houston for the Shriners Hospitals for Children College Baseball Classic.

When we got to the house, I had a letter from the Shrine Temple in Puerto Rico thanking me for making the visit to them after the devastating Hurricane Maria hit them. They were so thankful for a visit from the Imperial Potentate and expressed it really had a positive impact on their nobility.

Then in another envelope from the same group was a $500.00 check for Anne's Project, *"Love Grows Miracles."* This was so touching to both Anne and I, knowing all they have been through and continue to have to endure, to be so thoughtful. This defiantly made our day.

The letter they sent me was so touching. It was one of the most heartfelt letters I have ever received. I wish to share it with you here;

Dear Imperial Sir Gary,
On behalf of the Divan and all the members of Al Rai'e Saleh Temple we would like to express our deepest appreciation for visiting us during our most difficult times. We know about the great effort that you underwent in order to coordinate this trip. The hazards and frustration of not being able to spend more time with us due to the lack of hotel availability caused by Hurricane Maria, returning home late the night before from another trip, traveling to Puerto Rico at 4 AM the next day, having to return home the same day, etc... must be complex. But be assure, that your visit has made the difference between the collapse of our Temple and the continuance in helping our children in need and in serving Humanity. Now more than ever, your Leadership and Guidance has given us strength and inspiration to continue to strive for success. For this we are grateful to you, Imperial Sir.

May your endurance be an example for all of us in Shrinedom to follow! There is no doubt, that under your leadership and the help of the Great Architecture of the Universe, Shriners International will continue to grow!

Once again, may God Bless you and the members of your staff for the assistance rendered to our Temple when we mostly needed it.

Your generosity and compassion will never be forgotten!
Respectfully,

Romón L. Sierra Laporte
Ill Potentate Al Rai'e Saleh Shriners 2018

February 28, 2018 - Wednesday

Another early start, same routine, get ready and head to the airport. We got this down good. We arrived in Houston midafternoon and prepared for a few days here for the Shriners Hospitals for Children College Baseball Classic. We checked into our nice suite on the 23rd floor and settled in. Several of us went to dinner together and had a nice time. We talked about the Baseball Classic, the agenda, and the fun time we would have. Dustin Johnson has done a great job having everything set up and ready to go; a great young Shriner who I admire

"Trust is one of the highest forms of a compliment. It is said that trust is even greater than love when it comes to compliments."
GARY BERGENSKE

Chapter Nine
March 2018

March 1, 2018 - Thursday

After a relaxing morning we headed to Minute Maid Park for the First Pitch Luncheon. The luncheon was well attended by Shriners and their ladies, Coaches, Patients, and representatives of the Astro's Foundation. We had a really good lunch and then came the fun part. A panel of four of the coaches was set up and Alec interviewed them with some tough questions. Alec did great and we were all really impressed with the coaches as well.

After the luncheon we had a quick meeting of the board members present and then went down to watch batting practice by the teams who were in the tournament. You could tell the college players were excited to be playing in this Major League Baseball stadium of the current World Champion Houston Astros.

For dinner we all went to Jackson Street BBQ, an excellent place next to the stadium. This was some of the best BBQ I have ever had. Delicious! By the time we were done with dinner, we had a nightcap at the hotel and it was time for bed.

March 2, 2018 - Friday

After breakfast at the hotel all of us who were in town went to the Shriners Hospitals for Children – Houston, for a tour. The University of Kentucky Wildcats Baseball team were there as well. They interacted with the kids there and played some baseball with the patients in the indoor play area. During the visit at the hospital I presented Alec with an

Imperial Potentates MEDAILLION. I was so proud to receive it and it really caught him and his family off guard. Alec is a wonderful individual and was so appreciative, I love this guy.

In the afternoon the baseball games started. The teams invited to the tournament were Vanderbilt, Sam Houston State, Kentucky, Houston, Mississippi State, and Louisiana -Lafayette. Having the event in Minute Maid Park, Home of the World Champion Houston Astro's was exciting for the players and fans alike. We had dinner in the suite as we watched the games, a total of three for the day. Several of our patients were in attendance and are making a strong influence on the payers.

March 3, 2018 - Saturday

Early start and one busy day was on the schedule. It started with an 8 AM Board of Governors meeting with the SHC - Houston Board of Governors. Then we attended the Walk for Love around the baseball field inside of Minute Maid Park. During this time, I did some interviews as well. This was followed by another Board of Governors meeting with the Galveston Board. This was all in the morning.

At noon the first of three baseball games started, and they would run to nearly midnight. We spent the day at the stadium but left after the third game started. We head back to the hotel and got some dinner. We then proceeded to our room to pack and to prepare for our 5 AM wakeup call so we could head back to the airport again. This was a day packed with good activity.

March 4, 2018 - Sunday

Yep, 5 AM the alarm went off. We got ready and caught a cab to the airport. We missed the final day of the Shriners College Classic Baseball Tournament as I had another engagement for the following day.

This day was a little different, I was now headed to Kansas City to participate in a groundbreaking for the new DeMolay Centennial Courtyard, and Anne was heading back home to Orlando. We both flew to Atlanta together first and then would go on our different paths to our final destination. We got to the airport early enough to have a nice breakfast. We talked about plans for the upcoming Imperial Session, we will be the presiding couple in Daytona Beach. Hard to believe it will be here in only 4 months. Where has the year gone? It's gone way to fast in my opinion.

Upon arriving in Kansas City, I was picked up and we dropped my suitcases off at the hotel. Then DeMolay Grand Master Ron, Christian, Jody, and I went to downtown Kansas City to look for previous locations of DeMolay and for locations regarding Frank Land. We found Frank Land's home and a building that previously was occupied by their family restaurant. We also found locations that DeMolay previously had their offices in. Then we found the now empty lot where the Kansas City Scottish Rite was located, this was where DeMolay was founded. The building burned down a few years ago. Each of us found an old brick where the building once stood and took it as a souvenir.

After this we picked up two DeMolay International leaders, Chase and Mason and went to Strauds Chicken Restaurant where you get the best pan-fried chicken anywhere. I am so proud to have built this relationship with DeMolay, an organization that develops young men between the ages of 9 and 21 into better leaders of character. Although, as a young man myself, I was never a member, I had never heard of them, I'm happy to be able to help and assist them now. I feel good about the relationship I have been able to foster this year between the Shriners and DeMolay; it will have a long-lasting impact.

March 5, 2018 - Monday

The same six of us from last night met for an 8 AM breakfast where we talked about the day ahead of us. By 9AM we were at DeMolay International Headquarters and the weather was bad; rainy, windy and cold. Our whole purpose of today was to take pictures outside of a ground breaking for the "Editorial Without Words" statue that would be going into the DeMolay Centennial Courtyard. This statue, sponsored by Shriners International, was sponsored for two reasons: first, to enhance the Shrines relationship with DeMolay, and second, in memory of Imperial Sir Jack Jones who was a DeMolay Honorary Grand Master, and an Imperial Potentate of Shriners International. I take great pride that this is happening while I am serving as Imperial Potentate. Jack was a humble man, he would be so honored he is being remembered in this way.

Late in the morning the rain subsided so we moved outside to get some pictures. In the ground-breaking pictures were DeMolay Grand Master Ron, DeMolay International officers Chase and Mason and me as the Imperial Potentate. The rain may have stopped but is was still cold and windy. We got some sets of pictures, with a Fez on, with a hard hat on (they made me one with five stars on it) and one in our DeMolay regalia. Considering the cold weather, they turned out excellent. We then did some video's around the DeMolay Headquarters for future use.

We went to lunch, posted pictures on various Facebook pages, and enjoyed conversation. I was then dropped back off at the airport by 12:30 for a 2 PM flight back to Orlando for a day. This was another quick in and out trip where good things happened that should prove to provide great results. In all of the promotions we are asking people to consider buying a brick in the new courtyard. I arrived home by 9PM just in time to unpack and prepare to repack.

March 6, 2018 - Tuesday

Up early and off to work to catch up there. Of course, the day included Shrine conference calls and a haircut as well. When I arrived home after work it was again packing time. This time for several days in Tampa for the Oriental Guide and Assistant Rabban Seminars. Looking forward to spending some time with our up and coming Temple leaders.

March 7, 2018 - Wednesday

Up early and on the road to Tampa by 7AM. When I reached Shrine Headquarters there was work to be done and a few meetings with staff that were needed. The Grand Lodge line of Illinois was visiting and took a tour of Shrine Headquarters. Following their tour, we had a short visit in the Imperial Potentates office and took some pictures. We also made a video in support of working together and building membership. We then all had lunch at Bahama Breeze, John Piland joined us as well. After lunch there was still some additional items to catch up on at headquarters.

Late in the afternoon, I headed over to the Airport Marriott Hotel for the beginning of the Oriental Guide Seminar. Anne joined me later as she drove over from Orlando separately. Tonight, was the Opening Reception for the Seminar and there was a great turnout of excited Shriners and Ladies. After the reception we joined the Educational Committee for a nice dinner.

March 8, 2018 - Thursday

The opening session of the OG Seminar started at 8AM. The opening went great, Anne and I both made some of the opening comments and welcomed everyone to the exciting conference where they are expecting to learn many things. By mid-morning we were on our way to Sarasota for a luncheon at Sahib Shriners. When we got to the edge of town, the local Shrine Motor Corp met us and provided us with an escort to the Shrine Center. We were greeted by a large group of people. There were nearly 100 men there for the Men's Luncheon, and about 40 for the Ladies Luncheon. They treated Anne and I like Royalty and we had a great time.

By midafternoon we were on our way back to Tampa. We arrived about 5PM back at the Marriott just as the Seminar was wrapping up for the day. We had dinner at one of the restaurants there in the airport with several others. This was an early night back to our room and an early night to bed.

March 9, 2018 - Friday

Early start as the Oriental Guide Seminar continues. This is a very excited group who are showing great promise as future leaders. Anne's First Ladies Project items were a hit and over $5000.00 worth were sold during this event. The evening event was a Beach Party in the Ballroom celebrating "Back to the Beach" for the Imperial Session.

The Wedding - During the evening "Back to the Beach" event I was approached to see if I would escort the Bride in for the wedding. I thought they were kidding. But no, it was true, one of the couples who had been together for 20 years, decided tonight was the night they were going to tie the knot. They recruited a pastor from the group in the room and lined up for the wedding.

I escorted the bride in from the rear of the room to the dance floor and delivered her to the groom. A quick service was given, and vows were taken. We had our first ever Shriners Educational Seminar Wedding. Wow- this got the crowd going. For their first dance, it was a dollar dance and $230.00 was collected and it was all donated to Anne's First Lady's Project. What a night! Could it be that the *"Imperial Potentate of Love"* was involved?

March 10, 2018 - Saturday

This is the final day of the Oriental Guide Seminar and everyone was up early and off to class. The day went well. In the closing, Isabella did a great job and sang a song. She sang the one that was written for her and Emily for this year. I then gave the closing talk and we were all excused for a farewell party on the deck. Here everyone mingled and expressed how much they enjoyed the conference.

I had a call from David Ragan that Brad Paisley was doing a concert in Plant City, Florida and that he had some items for the Shrine Headquarters Memorabilia Room. Brads Dad was to call me the following day to set up a meeting time. This was exciting news as I've been working to get more relevant items in the Memorabilia Room for the younger generations.

Judy Burke had her birthday a couple of days ago, Richard invited Anne and I to join them for a birthday dinner. The four of us went to Capital Grill and celebrated her birthday. It was very nice to spend some time with them, as they have been doing an excellent job in the position as "Marshal" for Anne and me this year. Upon arriving back at the hotel, we stopped by the hospitality room for a night cap.

March 11, 2018 - Sunday

It was a lazy morning where we did not have to be up early. Late in the morning we all looked over the comments left by the Oriental Guide's and planned for the Assistant Rabban's conference starting later today. Jeff and Cheryl arrived as the Assistant Rabban's are their counterparts for 2020. They brought lots of shirts to sell and were excited to be there. Anne and I had lunch with them and caught up on things and talked about our trip coming up to the Philippines. We are all excited about what is happening there with regards to Membership, they are knocking it out of the park.

By midafternoon we still had not heard from Brad Paisleys father. We decided to head towards Plant City anyway as that is where the concert was tonight, at the Strawberry Festival. While driving their Brad's Dad, Doug Paisley called; he gave us directions where to meet to get back stage and told us he had tickets for the concert for us too. This sounded great! We arrived, parked, and made our way through the crowds to the stage side door. Doug met us there and took us to a room where he had some items from Brad, three of these were signed, most notably, one of Brads concert worn cowboy hats. This is going to be fantastic for our memorabilia room. Doug expressed their goal was to get us one of Brads autographed guitars for the room too. Wow- that would be outstanding! I then presented Doug with an Imperial Potentates MEDALLION for him to give to Brad. He expressed, it's in good hands as he is the keeper of all of Brads trophies and awards, and this Imperial Potentates MEDALLION would be added to all the Others. He then gave Anne and I great tickets for the evening show.

When we got to our seats, we were seated by two family friends of the Paisley's. They filled us in with some great stories as they all lived next door to each other as their kids were all growing up. This was really neat to hear. The concert starts, and it really was good, he goes nonstop. We were invited along with the neighbors to go on stage for the last 25% of the show.

Here we stood at a bar, offered Coke or water and watched the performance 15 feet away from Brad. Watching him and the crowd was amazing. When the show was over, he was quick to get on his bus and a police escort moved him out fast. They took him to the local airport where he caught his private plane home. This was a great night, only thing that could have been better would have been to meet him personally for a few minutes. I'm extremely proud he is a Shriner, he does a great job and was very generous to provide us some items for our memorabilia room. Hope our paths cross again soon.

March 12, 2018 - Monday

Up at 6AM, this is the first day of the Assistant Rabban Conference. Anne and I were part of the Opening Session and both did a welcome and shred some stories. Anne talked about her program, she did a great job, and people seem to support it. After the Opening, we packed our bags and hit the road home to get ready for our two-week Imperial Potentates Cruise in Europe. By midafternoon I was at work to catch up there on all I could. In the evening David and Marie Angie came by, they are good. After they left we got some packing done. It's a challenge, 16 days and we are only allowed one suitcase each, plus a carry on. Imagine Anne doing this. She bought the largest suitcase she could find, I never saw one this big, but it qualifies and "one" she says.

March 13, 2018 - Tuesday

Up early, for a full day at J&J Metro catching up and making sure all was in order for me to be out of the country for two weeks. Several Shrine conference calls as we were working hard on our messaging related to consolidating some of the hospitals. All of this is so important as the general nobility needs and wants information on our future.

When I got home I first worked on the sprinkler system as we had some broken heads and parts of the yard were drying out. I was able to fix most of them. The next order of business was us trying to get 16 days of clothes in one suitcase. Mmmmm, it just doesn't seem fair, but we'll get it. Are we getting excited or nervous about this riverboat cruise with 140 Shriners and ladies, well, I'd say a little of both? The neat thing is we sold out the entire boat, so everyone on there will be a Shriner or with a Shriner.

March 14, 2018 - Wednesday

Up early again to finish up our packing. Then off to the airport where we had lunch with our friends David and Jan prior to getting on the plane. When we got to Atlanta, we meet more of our folks who, were going on the cruise. We boarded the plane for our long trip to Brussels where we would arrive at 7:30 AM. Then our real adventures would begin.

Just before departure we received a text that the total sales for the OG and AR Conferences for Anne's project surpassed $9,300.00 dollars. This was exciting news, her project items did really well there. I have to say the selection she has this year, in my opinion, are really good and lend themselves to great sales. A big thank you to all who are supporting her program.

March 15, 2018 - Thursday

We arrived in Brussels at 7.30 AM. I was able to sleep some, but Anne not so much. Larry Lyons met us at the airport and got a cab for us to take to the ship. We had about an hour drive to Antwerp, Belgium where we boarded the *"River Melody"* ship. Everything was very nice; flowers and fruit were waiting for us in our room. Passengers arrived throughout the day. During the afternoon I had time to meet with some of the ship's leadership staff so we could talk about some special arrangements.

We made some adjustments to the agenda, created an Imperial Potentates table in the dining room where different guests would be invited nightly. The goal was for Anne and me to have dinner with every passenger on the ship at our table by the time we finished. Each passenger would get a personalized invitation delivered to their room by one of the ship's staff the night prior to invite them to sit with us. This turned out to be a fantastic idea and we got to meet and have great conversation with every passenger this way. We deeply appreciated everyone who traveled with us. The staff volunteered to place an Imperial Potentates pin at every place setting for dinner the following night.

By 6PM everyone was aboard ship and we had an orientation from the ship staff. You could tell that most were experiencing some jet lag. We then proceeded to the dining room for a delicious dinner and great conversation. Fallowing dinner there was entertainment in the lounge, but most went to bed early.

March 16, 2018 - Friday

Our first full day on the ship, high of 51 today and cloudy. After breakfast we split into three groups with individual tour guides and set out by foot to the city of Antwerp. Amazing old buildings and a Cathedral that is 500 years old. (It took 160 years to build) We had lunch in town today with the Zorians, Juetts, and Amicos. We visited some candy shops, clothing stores, etc. and then returned to the ship.

At 4:45 we set sail and immediately had our emergency/fire drill. This was followed by the intro of the ships staff and an open bar reception. We sat at the Captains table tonight with other Bahia nobles and ladies. The seven-course meal was wonderful. Anne and I continued to discuss our plan along with Robert, the hotel manager to have the invitations sent so that we will actually have dinner with every passenger on the ship by the end of the cruise. During dinner we went through the first of the 33 locks we will go through. After dinner we retired to the lounge for a nightcap. Not a big crowd, I think many are still adjusting to the time.

March 17, 2018 - Saturday

The alarm went off at 6:45 AM and we woke up in Willemstad, The Netherlands. We looked out the window; it was snowing, windy, and cold. The high today is only 30 degrees. The boat had made it into a safe harbor overnight, but due to the wind it was still rocking some. We were nice and warm inside. Soon we were off to breakfast. We skipped the morning trip as it was so cold and spent the morning in the ship's restaurant working on 2018 Imperial Session planning with Bob and Mikey. So much planning to do, we are so lucky to have such great support.

Soon after lunch we sailed to Kinderdijk, Holland. There we visited 19 windmills build around 1740 and learned how they operated and went inside one. Burr, it was cold but worth the walk.

Prior to dinner we sold Anne's project items in the lounge. ($675). Tonight, began our invitations to others on the ship to sit at the Imperial Potentates table for dinner. This was great, and we are so happy that by the end of the cruise we will have sat with every single person on the cruise for dinner. It's a nice touch that people are looking forward to and we are excited that we will be able to meet every person personally. Our expectations are being exceeded in every way.

Of interest, the 81-year-old noble sitting next to me at dinner asked me what I was going to do after my term as Imperial Potentate was done, I replied, "I'm not sure." He responded, "You always have to have a goal" he pulled out his phone and opened it and showed me a countdown clock with 90 at the top. He continued to say, "My goal is to live to 90, by this countdown clock I know exactly how long I have to go to accomplish it." It was a good lesson for me.

Remembering my Mom and her birthday today, the first one since she has passed. She sure would have enjoyed this trip if she was still around, she loved to travel.

March 18, 2018 - Sunday
Woke up today in Nijmegen and it's still cold out. After breakfast we met in the lounge where local people came in to speak to us about the areas involvement during World War II. We then set out on a walking tour of this 2000-year-old city overlooking the Wall River.

The area was heavily damaged during the war with the exception of the towns center that remained unscathed. It was so cold we were all anxious to make it back to the ship to warm up. When we arrived back the crew had warm towels for us and hot cocoa, this really hit the spot.

The evening was a dress in your favorite team's colors, and it turned out to be loads of fun and it got everyone talking. The music played, and the bar was busy as many stayed up dancing into the late evening. The ship cruised all night and the views from the lounge as we partied were wonderful. A comment was made, "When we got on the boat, we didn't know anyone, but because they are all Shriners, essentially we knew everyone." This added to everyone having a good time together.

March 19, 2018 - Monday

Woke up this morning and the ship was still cruising, now in Germany traveling down the Rhine River to Bonn. After breakfast we took a walk-through Bonn's Old Town where we saw some old church's and memorials. We visited the home of Beethoven, the renowned composer. Lunch was at a local restaurant, some of us ordered sausage and others ordered potatoes pancakes. The German beer was great, you pay for it twice, when you buy it and again when you give it back in the water closet. (Pay to use toilets)

After lunch Anne, Jan, and I continued to do some shopping. We returned to the ship about 4:30 and prepared for dinner. It was Mexican night and a good time was had by all. While we were eating dinner, the ship set sail again to move to a new location, Cochem, Germany. After dinner some of us gathered on the sun deck, in the dark for a cigar and a drink. The view of the cities we passed through was outstanding, we even saw some castles all lite up. This cruise is going so well, everyone is really enjoying it, Anne and I made a great choice on this one.

March 20, 2018 - Tuesday

We arrived in Cochem during the breakfast hour. Our morning starts off with a tour of the Reichsburg Castle, originally built in the eleventh century, then burned to the ground in 1689 by King Louis XIV of France. In 1868 it was purchased by Louis Ravene who converted the former Royal Residence in to his summer home. It was beautiful to see and the views from it were outstanding.

We then did some shopping and had lunch in a local restaurant, American hamburgers, they tasted good, with a group of eight. After lunch, a little more shopping and a walk back to the ship. During Happy Hour we showed Anne's *"Love Grows Miracles"* video and sold her merchandise.

Tonight, was the "Imperial Potentate and First Lady's Dinner." Everyone wore their Fez on this night, and we had them from all over the world present. Anne and I were escorted into the dining room to the Whitney Houston song, "The Greatest Love of All." This is the same song used when we were escorted to the stage in Daytona Beach for my Installation. It was a great day enjoyed by all. The ship's crew, who knew nothing about Shriners and what we do are now in awe of the great work Shriners do.

March 21, 2018 - Wednesday

Today we woke up to blue skies and sunshine, how nice. Still cold outside but beautiful. We are now in Trier, Germany after traveling through the night including passing through a number of locks. Our walking tour included seeing Roman Emperor Constantine's massive Basilica, erected in 310 AD. We also, saw the imposing Porta Nigra (Black Gate), a towering gateway built around 200 AD, now the largest surviving city gate of Roman times. We then had lunch at a restaurant with all of our group from the ship. The afternoon was spent with more shopping.

The evening started off with the Port Talk, an inspirational story by me about a patient, and then dinner. We had a great group at the Imperial Potentate's table with lots of laughter. This was the night Anne and I hired a private local band to perform for the Imperial River Boat Cruise Ball. It was well attended, and the dance floor was still full at 11 PM when it concluded. This was a real success that got everyone involved. SHRINERS - Having Fun and Helping Kids.

March 22, 2018 - Thursday

Today is a day we have been looking forward to, our optional trip to Luxembourg, a constitutional monarchy located between Belgium, France, and Germany. With a territory of less than 1000 square miles, the country is one of the smallest in the world. Our walking tour of Luxembourg City included the market, the Paladins of the Grand Duke of Luxembourg, and the Notre-Dame Cathedral. Again, we had lunch at a local restaurant.

In the afternoon we went to see the Luxembourg American Cemetery, it was covered with an inch of fresh snow. This was a touching and emotional time as we had a tour guide take us through the cemetery and also tell us some personal stories about some of the soldiers. General George Patton is also buried here and has a special, place, something very rarely done in a military cemetery. This cemetery gave me the same feeling that Arlington National Cemetery gave me when I visited there.

We than visited the nearby cemetery of the German soldiers. This was nicely done but not close to the beauty of the American one. The interesting thing here was that many of the graves had flowers on them. I found this nice as these graves were over 70 years old and were still being visited by local German families.

In the reception prior to dinner during my talk I made a special presentation. An Imperial Potentates MEDALLION award was given to Illustrious Sirs Bob Amico and Mikey Juett. This caught them both by surprise and made me very happy to present them. Both of them have worked so hard assisting me over the past years, we have been friends for 25 years. After a delicious dinner we all retired to the lounge for a nightcap. Wonderful day.

March 23, 2018 - Friday

After breakfast we went on a guided tour of Bernkastel, Germany. We visited the small riverside town with quaint stores and homes. We then visited one of the area's most famous wineries for a wine tasting. It took place in a wine cellar that was dug into a mountain side over 400 years ago. It was really cool. There we tasted four different wines in a most unusual place. (Like a cave). Following that we returned back to the ship for lunch.

We set sail at 4PM down the Rhine River. On this night we had a wild onboard Karaoke night with a full lounge. We did team song competition and had numerous individual singers. It was really a fun night.

Of special interest, on this night I was given information on a child here in Germany we may be able to help at Shriners Hospitals. An inquiry is being made and I should know something before we leave the ship. The ship's crew is so impressed with our work and is going an extra step to be sure we are all having a great time.

March 24, 2018 - Saturday

This was a special day about half of the ship has been looking forward to. This was the day of the optional trip to the Marksburg Castle. It is the only castle in the country from the 13th century unchanged by war or reconstruction and offers a glimpse into the daily life of the time. It was amazing to see how they lived and protected themselves during that time. The views from the mountain top were beautiful. Following this we did a guided tour through Boppard, Germany visiting its marketplace and stores.

By midafternoon we were again cruising down the river. This afternoon the sun was shining, and the temperatures had warmed up. Many of those onboard headed to the sundeck. As we cruised down the Rhine we saw numerous old castles, small towns, churches and electric trains were often buzzing by. It was a magnificent afternoon for site seeing.

In the afternoon Anne and I also worked in our cabin on plans for the upcoming Joint Board meeting in Mexico City. Our planning never stops; however, it is really important to us as we both strive to do our best for others.

Prior to dinner I gave a talk about the European Shriners and of our experience with the clinics that have been taking place for 36 years in Cyprus. After dinner and during the evening there was another cigar smoke out on the sundeck where several smokers gathered. In the lounge an exciting Disco night was taking place with the ship's crew leading the way. Great fun! Everyone was reaching their personal relaxed stage this far into the cruise and they were enjoying the evening. We have made so many new friends on this ship, how nice.

March 25, 2018 - Sunday

We woke up in Speyer, Germany today, with blue skies and sunshine. After breakfast we headed into town for the sites of Speyer, a town founded by the Romans in 50 AD. The highlight was a Romanesque Cathedral built in 1030, a magnificent structure. It is Sunday and the people were arriving for Palm Sunday. The stores in town were closed, but we enjoyed the walk.

After lunch we had the pleasure of hosting several European Shriners from Emirat Shriners and their Ladies on the ship. A small group of us went to meet the Mayor of

Speyer at City Hall where he gave us some history of the city. Our small group then proceeded to the burial site of Helmut Kohl, the former Chancellor of Germany. He was involved with bringing down the wall in Germany.

We then went back to the ship where we had a reception with all of our visitors from Emirat Shriners. It was a fun time and they were so appreciative and gracious to be on the ship with us for a few hours. We recognized the new Daughters of the Nile members on board who are members of the Orlando Chapter, Athaliah, and took many pictures. They all left the ship about 6 PM. As there are not that many Shriners in Europe, I know this was special for them to be able to associate with other Shriners. Those of us on the ship all felt good about the visit.

After a nice dinner we had Karaoke - Round 2 in the lounge, it was great fun and the ships staff joined us on this evening. Let the good times roll!

March 26, 2018 - Monday

We have arrived in France, Strasbourg, France. Swans were swimming all around the ship where we were docked as we had our breakfast, pretty cool. Our day started with a walking tour of Strasbourg, a larger city with lots of history and sites to see, including neat canals. We also took a ride on the public tram to the downtown area and saw homes that dated back 400 years. This city dates back over 1000 years and we saw the magnificent Strasbourg Cathedral regarded as one of Europe's great Gothic Cathedrals. By noon we were back on the ship for lunch.

We then took a bus about an hour away for the optional Alsatian Highlights excursion through the famous wine region. We visited the Stork Park where many strokes come during this time of year to lay their eggs. Then we visited the quaint town of Kaysersberg, France and browsed through the stores. Dinner was back on the ship followed by entertainment by a local accordion player in the lounge. On this night most seemed to retire early.

March 27, 2018 - Tuesday

We are still in France, but we all boarded three buses and drove up into the Black Forrest. It was beautiful, and when we reached the top there was snow on the ground and a couple of ski resorts were there. We then proceeded down out of the hills to Baden-Baden, Germany. Here we walked through the town that is famous for its thermal spa baths since Roman times. While the girls shopped, Mikey, Bob, David, and I had a beer in a cool German Beer Garden.

The buses got back to the ship in time to have a late lunch onboard. As we were eating the ship set sail for Switzerland, our final stop. During the afternoon we began to pack as we will be leaving the ship in two days.

The evening was entertainment by the crew as they provided a "Crew Show." It was outstanding. At the conclusion I presented an Imperial Potentates MEDALLION, one collectively for the entire crew, to show our appreciation for the tremendous job they did taking care of all of us for the past two weeks. After the show concluded, we did a picture with the Captain, Robert, the Hotel Manager, and me in the wheel house with the Imperial Potentates MEDALLION. This really is one of the highlights of this Imperial year for Anne and me. The trip was great, but even better than that was all of the wonderful people we were able to spend quality time with. Being a Shriner is so great.

March 28, 2018 - Wednesday

Today, our last day, we woke up in a port in Basel, Switzerland. This is to be our warmest day of the trip, going up into the mid 50's. After breakfast we first did a group photo of everyone on the trip up on the sundeck. We did an I AM – RU Committed to Membership video too. Then we started our Basel explorations, in Switzerland's second largest city. We took a bus downtown and did a walking tour through parts of the old town. This again was very interesting. After the tour our smaller group had lunch in town and did some shopping afterwards. By 3 PM it was lightly raining, and we decided to head back to the ship. Prior to dinner we did a photo of all Bahia Shriners and Ladies who joined us on this wonderful trip.

On this final night some of us were invited to have dinner at the Captains table. On this night we completed Anne and my wish to have dinner at least one night with everyone on the ship. Mission accomplished, and it was a great success as we were able to get to know everyone personally. Following dinner, most went to their rooms early to pack for our early departure off the ship, the next morning. Most will be flying home, but about 40 will be staying for an extended road trip in Switzerland.

This entire experience of a river boat cruise in Europe exceeded Anne and my highest expectations. It was a great success that all enjoyed. We are very happy with it. Of interest, the fourteen consecutive nights Anne and I slept on this ship were the most we slept in any one place all year long. Although the ship moved every day, we remained in the same bed.

March 29, 2018 - Thursday

Whew, alarm went off at 5:30 AM. We got ready and then finished up our packing. After a quick breakfast in the dining room and some last-minute goodbyes, it was time to jump on the bus to the airport. Again, our Program Directors were with us all the way to the gate. This was a long day of travel with three plane changes. We arrived home about 10 PM, with a 6-hour time change. A long 22-hour day for sure. Many thoughts of the trip went through our minds as we traveled home, all of them good. The important thing was that everyone had a wonderful time and enjoyed themselves. We feel blessed it turned out so well.

We went through our mail, unpacked a few things and went to bed. I had to be back at the airport at 9 AM for another flight out.

March 30, 2018 - Friday

Early to rise, every day. To start the day, I needed to finish unpacking and then repack for my trip to Washington DC. I was going for the York Rite, Grand Encampment of Knights Templar Easter weekend. By 9 AM I was right back at the airport ready to go again, but this time I was on my own as Anne was home catching up on things there.

I arrived in Washington DC at 4 PM to cool weather. After getting to my room and settling in it was time to attend a special invitation reception and dinner of VIP Guests. I only knew 3 people at the event to start but soon became acquainted with others. Sitting at my table was George Seghers, the Executive Director of the George Washington Masonic Memorial. I expressed to him my desire to get a Shriners display back into that building, he agreed. We made an appointment to meet on Sunday after the Easter Service to tour the building and to discuss how we can get collaboration between our two organizations.

After dinner I stopped by the hospitality room for a Diet Coke and proceeded to my room. I was still having some jet lag from our trip back from Switzerland a day earlier.

March 31, 2018 - Saturday

Today was a free day mostly, after getting up a little later and having some breakfast I headed to the Smithsonian Museum of American History. This was my first time attending a Smithsonian Museum. It was outstanding. In particular, because of my interest and collection of United States Presidential memorabilia I especially enjoyed the area on Presidents and First Ladies. I enjoyed seeing items of my friends Jimmy and Rosalynn Carter there as well as some of the old cars.

After returning to the hotel midafternoon it was soon time for the Grand Encampment Reception and Dinner. Dressed in my Imperial Divan suit, I felt like the most underdressed man in the room. All of the members of the Knights Templar were dressed to the hilt in their decorated uniforms. I was impressed. The dinner and company were delightful and enjoyable. Following dinner, it was a short evening as the following morning was the Easter Sunrise Service.

Chapter Ten
April 2018

April 1, 2018 - Sunday

The alarm went off at 5AM. After getting ready and a quick breakfast we loaded up on busses and headed to the George Washington Masonic Memorial in Alexandria, Virginia.

With 50-degree weather we marched up the hill to the steps of the building where the outside service was held overlooking the city. Here all of the Knights were dressed in their most ornate and prestigious attire and a beautiful Easter Service was given. It was nicely done in a most respectful way.

Following the Service, George Seghers gave me the tour of the George Washington Masonic Memorial we had planned. I had not been in the building in several years and was now in total awe of the tremendous amount of work and improvements that had been done. The building had transformed back to the distinguished honor it had once held and was updated to today's standards. Again, I was extremely impressed. After taking the tour I was even more desirous of having the Shriners represented again in the building. George will be putting together a presentation for me to present to our boards at our meeting in Mexico City in two weeks.

It was then a quick trip to the airport to head back home for a day. Upon arrival back home, I was able to have Easter dinner with some of our family. It's always great to spend some family time, especially on a holiday.

Gary Bergenske's Shriners Diary - Our Mission – Our Members – and Me

April 2, 2018 - Monday

Catch up day at J&J Metro, and there was a lot to catch up on. I had not been at my office here for three weeks. It was good to see all of the employees here and to spend some time with them.

By late afternoon I was on my way to Tampa for Committee week. This will take up the remainder of the week as we prepare for our Board meeting coming up in Mexico City.

April 3, 2018 – Tuesday

The morning started with a 7 AM Executive Team meeting followed by an 8AM Committee meeting, both at Shrine Headquarters. Meetings lasted until five, but I was able to sneak in and out as I had many other individual meetings I needed to attend to. The day ended with dinner with some of the finest men I know, other Board members.

April 4, 2018 - Wednesday

Another full day of committee meetings. All of these meetings are in preparation for our upcoming Board meeting in Mexico City in two weeks. Again, I was able to accomplish much more by being at headquarters with many other important issues. Already we are working on the upcoming Imperial Session in Daytona Beach. Where does the time go? I talked with Anne several times during the day, she is sick at home and really under the weather. After another dinner it was off to bed rather early this night.

April 5, 2018 - Thursday

Another full day of Committee meetings starting at 8 AM sharp. I spent some time with Jessica as well going over upcoming schedules and flights. We also worked on a letter to send out to all Board members about the I AM - RU Committed to Membership program; to remind each of them on their commitment to top line sign a new member this year. Although we are behind on meeting my personal membership goal, I'm proud to say creations are up and suspensions are down. I'm hopeful the report I give on this at the Imperial Session will be very positive. I'm confident we can change the culture with the right attitude. Still, Anne is sick at home, hope she feels better soon. She has been trying to do too much, a few days of rest will be helpful.

April 6, 2018 - Friday

The final day of Committee week and I was glad to be on my way home by noon. It took me three hours to get home due to the bad traffic caused by accidents and construction. Once I got in town, I went by my office and worked for a few hours. Anne was still not feeling well so I picked up dinner on the way home. Unpacked and did some laundry and soon I was ready to sleep in my own bed for a night.

April 7, 2018 - Saturday

Up early and off to J&J Metro for the morning to get the crews off and to catch up on some work. Things are in good order, even with me gone so much.

Bahia Shriners, my own Shrine Center, was having a Car Show at their new Building, so I drove my 1999 Corvette over, looked around and had lunch. This was great for me as I had not seen the new place since its completion. Everything was done and looked great as it was all new. We should not have any problems there for a while. We will be able to just enjoy it. The Car Show turned out great, we had more participants than expected. Looking forward to enjoying this new place over the coming years. It was nice to casually visit my own Shrine Center as the Imperial Potentate.

I was able to get some things done around the house and then prepare for our trip to Daytona Beach. We are going for a Pre-Con meeting for the upcoming Imperial Session just three months away. Time flies when you're having fun.

April 8, 2018 - Sunday

We were up and at it early, lots to catch up on around the house. I spent some time on the pool and in the yard. Soon it was time to get those suit cases packed for our trip to Daytona Beach for Pre Con. I drove over ahead of Anne and she joined us in time for diner. It was great to see our convention team and the Daytona Beach CVB Team for diner. We had some catching up to do and then a lot of talk about our plans for our second consecutive Imperial Session in Daytona Beach. The Hilton Team as well gave us a warm welcome and expressed how excited they were we would be returning again in July. We are so blessed to have so many great people assisting us with this.

April 9, 2018 - Monday

After a 7:30 breakfast we started our meeting promptly at 8:30. It was like an old coming home week. We also had the 2019 Nashville Team join us and we all worked together on planning the session. Throughout the day different convention committee chairmen came in to give their reports as did many local officials.

We presented each of them with a 2017 Imperial Session Medallion they all loved. The weather was windy and rainy, but we were all dry in our meeting. For diner we walked over to Sloppy Joe's, the rain even stopped for our walk. It was a good day of planning and of confirming our agendas. We enjoyed having the 2019 Nashville Team with us and we are hoping we are giving them some good information to assist their future planning.

April 10, 2018 - Tuesday

We woke up to more rain. Anne got up early and was on her way to Atlanta by 7AM to go help daughter Jami with the grandkids as Jami just had surgery. Anne had still not recovered from being sick herself the week before but drove up to be of help. She is an amazing woman.

Our Pre-Con meeting again started at 8:30 and we continued to work through our planning. We completed all of our tasks by noon, had lunch, and departed for home. I was able to get back to my Orlando office to work a couple of hours there before going home. A quite night at home, almost forgot what that was like, it was wonderful. The Imperial Potentate home alone, could be dangerous.

April 11, 2018 - Wednesday

Into work at J&J Metro by 7:30 for a full day of work including a few errands I was behind on. And of course, a few Shrine conference calls during the day. I was able to get a lot done and reflected on the past 9 months of serving as the Imperial Potentate. What an honor it has been, to meet so many wonderful people and to have the opportunity to go to so many places. Anne and I will be forever grateful.

After having a bite to eat out by myself, as Anne is in Atlanta, I headed home. I had a lot of packing to do, an eleven-day sprint to Las Vegas and then to Mexico City for the Spring Board Meeting. We all were as well taking children's books to Mexico City to give to the patients there. I was taking part of Anne's luggage with me as she would be meeting me in Mexico. So, I had a fun night packing.

I've been looking forward to the Mexico City Board Meeting for a couple of years. It became apparent to me a few years ago how important it was to me personally that every board member and staff member see what goes on there. As our busiest hospital that is bulging with patients, it's amazing and extremely touching what you see. If this trip touches the others half as much as it has Anne and me, it will be a big success. Can't wait to get there.

April 12, 2018 - Thursday

After loading up the car with a bunch of luggage I was off to the airport by myself. The first stop as usual was Atlanta. There I was joined by our outstanding Marshals, Richard and Judy for lunch. We proceed on to Las Vegas to attend the Western Shrine Association meeting that should be a great time in Vegas.

We were picked up at the airport by a friendly Shriner who brought his pickup truck because he heard we had a lot of luggage, a lot of which was books to give out at the Shriners Mexico City Hospital. We did fill his truck bed up with luggage and headed to the Golden Nugget Hotel. The place was great, and I had a nice room. We greeted people in the hospitality room where a good time was had by all. Then the Imperial Officers and their ladies had dinner with the Western President and his lady, Ray and Sharon. Following dinner, it was off to bed, the three-hour time change was catching up to us.

April 13, 2018 - Friday

Friday the 13th, wow. The day started early with a meeting of the Western Association of the Legion of Honor, starting a 7 AM. During the meeting I installed the newly elected officers. This was a good group as they talked of plans on how to get more membership and ways to get them more involved.

At 9 AM the main meeting of the Western Shrine Association started. This was a good meeting as well. The three Imperial Officers attending, Ed, Richard, and myself all had good presentations. They were all well excepted. We did a great I AM - RU Video too.

The evening started off with a Shrine nightshirt parade and competition. Some of these folks really got into dressing in their nightshirts, pretty funny. Their parade went down through the casino and out onto Fremont Street and back. We awarded trophies for the best dressed, drank, ate, and had a good time.

A Year as the Imperial Potentate of Shriners International

After this completion a few of us walked around Fremont Street and took in all the sights, and they were something else. It was real fun. Following this the Imperial Officers and wives (I was still missing Anne) had a nice dinner and then retired for a night's sleep.

April 14, 2018 - Saturday

Again, an early start as they had Motor Corp competition across from the hotel in a parking lot. It was the first time in many years they have had this the Western meeting, it was small, but a great start to getting it going again. I'm proud of their efforts and expect it will continue on, adding more value to attending their sessions in the future will bring more people.

By 10AM we were in a car and on the way to the airport. Richard, Judy, and I had Delta tickets but soon found out we were flying on Aero Mexico, their partner, and were in the wrong terminal. This caused some frustration, but we eventually found our way. Somehow, we left one of Judy's bags behind at the other terminal. Richard went back for it and fortunately it was still sitting where she left it at the other terminal. After grabbing something to eat we were on the plane and on our way to Mexico where I would again meet up with Anne.

April 15, 2018 - Sunday

We were able to sleep in a little today. There was a fantastic brunch in the hotel we all went to and enjoyed a moment of rest and relaxation. Following brunch, we all finished setting up of the hospitality room. Soon we began receiving the guests that would be attending the Board Meeting as they checked in. Everyone was impressed with the hotel.

We had a spectacular dinner at the hotel that was a Mexican buffet. Really good. We were serenaded by a wonderful Mariachi band and the atmosphere was very festive. Joining us for dinner was the entire Shriners Hospitals for Children - Mexico Board of Governors.

On this evening I presented my longtime friend, fellow Bahia Shriner and current Mexico City Shriners Hospitals for Children board member, George Barfield an Imperial Potentate's MEDALLION. He was overtaken with emotions in front of the many people in attendance. I was happy to be able to make this presentation. After dinner it was some time in the hospitality room and then off to bed.

April 16, 2018 - Monday

After breakfast, Monday started off with a Bang; all of the Joint Board Members along with the Executive Staff headed to Shriners Hospitals for Children - Mexico City. We were greeted by patients as we entered the building where many hugs were given. As we proceeded through the building, we witnessed a busy hospital full of children. We toured the clinic area and also the in-patient wards.

I approached a young boy sitting up in his hospital bed, his Mother at his side. I asked him, "How are you doing!" He replied, "I'm okay, yesterday they cut both my legs off." I didn't know what to say, I was speechless and began to feel a lump growing in my throat. With that he pulled back his covers an exposed his two amputated legs. He said, "I'm getting new legs and soon I'll be able to run and play." His legs were amputated because the deformities were so bad, he was unable to walk. By now, you know, I was crying. My tears were of sadness, but also of pride as I knew we were making a tremendous difference in this child's life. These moments touch me ever so much, it's things like this that keep me going strong every day.

Many tears were shed by others too as we walked through the hospital, the families of the patients were so outwardly grateful. They wanted pictures with us wearing our Fez and many would hug us. It was such a touching experience.

A Year as the Imperial Potentate of Shriners International

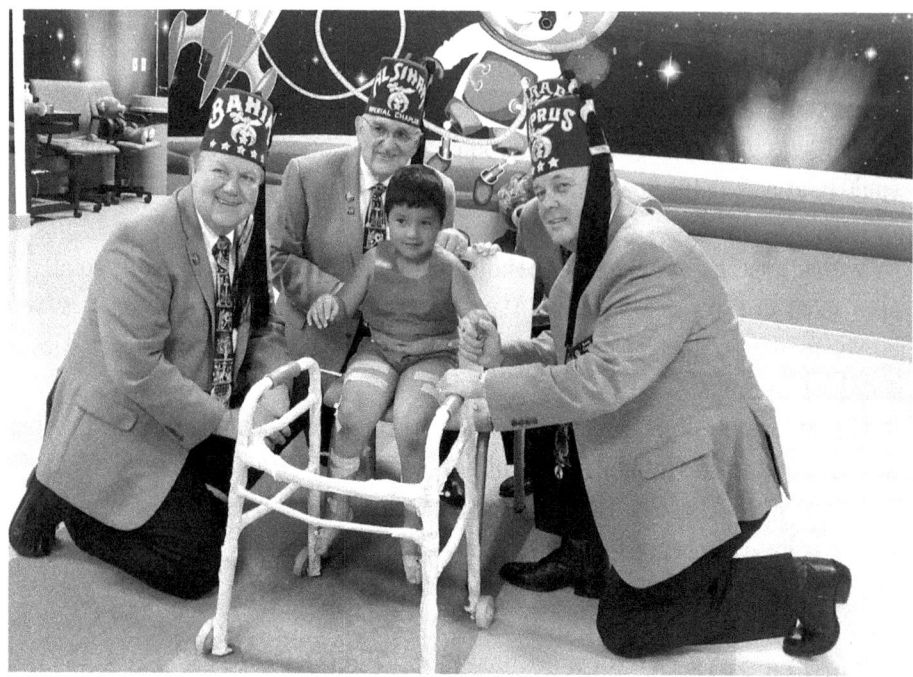

As we left the hospital and walked through the parking lot, families and patients followed us to the bus, still asking for pictures. To think they looked up to us so much

and are so appreciative of the work we do is incredible. It's a humbling experience to know each of us has a small part in changing the lives of children and their families.

We headed back to the hotel to begin our Board Meeting. After the bus dropped us off, it loaded up our ladies for a hospital visit and to have lunch there. The ladies took with them all of the children's books we all brought with us to give to the children. Most of the ladies had never been to our busiest hospital before. They too were touched by the patients and their families. I'm so glad Anne and I brought everyone here to see this during our Board Meeting.

Back at the hotel our meetings progressed nicely, and we were able to complete some good business. The hotel staff was extraordinary and went above and beyond to make sure we were all doing well.

For dinner we all loaded up on two buses and headed to Hacienda de Tlalpan Restaurant. As we entered into the grounds we were greeted by beautiful peacocks and gardens. We started with happy hour on the roof top and then proceeded to the dining room on the first floor. This was a wonderful meal with great company. Here I presented Dr. Hasis an Imperial Potentate's MEDALLION for his 30 years of service including 20 years as the Chief of Staff. He was surprised and broke down in tears as he accepted the Medallion. He then gave a nice talk and reflected on his service with Shriners. Following dinner, we were bused back to the hotel for some needed sleep. The ladies were still talking about their hospital visit.

April 17, 2018 - Tuesday

Another great breakfast that is included in our room rate and our meetings started at 8 AM. I'm happy to say we have been moving through our business in good time and that everyone is working together. During lunch we had three local patients join us. By having patients around, it sure keeps us focused on our mission. One of these patients, a young boy with cerebral palsy played the piano for us and sang. It was very touching, and he was very good. Our meetings continued throughout the afternoon.

Our ladies had a nice day visiting the Presidential Palace and some old Ruins. They then had lunch at the Grand Hotel, a 100+ year old beautifully kept place. They are all having a good time, this is good as every one of them provide a tremendous support system for us.

For dinner we all went to the Amatista Room in our hotel for a delicious dinner and drinks. I could not be more pleased on how things are going, everyone having a good time and our meetings are moving along good.

April 18, 2018 - Wednesday

This was a big day during our trip. After meeting for a couple of hours in the morning we prepared for our day trip. We all loaded up on a couple of buses and took our two-hour ride to the Teotilhuacan - Guanajuato; Pyramid of the Sun adventure. It is an incredible city built 2000 years ago, discovered again in the early 1900's. It's hard to imagine how they could have built something like this so long ago with no tools or electricity. Amazing!

We walked around the pyramids and several of our group climbed all the way to the top, not an easy task, I know as I've done it before. On the way back, we stopped at some gift shop type places and learned more about the area. This proved to be a great team building day for our boards, staff, and ladies. They all intermingled so well. We had a dinner at the hotel when we arrived back. Everyone was tired from a busy day and retired early.

April 19, 2018 - Thursday

Another early breakfast and an 8AM start to our meeting. We moved through a lot of business on this day that was very productive. I'm so proud everyone is so respectful of each other in our meetings, nice to see everyone pulling in the same direction for the betterment of our organizations. Long day of meetings and discussions on this day.

Our ladies went to the market, Plaza Ciudaldela for a day of shopping for traditional Mexican items. They had a great time and were able to purchase some nice items, shirts, etc. when they arrived back at the hotel it was time to get ready for dinner.

Again, we all boarded a couple of buses for dinner, this time we were off to Restaurante Arroyo, a festive Mexican Restaurante. Upon arrival drinks were served and we experienced an official Mexican band complete with dancers for an hour. We then moved into the dining area for diner. The Anezeh Shriners Divan from Mexico City joined us, and this was a wonderful experience for all of us. The Mexican Shriners do not often have an opportunity to see other Shriners. I had the pleasure along with the Anezeh Potentate to present a Charter for a New Shrine Club prior to dinner. Lots of Tequila was being served and it was beginning to show. Our dinner was a true Mexican one and was so good.

After dinner, I was privileged to recognize Illustrious Sir Edaurdo, the Anezeh Potentado for his heroic efforts in helping with the transfer of 9 young girls who had been badly burned from Guatemala to Shriners Hospitals. He assisted in raising the money for transferring the girls to the United States for care in just a couple of days. Through

his efforts 8 of the girls survived and are back home now. The crowd gave him a standing ovation, he then told his heartfelt story. Another amazing moment.

On the way back to the hotel there was a lot of singing on the bus, I think the tequila had something to do with it. As I say, success comes from working hard and playing hard.

April 20, 2018 - Friday

Our final day of the Board Meeting. We again started at 8AM, and on this day we completed at noon. We invited as many hotel staff as was available into our meeting room, so we could give thanks to them for the over the top treatment they have given us. They truly did an excellent job and we all appreciated it, often referring to it as the best service we have ever had. The hotel staff had a special surprise for us too, they had our lunch beautifully set up pool side for us to enjoy. It was fantastic! The rest of the afternoon was free, and we all needed a little down time to catch up.

Our final dinner was held at the hotel in the Tezka Restaurant. The room was set up for Kings including Mexican dressed men and ladies. Happy hour was a fun time. When dinner started, we had a blind saxophone player providing quiet music for us. That is until the lower 5 on the line began singing. They actually did really well. Everyone had a great time on our last night together and we had many compliments on the week. It really was a good and productive week.

April 21, 2018 - Saturday

Up early, time to head home for a couple of days. We got ready, finished up our packing and headed to the airport with Richard and Judy with a driver. After getting our bags checked and through TSA we grabbed a bite to eat in the Areo Mexico Sky Club. Anne and I are so proud of the work Richard and Judy did this week as the Marshals, awesome. They pay attention to every detail, we are very lucky.

When we arrived in Atlanta and got through customs, Anne left the airport with the Burke's and I proceeded on to my flight to Orlando. Anne's car was still in Atlanta from her visit to help Jami after her surgery. I arrived home, all was well at the house. After unpacking I did some laundry, watched a little TV and crashed into my own bed. That sure felt good.

April 22, 2018 - Sunday

A day to sleep in some, how nice. After getting up and getting a few things done around the house I met Jason and Avery for lunch at Chucky Cheese. Our original plan was to go boating but the weather turned out to be rainy. A little family time was enjoyed for a change. I then spent this Sunday afternoon at work catching up on mail, paying bills etc. for our business. Fortunately, everything there is running well even with Anne and I being gone so much. A big thank you to our staff there.

We are now officially into the final quarter of this Imperial Potentate year. It has flown by and we are so appreciative of all the other people who have helped us. We hope to finish strong, especially with our I AM - RU Committed to Membership Program.

April 23, 2018 - Monday

A full day of work coupled with Shrine Conference calls at J&J Metro. Planning for the Imperial Session is beginning to pick up too. The committees are all up and running with an attitude to even improve on what we did last year. We are so lucky to have such a committed team.

Anne arrived back home after driving in from Atlanta today. She is feeling a little under the weather and tired, the past couple of weeks have been a lot for her with the traveling and helping the kids. We had dinner out and went home for a quiet night.

April 24, 2018 - Tuesday

The morning started off at work for a few hours. I picked up Anne at 11:30 and we headed to Daytona Beach for a meeting at the Daytona Hilton. Our meeting was with regards to Anne's Ladies Luncheon, with committee people and Hilton staff. We spent 3 hours tasting wonderful food, and planning the menu, decorations, the program and more. By the time we were done the plan was all in place. This was a big relief for Anne to have this behind us, everyone was so helpful. It was a pleasure to work with this wonderful team.

After returning back to Orlando we had dinner with David and Marie Angie for an early celebration of Marie Angie's birthday. This was again a nice evening.

April 25, 2018 - Wednesday

Wow - three days in a row of going into my office, not sure if this has happened before this year. Was able to get several things done along with more Shrine conference calls. Did some planning with Jason with regards to Move it Pro and on building out more office space to accommodate the growing need for more employees. This has been growing fast and is exciting to watch.

We ate dinner at home and packed for an early departure in the morning to the airport. This is daughter Lisa's birthday today, we finally contacted her about 9:30 to wish her a Happy Birthday and to catch up on some things.

April 26, 2018 - Thursday

Up at 4:30 AM, shower, finish packing, load the car, and off to the airport by six o'clock. An early start for our trip to the Pittsburg area for Mid Atlantic Shrine Association, always one of our favorites. We have met so many nice people in this association that we have become good friends with, this makes for great fun.

At the Atlanta airport we met up with Richard, Judy, and Kevin on our way to Pittsburg. Upon arrival at the Pittsburg airport we were greeted by Nobles and Ladies who loaded us up and took us to the hotel. On the way we saw beautiful cherry trees in full bloom, what a sight. A group greeted us as we arrived at the hotel. We were handed the keys to our room that was a very nice suite.

That evening we visited the hospitality room and then went for a great meal right there in the hotel. Good food and great friendships continued through the night. By now Imperial Sir Jim and Patsy had joined us as well. Patsy, as she always does, was again doing a tremendous job selling First Lady's Project items.

April 27, 2018 - Friday

The morning started with a great breakfast buffet at the hotel and the Mid Atlantic Shrine Association meeting started at 9AM. The morning session was for MASA business and then again, we had a good lunch. The afternoon was spent with the four Imperial Officers providing education and reports to the Nobility. This made for a good full day of meetings.

The evening was a nice MASA Presidents Banquet with everyone in attendance. During my remarks prior to the dinner I presented Illustrious Sir Dick Wright PP an Imperial Potentate's MEDALLION for his service to the Shriners organizations. He is a Past Potentate of Khedive Shriners, a Past President of MASA, the current Treasurer of Khedive for the past 32 years and has been a Shriner for 56 years.

I told the story of how he and his wife Thelma had welcomed Anne and I on our first trip to MASA 13 years ago when we were campaigning. How they made us feel so welcome and continued to do the same through the years. Although Thelma passed away a few years ago, this presentation was for her as well. Dick and I both choked up with tears as the presentation was made.

I was so proud to present this to him as he is so deserving and humble. The crowd rose to their feet in applause as he accepted the award and shared his memory as well about the first time we met. It was a touching moment as he too, remembered his wife.

After diner it was drinks and dancing in the hospitality room, and some shots of Fireball before heading upstairs to bed. That evening as I was lying in bed thinking about the day's activities, it became clear to me what one of the most prestigious honors of being the Imperial Potentate was. It is the honor of holding this high office which affords you the privilege to recognize others in a way that is so impactful, so appreciated, and so emotional. When I think back of the Imperial Potentate's MEDALLIONS I have presented this year, they have all been very emotional and most involved tears of gratitude. I'm so grateful to have the privilege of recognizing others so they know their efforts are appreciated.

April 28, 2018 - Saturday

After breakfast the meetings resumed. First thing, we made an I AM – RU Committed to Membership video, and this time I was able to hold one of our beautiful patients, Sarah while we did it. We then had a report from one of our Doctors from the SHC Erie hospital. Very good. We left prior to the conclusion of the morning meeting for the airport.

When we arrived in Atlanta, we exited the airport as we now had a function there. Richard and Judy had their car there and dropped us off at our hotel. We had a couple of hours to rest up and then it was off to the Golf Tournament Banquet, a fundraiser for Shriners Hospitals for Children at a local Golf Club in Atlanta. They had many NFL Alumni who were going to play in the tournament in attendance. There was a silent auction, BBQ dinner, beer tasting, and a trick golf hitting expert. Alec and his mom and sister were also in attendance and we spent some time talking with them. I had my picture taken again with Heisman Trophy winner George Rogers and his 1980 Heisman Trophy. It was a nice relaxed evening.

April 29, 2018 - Sunday

Had a great breakfast with Alec and Kevin Butler, the former place kicker of the Chicago Bears who played on their 1985 Super Bowl Team. Our discussions were all about sports and I'm always impressed by the knowledge and enthusiasm Alec has when the topic is sports. He has an incredible ability to carry on great discussions with anyone regarding sports.

Later on, we were with Richard and Judy and had lunch along with Jami, Jason, and the kids. Following lunch Richard, Judy, Anne, and I went to visit Gene Bracewell at the hospital. He was still in ICU and not accepting visitors. Catherine was there, and we were able to spend some time with her. Gene is not doing well at all and Catherine is very worried as we all are about Gene. Unfortunately, he has not been doing well for some time, our prayers are with him and his family. Gene is one of the finest men, particularly as a Shriner I have ever met. Wishing for the best for him.

When we left the hospital, we were off to the airport again to head home, back to Orlando for a couple of days. Once we got through security, we ran across two Shriners I knew from the Philippines from my last visit there. That was a surprise, they were heading home from the Jesters Annual meeting. We will be seeing them again in three days in their country, half way around the world, in the Philippines. We arrived home safe and sound. David and Marie Angie prepared diner for us at our house, this was a nice treat.

April 30, 2018 - Monday

A day home in Orlando and it was spent at J&J Metro working. Business is good there and starting to pick up for our summer season. Most of the day was spent catching up on mail, payables, and planning for the next 30 days as we will be gone most of the month of May. Anne and I had dinner out, then went home to begin packing for our 16-day trip.

Chapter Eleven
May 2018

May 1, 2018 - Tuesday

Although I spent the day at J&J Metro, I was on a Shrine conference call for 8 hours. We did interviews for the position of Chief Membership Development Officer; interviewing five different finalists. All five were excellent, however at the end of the day we narrowed it down to three for face to face interviews later in the month. I feel good that we will find a great leader to take our membership efforts to a new level.

We celebrated Avery's birthday in the evening a day early. Jason, Avery, Anne and I went out to eat and gave Avery a few gifts. Her actual birthday is tomorrow but we will be gone. After diner we headed home to finish packing for our long trip to the Philippines and Honolulu. What a task! It was nearly midnight before we went to bed and our alarm was set for 4:30 AM.

May 2, 2018 - Wednesday

Yep, 4:30 AM and the alarm goes off for the beginning of a long two days. We don't arrive in Manilla until 8 PM the following day. We were on the way to the airport early and boarded our flight to Detroit. Our next flight is Detroit to Tokyo, and then on to Manilla. A long trip for sure. Jeff and Cheryl are going with us to attend a Mabuhay Shriners Ceremonial, this is exciting as they are anticipating over 200 new candidates.

A little sleep, lots of TV, some work on the computer, and three meals later we landed in Tokyo. Eastern time it was 1 AM in the morning, but Japan time it was 1 PM Thursday afternoon. We lost a few hours going over the time line.

May 3, 2018 - Thursday

With the time change and going over the time line we were all out of whack. Our flight from Tokyo to Manilla was five hours. We arrived in Manilla at 8 PM and were greeted inside the security area where we got off the plane by several Shriners. They escorted us through immigration and out into the public part of the airport. After getting all of our bags, we along with the Sowders loaded up in a van for two-hour police escorted trip to Clark. Clark is a former United States Air Force Base where the Ceremonial will be held.

When we first arrived, we were given a tour of the hotel and were greeted by the 205 Novices (new candidates) who were soon to become Shriners. It was amazing, they were all dressed in matching outfits and had a camel with them. They sang the "Bubbles" song for us and we recorded it. We also did an I AM - RU Committed to Membership video outside near the pool. It's hard to even explain what was going on here, with so many new candidates, all the preparation, the excitement in the air, it was incredible. They had been waiting for us to eat, even though it was late. It was eleven by the time we checked into our room and we were exhausted. We fell asleep quickly, but it was hard to continue to sleep with a 12-hour time change.

May 4, 2018 - Friday

Jeff and I were up early for a 7 AM breakfast, Anne and Cheryl had until nine before they had to meet the ladies. After breakfast all of the men along with the 205 candidates headed to downtown Clark for a Shriners Ceremonial Parade.

The excitement continues as they prepare for this parade line up. The nearly two-mile walking parade went through the town. The Novices, all dressed alike in yellow T-shirts and white covers on their head sang the bubble song the entire way. Along the way we placed a large wreath at the statue of one of the Philippines former Presidents who was a Mason. This was a touching moment.

The highlight of the parade took place when all of the Novices were showered with water from a Fire Truck. I was invited to the truck, climbed up on top and took part in spraying all of the new guys. It was pretty neat.

Gary Bergenske's Shriners Diary - Our Mission – Our Members – and Me

A Year as the Imperial Potentate of Shriners International

I then took off my Fez, emptied my pockets and joined all of the Novices in being hosed down by the fire truck. We were all soaked to the bone. It was so hot out it felt good, but there was not a dry spot on us. The dress shoes I had on were full of water and squeaked with every step. The new guys were so happy I joined them, they picked me up and carried me. Singing, "We love our Potentate, we love our Potentate." After a few more blocks the fire truck showed up again, and again we were soaked. As we proceeded through the streets we came upon an area where there were many kids, the Shriners had toys to pass out to them there and the kids went wild.

The parade eventually ended where it started, and they had a great sound system set up with music playing. Soon a program started that included speakers, the Mayor, Potentate, Jeff and me. In addition, during this time 15 children's wheelchairs were donated for local needs. Good program that lasted a half hour and ended with the fire truck again spraying all of the new guys. Interesting, the Novices were transported to and from the parade in large Police trucks. Many police officers are Shriners here and they are willing to assist when they can.

After getting back to the hotel it was time for lunch. This was an experience too. Outside they set up 20 or so banquet tables lined up in a single row. The tables were covered with large banana tree leaves, then on them was rice, chicken, noodles, sardines, peppers, boiled eggs with the shells still on, and more. All 205 Novices lined up around this table and ate with their hands only. What a sight, watching them eat as I was at the head of the table eating too. At the end of lunch, about 15 minutes, all that was left on the table was the banana leaves, chicken bones, and egg shells. The afternoon was some free time for us, we had a tour of Clark Air Force base and got some needed rest.

While we were at the parade and lunch, the ladies went shopping and then to a poor part of town where they met with many poor children. They taught them how to properly wash their hands and brush their teeth. They then gave them gifts. It was a moving experience for all of the ladies, they shared their stories with us.

In the evening was the Imperial Potentate's Banquet attended by about 500. It was a spectacular affair with a nice meal and entertainment by the Novices. They also auctioned off the Novices, mostly their Shrine Clubs bought them. They raised $26,000 US dollars doing this for Patient Transportation.

I gave a speech on the difference between Good and Great. Then I proceeded to compliment them on reaching "greatness" and expressed my thanks and gratitude to Mabuhay Shriners for reaching "Greatness" with their membership efforts.

I predicted their greatness would lead them to becoming the largest Shriners location in the world within five years in membership. Everything was being videotaped and the crew doing it was excellent as they would turn around videos to view in hours.

May 5, 2018 - Saturday

This morning started off with a 7 AM breakfast again. The Sowders and us along with some of the Shrine ladies were going to a Spa day up in the mountains to be buried (with our head out) in hot ash from the Volcano. We also visited hot springs where the pools had natural hot water. It was some of the most beautiful scenery we have ever seen. To get there we had to take four-wheel Jeeps up the river bed. In some areas there was some water flowing we had to drive through. For four to five months per year this place is not even excisable. During the rainy season the river bed becomes a raging river. Glad we were here at a time of year we could see this. So, Jeff, the ladies, and I experienced the hot sands, being buried in the ash of a volcano with ladies walking on top of us to massage us. The final step was a mud bath. All of us covered in mud proceeded down the mountain in the Jeeps where we were able to take a shower. We were then treated to a nice lunch in this paradise. We then headed back to the hotel. We found the people of the Philippines to be so good to us, they went above and beyond to make sure we were enjoying our time in their country.

After a quick change it was time to attend the graduation and Fezzing Ceremony for all of the new Shriners. First, we presented the Charters to the officers of the four new Mabuhay Shrine Clubs. Then we installed the officers of the newly formed Mabuhay Legion of Honor. Next, Retired Major General of the Philippines Marine Corps, General Alexander Balutan was made a Shriner at sight, this really excited the crowd. Following this I personally Fezzed all 205 new Mabuhay Shriners and then Imperial Sir Jeff presented them with an Imperial Potentate's Pin. This was a real honor to Fez 205 Shriners. The celebrating was running high with passion.

Imperial Sir Jeff and I received numerous gifts and Accolades for attending. At the closing, I presented an Imperial Potentate's MEDALLION to the entire membership for their efforts on building membership. The Illustrious Sir Graciously received it on behalf of his entire membership. By the time this was all done it was 4 PM. We packed and loaded our things into the van and headed back to Manilla with a Police Escort where we checked into the Fairmont Hotel, a beautiful hotel in downtown. These Police escorts we had the entire time we were here, cut our travel time in half because of the busy traffic everywhere.

After checking into our rooms, we walked across the street for some American food at TGIF Friday's with our Filipino friends. We were exhausted and headed off to bed soon after dinner.

May 6, 2018 - Sunday

Finally, we were able to sleep in a little. After a 10 AM breakfast we headed out to a Mall and then to a market. Paul was our driver and has been doing a great job our entire visit. We all enjoyed the market, it was big and had some of everything at reduced prices. We had an early dinner with the Sowders, and the Potentate along with other Divan members and ladies. After dinner they then took us to a spa for a massage. This place was something else. There was a movie theater inside where we all watched a movie while having a lady massage each one of us individually during the entire movie. Wow did that feel good. They have really gone overboard taking care of us here, it's been so nice.

By the time the movie was over it was time to head back to the hotel and turn in early. This has been a tremendous trip, everyone has been so nice, and 205 new Shriners have been created. I'm also thankful that Jeff and Cheryl came along too, it's been a great experience for them as well for the future of Shriners International.

May 7, 2018 - Monday

This is our last full day in the Philippines. After breakfast the ladies did some shopping. The men went to the Philippines Grand Lodge. It was the first day in office at the Grand Lodge for the new Grand Master.

At 8 AM they did a ceremonial flag raising on the grounds followed by a fellowship breakfast. The new Grand Master, who is also the Oriental Guide of the Shriners, makes for a great connection. We were then given a personal tour by the Grand Master of the very impressive Grand Lodge building. During the tour there was a Catholic Priest who was blessing the building and sprinkling Holy Water everywhere in honor of a new administration beginning.

We then visited the Masonic Museum and DeMolay offices that were also on the Grand Lodge property. This was exceptional as we also met the DeMolay Grand Master who provided us with token gifts.

Next was a visit to the offices of Mabuhay Shriners, also on the Grand Lodge property. Here we had a short tour and a meeting with some of the Shrine officers. They are really upbeat with all they are doing. They also presented Imperial Sir Jeff and I with some token gifts and a Mabuhay Fez. On the Grand Lodge property was also a small hotel for visiting guest to stay in.

From here we proceeded to a special luncheon at the invitation of the Grand Master at an elegant restaurant. There were about 20 in attendance, all of the top Masonic and Shrine leaders. I sat next to a Past Grand Master who had been totally blind for the past ten years, he reminded me of my Grandfather who I never met but was also totally blind in his later years. In our discussions he shared with me that although he is blind, he now knows all of his friends much better as their conversations are much better and deeper since becoming blind. How interesting. At the conclusion of the lunch, the Grand Master presented Jeff and I with a wooden plaque made by prisoners, and a paperweight made from volcanic ash. He even gave us a gift to take to our wives.

Our final dinner was with part of the Mabuhay Shriners and their ladies at a nice Italian Restaurant. The food was good, and the company was even better. Again, they had gifts for us that they presented. Necklaces for the ladies, and a box of Masonic items displayed in a nice wooden box for Jeff and me. They have been just so nice to us. Following dinner, it was back to the hotel to finish up our packing for an early departure for the airport.

May 8, 2018 - Tuesday

Up at 4:30 to shower, finish packing and to head to the airport for an 8 AM flight. Our first leg was to Tokyo along with Jeff and Cheryl. From there Anne and I headed to Honolulu and the Sowders headed back to Kansas. Anne and I had a six-hour layover and were dragging. On our flight to Honolulu we flew over the International Time Line and landed in Hawaii at 7:50 AM Tuesday morning. Confused, that's right, we gained a whole day as we actually landed in Hawaii before we took off from Manilla. Figure that one out.

We made our way to the hotel where the Annual Meeting of the Ladies Oriental Shrine would take place in a couple of days and checked in. The hotel was on Waikiki Beach and just totally remodeled, very nice. We spent a lazy day resting and trying to catch up on some sleep. We walked down the beach for a quite beachside dinner with just the two of us.

May 9, 2018 - Wednesday

This was a free day for us, a day to just relax, imagine that. Anne and I both could not remember the last time we had a day like this. We were able to sleep in and enjoy the day. Later we walked around the beach area, visited some of the local shops, and had a bite to eat.

Anne and I took a sunset cruise ride on a catamaran sailboat off the shores of Waikiki Beach. It was fun and outstanding as we sailed around Diamond Head on a warm night watching the sun set. After returning back we grabbed a light dinner and headed to our room at the hotel.

May 10, 2018 - Thursday

After getting up and getting caught up on some Shrine work and also with my office back home it was again time to spend some more free time. Anne and I rode around the Hawaiian Island and visited the Dole Plantation. This was interesting and had some fine pineapple ice cream we both enjoyed.

By now members of the Ladies Oriental Shrine of North America were arriving and we were visiting with them. Their pre-week of board meetings were taking place and the excitement was beginning to build. It was great to spend time with these ladies and to thank them for all of their work and support. They do a tremendous job supporting Shriners Hospitals for Children.

May 11, 2018 - Friday

After breakfast I meet with some of the men who were attending this session along with their wives. They are from all over the United States and are enjoying their time in Honolulu. I also worked with home office on upcoming plans for the Imperial Session.

A Year as the Imperial Potentate of Shriners International

In the evening Anne and I went on a dinner cruise off the shores of Waikiki Beach. This was a nice time to relax, have something to eat and watch the sunset again. After the sun was down there was a really good fireworks display we watched from the ship.

May 12, 2018 - Saturday

Again, during the day there was time to relax for a while, plus, Anne and I are celebrating our 15 Anniversary today. The big daytime event was Hula Dance class with Ladies of the Oriental Shrine. This was practice for a Monday night performance given by Hawaiian ladies of the Oriental Shrine. I participated and got a lot of help including my own grass skirt. They had a lot of work to do with me as I'm not much of a dancer and have little to no rhythm I'm told. I did the best I could.

The evening event was a big one. The first annual Gala for Shriners Hospitals for Children - Honolulu was on the agenda. The emcee for the evening was Mahealani Richardson, the anchor/reporter of Hawaii News Now evening news. Mahealani is the former Communications and Marketing Director at the Honolulu Shriners Hospitals and is a fantastic supporter of Shriners. The event was a dressy affair with a big silent auction and also a live auction. A great meal was served and there was good entertainment by a Grammy Award winning local female singer.

For me the best part of the night was being able to Fez Nick Rolovich, former Denver Bronco and current Head Football Coach of the University of Hawaii. He took his Shrine obligation earlier in the day and I had the honor to Fez him in front of nearly 400 people. He gave a nice talk on why he wanted to be a Shriner. I then presented him an East West Shrine Game jersey he plans to display at the University. He is a BIG supporter of Shriners. This was a highlight for the evening for me.

On a sad note, on this day our good friend and Imperial Sir, Gene Bracewell was laid to rest in Atlanta, Ga. Gene was the finest Shriner I ever knew, he worked hard and played hard serving on the Shriners Joint Boards for 36 years. My heart was broken that I was to far away to attend his funereal. I always enjoyed my time with him, he was a great mentor to me over the years. He will be missed by many.

May 13, 2018 - Sunday

The morning started off with a wonderful Ladies Oriental Shrine church service. There was a large attendance and a nice sermon was given by a local lady preacher on "Blessings." It was a great message.

In the afternoon Anne and I took a ride up to the north side of the island to see the sites there. It's nothing like the Waikiki Beach area for sure. That evening we enjoyed dinner with Imperial Sir Ralph and Lady Pat along with some of their friends from back home. It was a nice evening as we learned more about the Ladies Oriental Shrine.

May 14, 2018 - Monday

My morning started early as I had two back to back conference calls early in the morning with the Joint Boards. This took a couple of hours first thing in the morning. Anne and I then proceeded to the Royal Hawaiian Hotel where we had lunch. During lunch a pigeon crapped all over me, oh what a thrill.

I also received word our invitation to the White House had been confirmed. Our plan is to present an award to the United States Government for their assistance in transporting 9 young girls on a C-17 medical plane who had been badly burned in Guatemala to our Galveston Hospital. As this was the first time Shriners Hospitals for Children and the US Government had ever collaborated to take care children, this was special and hopefully something that will continue in times of disaster. The presentation will be made to President Trump to share with the Military, US Medical Team, Health and Human Services, and others involved.

This evening was the Ladies Oriental Shrine Fun Night. This is where those Hula Dance lessons helped out. All of us in the class performed three dances in our grass skirts. Oh, what fun we had. The evening featured a good meal, dancing, and fun. At the conclusion of the Fun Night we headed up to our room to call it a day.

May 15, 2018 - Tuesday

First thing in the morning I had some Shrine conference calls. At 9:30 Anne and I were picked up from the hotel by Ill. Sir Mark Leo, Potentate of Aloha Shriners and Ill. Sir Lee Gordon, Chairman of the Board of Governors at Shriners Hospitals for Children - Honolulu. They took us for a tour of "Iolani Palace" the former official Royal Residence of the Hawaiian Monarchy. Built in 1879 this Palace was beautiful, large, and well restored. King Kalakaua was the King at the time and was a Mason and he also became a Shriner shortly before his death in 1891. The Kingdom was overthrown a few years later. The Iolani Palace is a treasure to see. Many of the original furnishings can be seen along with jewels from the Royal Family and even many of the Kings Masonic items. From here we went to the Pacific Club for lunch.

In the afternoon we visited the tomb and grave sites of the Royal Family. This private cemetery is extremely nice, and the tombs of the Royalty are of course, exceptional and well-kept. They dated back into the early 1800's.

We then visited the grave site of Imperial Sir James McCandless, who was the Imperial Potentate in 1922, and a member of Aloha Shriners. No doubt he had a lot to do with the hospital being built in Honolulu. We then walked over to the gravesite of Alexander J. Cartwright, Jr. who was the inventor of baseball. He passed away in 1992, but tradition still has people leaving signed baseballs on his grave. There were a hundred or so balls there, Anne and I both signed one and left them as well.

The Ladies of the Oriental were all in meetings during the day. The evening was a big event, it was the Official Opening of the 104 Session of the Ladies Oriental Shrine of North America. It was a dressy affair full of pageantry and flair. Anne and I were escorted to the East for the evening that lasted nearly four hours.

When I was given the opportunity to speak, I thanked the ladies for their support and love and for the great work they do for Shriners Hospitals for Children. I thanked them as well for the support they give to all Shriners. I then told them my story about Hero's, and how each of them is a Hero to someone.

I finished it up by presenting an Imperial Potentate's MEDALLION to their entire organization for everything they do and will continue to do. I placed it in the hands of the Grand High Priestess, Janet, on behalf of our 240,000 members, 1.3 million patients, and 6,000 employees. The room all stood and erupted in applause. I was very proud as I had planned on presenting this one to them for a few years. The evening ended late, but a good time was had by all.

May 16, 2018 - Wednesday

We got up early and caught a ride to our adventure for the day. Anne and I were going Parasailing, going to go up 1000 feet. We arrived at our boat and went out along with three other couples. It was a blast and so peaceful once you got way up in the air. All you could hear was the wind blowing in the parachute. Although the thought of it is scary, it's not. Anne actually got to go twice as one lady was by herself and two need to go to balance out the weight. She loved it!

In the afternoon we attended the Ladies Oriental Shrine activities. Each of the Courts put on a little skit or would sing a song, or something clever. They were all dressed up in costumes and having a grand ole time.

We had dinner with our hometown local ladies from the Orlando Court, Kismet, compliments of Ill. Sir Michael T. Rudd and his lady. It was at "Rock a Hula" dinner club. After dinner there was a great musical Hawaiian show we all enjoyed. Fun times!

May 17, 2018 - Thursday

We were up at 5:30 AM and headed to the airport for our long flights back to Orlando. Our first stop was LA where we have a long layover before our second flight into Orlando. When we arrived in LA the airport was so crowded and it was hard to even get something to eat. We boarded our red eye flight at 11PM, headed home to Orlando.

May 18, 2018 - Friday

We landed at 6:30 AM in our home town. By the time we got our bags and the car it was nearly 9 AM before we arrived at the house. Anne unpacked and started washing clothes. I laid down for a three-hour nap and then headed into work for the afternoon. When I arrived at work, they had started on our expansion of adding twelve more offices to accommodate the additional space we needed. A lot had been done since I left. I spent the afternoon catching up on mail, bills, planning, etc. for the company.

Jason had me go pick up Avery from her Moms, so he could work. It was great to see my granddaughter, and then I dropped her back off at the office. By the time I got home it was nearly eight and Anne had a light dinner made. After we ate and cleaned up we were both ready for a good night's sleep. Although we were still on Hawaii time we had no problem going to sleep.

May 19, 2018 - Saturday

I went to work mid-morning and spent most of the day trying to catch up. Jason stopped by with Avery. I took her home, so he could work a while. Anne and I took Avery out to Steak and Shake for dinner and had a blast with her. After that we dropped her back off and I went home, Anne went to do some shopping. During the evening we watched some replays of today's Royal Wedding and then turned it in for some sleep.

May 20, 2018 - Sunday

Lazy start to the day, we did not have anything we HAD to do. Got some work done around the house and worked on the planning of upcoming events and trips. By 2:30 I was on my way to Tampa in a torrential rain storm, so I could be there for meetings first thing Monday morning. I arrived in Tampa in time to have dinner with some of the other board members before checking into the hotel and turning it in for the night.

May 21, 2018 - Monday

Up early for an 8 AM start. Today we are interviewing candidates for the new Corporate Director of Membership position. We had three excellent candidates who we spent one and a half hours with each. By the end of the day we had a unanimous decision on one candidate and decided to offer him the job. He will be contacted soon. This left me some time to work with other departments like, membership and Public Relations on planning for the upcoming Imperial Session and our I AM - RU Committed to Membership Program. I as well worked with Jessica who does a great job, on upcoming trips and Imperial Session planning.

After a dinner with other members of the board present, we headed back to the hotel and called it a day.

May 22, 2018 - Tuesday

Another 8 AM start at headquarters for a Strategic Planning meeting and the review of upcoming legislation for the upcoming Imperial Session. This was a busy meeting with the entire Joint Boards in attendance. After lunch we had a called Joint board meeting where we discussed and voted on several pending matters. The meeting was over by late afternoon, but I still had work to do around headquarters.

When I finally left for home at about 5:30 it was raining like cats and dogs aagain. I knew this was going to be along ride home with rush hour and the rain. After a three hour drive I stopped by my office for an hour and then headed home. It was late, but I had to unpack and repack as we had an early flight in the morning. It was about 11:30 by the time we went to bed.

May 23, 2018 - Wednesday

The alarm went off promptly at 5 AM. We were soon up and ready to head out the door to the airport. Our flight was delayed, and this caused us to miss our connection in Atlanta. We were rescheduled on a later flight and arrived into Indianapolis a little after 4 PM. We were picked up and taken to a nice Hilton in the downtown area. This is the beginning of our trip to attend the Indy 500 race with the Murat Shriners. We are excited to be attending this iconic event as the Imperial Potentate does each year.

On this night the men went to a dinner and the ladies had their own dinner. At the men's dinner over 30 men from Al Malikah Shriners in LA joined us. They are here for the race also. We had a nice evening of fellowship and fun, great food, and fine drinks. The lady's dinner was nice too Anne said. We were provided a nice suite for our visit and we turned the lights out about midnight.

May 24, 2018 - Thursday

We woke up in Indianapolis and got ready to go to Murat Shriners. We left mid-morning, they had a very nice Memorial Service where I was given a few moments to make some comments. Following the service there was a nice lunch in the same room. We then were taken on a tour of their entire building. Wow- what a large beautiful place filled with history.

In the afternoon Anne went shopping with the ladies and I stayed in the room to work on catching up on many upcoming Shrine activities. With all that is going on and now the Imperial Session was getting close it seems there is more and more to do.

In the evening the men went to Murat Shrine for dinner and fellowship. One of the Shrine Clubs cooked large delicious steaks for us. When I say large, I mean they covered the entire plate and they had great seasoning on them. The Shriners from Al Malikah also joined us, and it was a wonderful evening. Some gifts were exchanged between the two Temples and the Grand Master made some presentations to the Potentate's and myself. Anne had dinner with the Divan ladies at a nice restaurant. After we arrived back at the hotel, many of us had a nightcap in the hospitality room.

May 25, 2018 - Friday

Our day started off with a police escort to the Indianapolis Speedway with about ten of us in a van. After getting inside we toured around in the garage areas and then went into the stands where we watched all of the race cars during their last one-hour practice time prior to the big race on Sunday. The weather was perfect, and the race teams practiced pit stops and the drivers practiced high speed driving in excess of 225 MPH.

We then proceeded to a suite for lunch with some other Shriners. During the afternoon we again went through the garage area and also the gift shops. We then had a great police escort back to the hotel.

I spent the rest of the afternoon working on Shrine planning and two conference calls. With 49 items submitted for the call (legislation to be voted on) at the Imperial Session we are worried on how we will get through all of them. We are considering using electronic voting devises. It has never been done before at an Imperial Session and would itself have to be voted on to allow it.

The evening found us back at Murat Shrine for dinner and entertainment from a great band. During the evening we created a new, young Shriner and did an I AM - RU video. Anne was able to sell some products that support her First Lady's Program. In addition, Anne was presented a check for $1,000.00 from the Murat Ladies for her program, how nice is that. By 11 PM we were back at our hotel ready for some sleep.

May 26, 2018 - Saturday

Our day started at 10AM back at Murat for a brunch before the parade. After eating we proceeded to the parade route where our bleacher seats were waiting for us. This was an awesome parade with many great entries. All of the Drivers of this year's Indy 500 were in the parade with their families. In addition, many of the former winners of the race were in the parade. Although it was a hot day, most of the time during the parade we had some cloud cover. After the parade we went back to Murat Shrine for a lunch.

We then went back to the hotel I had an hour conference call regarding planning for the upcoming Imperial Session. We had an hour or so to rest and then it was off to dinner with the Murat Divan.

We walked to dinner at the Columbia Club, an exclusive private club about a block away. This was a fancy place with lots of history. An item of interest was the "Lincoln Eagle" that was one of a pair from President Lincoln's funeral procession and that hung above the casket of President Abraham Lincoln in the rotunda of the old Indiana State Capital. The dinner was fantastic, and they celebrated my Birthday two days early during the evening. The meal was delicious, but the best was the banana foster dessert they prepared in front of you. After a walk back to the hotel it was time for bed.

May 27, 2018 - Sunday

We were up at 6 AM to get ready for the Indy 500 Race. We caught a bus ride over to Murat Shriners for breakfast and then proceeded on to the Speedway. A few of us had credentials to go onto the track and look at the actual race cars and pace car up close. The area was very crowded, but also exciting. The weather was approaching 90 degrees and felt much warmer than that in the sun.

We next made our way up into the stands to our seats in the upper deck near the start/finish line. The view was excellent, and we could see much of the track and all of the pits. The pre-race show was spectacular with music, singing, introductions, and a fly over. As the race started the sun was baking us, but we knew as the sun continued to move we would soon be shaded by the roof. Having never been to an Indy 500 Race before this was fantastic. Very exciting! With the cars running at speeds over 225 MPH their roaring engines made lots of noise. Several accidents happened which eliminated cars as the afternoon went on. The race was completed by about 3 PM and then the real race began, getting 300,000 people out of the Speedway and onto the roads.

We had a long walk back to our bus that started with a couple of flights of stairs to walk down with thousands of people, all trying to get out of the stands. There was an elderly, heavy man in front of us who was having real troubles with the stairs. He was sweating profusely and barely able to make each step. He was holding onto the stair railings on each side and stopped anyone from going down. When he reached a landing, he paused and let others go by. When I reached him, I asked if he was ok and if he was going to be able to make it. He was concerned and not well. I told him not to worry about anyone behind him, they will just have to wait. I got in front of him and let him know if he began to fall, I'd be there to catch him. We proceeded down the steps one at a time until we reached the bottom. We then got him to a seat where others took over to assist him. Glad we were there to help, everyone else was in such a rush they just passed him up.

Soon we all arrived at the bus and were loaded; we actually got out of there fairly good with our police escort and headed back to the Shrine where several left their cars.

By the time we got back to the hotel we were exhausted and ready for a shower. Around 7 PM those of us still staying at the hotel had pizza in the hospitality room along with a couple of drinks. We reminisced about our days together, how much fun we had, and said our good byes until the next time we meet. Everyone treated us so nice, it was a fun time.

May 28, 2018 - Monday

My Birthday! We were up at 6AM, showered and finished packing so we could catch our flight back home. Ron took us to the airport and dropped us off at Delta. Ron and Sally Jo along with Scott and Karen really took great care of Anne and me on this trip. They had every detail covered. This was a long trip but so enjoyable and fun.

We grabbed something to eat and took our flight to Atlanta. Our second flight was delayed an hour or so, however we arrived home in time to have dinner with Jason, David, and Marie Angie at Outback for my Birthday. It was good to be with some of the kids, and to be home for a couple of days.

May 29, 2018 - Tuesday

Off to work early in the morning at the moving company. Things have been busy there plus we are in the process of building out some more office space. Lots of moving parts there. It seems it has not stopped raining in Florida for about two weeks. Rain makes the work difficult in the moving business. During the day a couple of conference calls related to planning for the Imperial Session. We have over 45 pieces of legislation now, which will make the time very valuable to get it all done in the time allotted. We are looking into using electronic voting devices again, as they will save time when it comes to counting votes. It will however take a bylaw change at the beginning of the Session to allow their use.

I picked up Avery and she had dinner with Anne and me. She spent some time with us and then I took her back to Jason.

May 30, 2018. - Wednesday

First thing in the morning was my 6-month physical with my Doctor. She was proud of me that in my 11 months traveling as the Imperial Potentate I only gained 7 pounds. I'll be able to lose that easy once I'm back home on a regular schedule again.

We had a conference call with the Daytona Beach CVB and part of our Executive Committee with regards to Housing for the Session. We are getting close to Session and some of the Temples still do not have their contracts in. We will begin taking a proactive approach to getting this done.

We invited David and Jan, and David and Marie Angie over for dinner. After dinner we framed 825 of the 1300 pictures needed for Anne's Ladies Luncheon. Actually, it went fast, took about 2 hours. We need more pictures to finish up. These individually hand colored pictures by Shrine patients are going to look great on the tables for Anne's First Lady's luncheon.

May 31, 2018 - Thursday

Wow- three days in a row at work, been over a year since that has happened. Actually, getting caught up on a few things. Today we got further confirmation on an invitation to the White House to meet President Trump on June 21st. Our plan for our meeting is to recognize the United States Military and the US Department of State, and more for their assistance helping with the children we treated from Guatemala last year. This is exciting, I hope it goes through, I'm sure the President has many things on his schedule and this could get cancelled.

In the afternoon I had a dental appointment. Trying to get caught up on all appointments. After work a couple of visits to some stores were made and then home for dinner. After dinner it was time to pack for our trip to Canada, and to get some sleep; going to be a short night.

Chapter Twelve
June 2018

June 1, 2018 - Friday

Up at the stroke of 5 AM and on the road to the airport by 6:15. We are on our way to Ottawa, Canada to place a wreath on the Tomb of the Unknown Soldiers with Tunis Shriners. After flying through Detroit and landing in Ottawa we were whisked off to our hotel, the Lord Elgin. We checked in and soon it was time for dinner. There was a cocktail reception in the lounge with a warm welcome from many members and their ladies. Following that was a nice dinner in the hotel with the Tunis Divan. We stopped by the hospitality room for a nightcap. Soon it was getting late and we were ready for bed.

June 2, 2018 - Saturday

We had a relaxed start for the day and met those going to the Canadian Tomb of the Unknown Soldiers at 10:30 in the hotel lobby. We had a short 3 block walk to the Tomb. It was beautiful, placed on a hilltop right in the middle of Ottawa, Canada's capital city. There were about 50 Shriners present all wearing their Red Fez for the occasion. In addition, most had their ladies were with them and there were also many others looking on.

The ceremony was wonderful as all Shriners participated, marching up to the Tomb where the wreath was laid by the Tunis Potentate, the Commander of the Legion of Honor and myself. There was bagpipe and bugle music being played, along with a prayer. Each Shrine member placed a Poppy by the Tomb as well. Following the ceremony, we did many pictures, it was really a perfect morning with blue skies and sunshine. The Grand Master gave me special dispensation allowing me to wear a Masonic Shrine Apron along with my Imperial Potentate Fez for this event. I appreciate how well Anne and I were treated, this was an extraordinary event of tradition and respect.

By now it was lunch time and we all walked down to the Old Military Armory where a catered lunch was waiting for us. After lunch we returned to the hotel, changed clothes and headed back out. We were taken a few blocks away for a tour of the Canadian Parliament by one of the Shrine members who works there. It was a great private tour in the building and up to the clock tower. There is tremendous history here in the nearly 200-year-old building.

It was then time to head back to the hotel again and change into our formal wear for dinner. First was cocktails in the hospitality room and then a short walk to the banquet room. Here we were escorted in by a piper playing his bagpipe and introduced. Following dinner a few speeches were given and they donated $1000. to Anne's project and purchased another $1000. worth of her products. As the banquet came to a close, I shared some stories about our many travels they enjoyed. On this evening I then presented an Imperial Potentate's MEDALLION to the entire membership of Tunis Shriners for their efforts in turning their membership numbers around. They recruited and added to their membership rolls more than 10% in new members. This was a great job and they became a GOLD Temple as a result. We wrapped it up by doing an energized I AM - RU Committed to Membership video.

The hospitality room was open after dinner and we stopped by for a drink before heading off to bed. This was a wonderful day filled with great events, one of those, Proud to be a Shriner days.

June 3, 2018 - Sunday

Our final day in Ottawa, we were up for a breakfast with the Tunis Potentate, Gary, and First Lady in the hotel restaurant. Following that they did a video interview with me with regards to a patient that was paralyzed in a bus accident due to a spinal cord injury. He was just sent to Shriners Hospitals for Children - Philadelphia. They will use this video on social media to create more awareness.

We were then taken by the Recorder, Perry and his wife for a car tour of the city that ended at their Temple that is in the Ottawa Masonic Building. It was a great setup for them and the cost is low. We had a tour of the building, the Oriental Band played for us and we had a hamburger. On the way to the airport they drove us by a commercial piece of property the Shrine owns that generates a lot of money for them.

Our flight was through Detroit again and we did not land in Orlando until 11PM. By the time we got home it was well after midnight and I was ready to crash. I was planning to be at work early in the morning. This was a fast-paced trip.

June 4, 2018 - Monday

Up early and off to work. The office is somewhat in disarray as the addition to the office space is going on. Can't seem to get away from the drywall dust. But, we are about half way done. There was lots to catch up on at my company today, plus a couple of Shrine conference calls. A large volcano erupted last night in Guatemala and we are working to identify children that were burned so we can bring them back to our hospitals for treatment. We had a "Go Team" from SHC - Galveston go there.

With only five hours sleep last night and so much to do, I don't know where the day went. Soon it was almost 4 PM and I had to head out to Stumpy's when I realized I had never stopped for lunch. One of the office girls shared some of her left-over sandwich with me.

I arrived at Stumpy's for our Executive meeting of the 2018 Convention Corp. We had several people call in to report on their part as we reviewed and adjusted plans for the session that was now only six weeks away. Wow- where did the past eleven months go? It seems like we just started. The meeting went well as we identified problem areas and planned to make them better. Our goal is to have another great session, "Back at the Beach." I then proceeded home to pack for an early departure to Panama City, Panama.

June 5, 2018 - Tuesday

The alarm went off at 4 AM, Anne and I both jumped up and got ready to head to the airport. We flew on Copa Airlines to Panama with Peter and Vicki for Abou Saad's 100th Anniversary. This is going to be a great 5 days, I'm sure.

We were picked up by Ill. Sir Ricky at the airport and immediately taken to lunch where we met some other Shriners at Yimmy's Restaurant. We had a great meal and went over the activities for the next few days. We then proceeded to the Golden Hotel where a suite was waiting for us on the 23rd floor. We had a couple of hours to rest and unpack. Then at 4 PM Peter and I were picked up and taken to the Temple for their Centennial Ceremonial. They brought in 32 new Nobles and did a tremendous job doing so. By the time it was over it was 10 PM. We then had some pizza and a beer and headed back to the hotel. Anne and Vicki remained at the hotel and had dinner there.

It was a long 20-hour day by the time we got in bed, but an exciting one. The Abou Saad Shriners are excited and proud to be celebrating 100 years. The 32 new candidates have them reaching their I AM - RU Committed to Membership goal and gives them GOLD Temple status for the third consecutive year. GREAT job!

June 6, 2018 - Wednesday

We were up at 6 AM and headed to the Temple by seven. The morning started off with a flag raising ceremony in front of the Temple, along with the presence of the Fire Dept, two fire trucks and several men. With six flags to raise and the Fire House band playing it was really a neat event. The new candidates watched in amazement. When this was completed the firemen pulled out the fire hoses and watered down the candidates, soaked them to the bone. The candidates continued on for a few hours with the second section.

Peter and I, along with Anne and Vicki proceeded to the Panama Rehabilitation Clinic (Instituto Nacional de Medicina Fasica y Rehabilitacion' in Panama City, Panama) with the Abou Saad Shriners. This facility treats Shriners kids for us by providing rehabilitation. A few years ago, they placed an "Editorial Without Words" statue in front of their building, the most detailed one I have ever seen, made of bronze. Today, on the 100th Anniversary of Abou Saad we were there for the unveiling of a plaque to celebrate this monumental day. When the cover was removed, a beautiful plaque appeared, and it included my name as the Imperial Potentate, I was speechless. The plaque read;

ABOU SAAD SHRINERS
ABOU SAAD 100 Years SHRINERS

Jamie Zelaya L.   Gary J. Bergenske
Potentado 2018   Potentado Imperial

Esta placa marca con alegría cien años de Noble labor Filantrópica a beneficio de nuestros niños.

1918 – 2018

(Translation - "This plaque marks with joy a hundred years of Noble Philanthropic work for the benefit of our kids.") This was a surprise to me that my name would be included on this plaque that will be here for the next 100 years. I was so appreciative of them including me. They will be installing a second one at their Shrine facility as well. This is really wonderful for them to be having such an enthusiastic 100 Year celebration.

We returned back to the Temple where the second section of the ceremonial was still going on bringing in their new Shriners. Boy were they having some fun. They asked me if I would be willing to take a pie in the face to raise some money, and I said yes. When it came my turn, we had an auction for those who wanted to participate, and we raised a little over $1000.00.

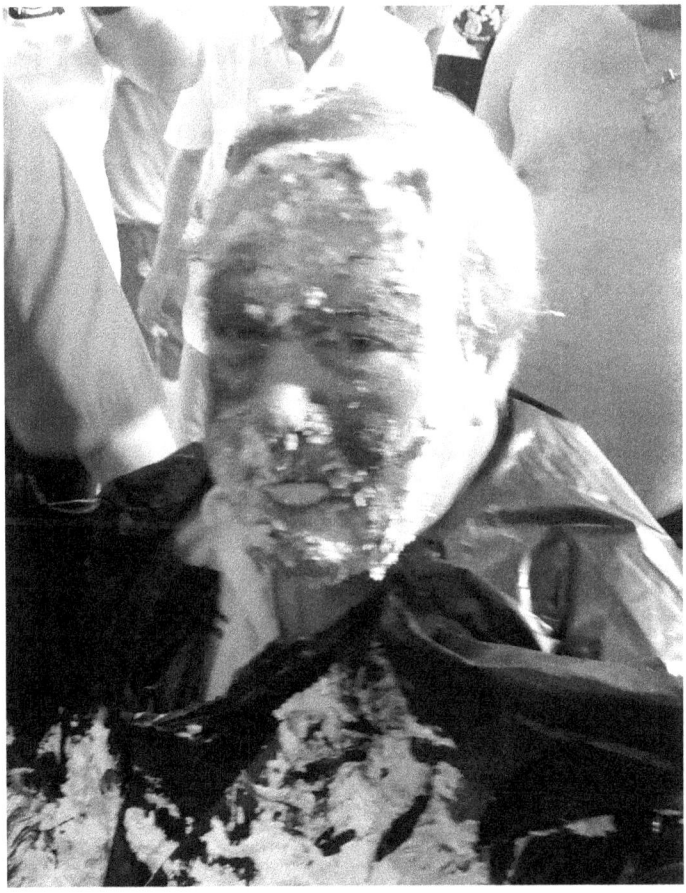

Boy did they give me a hit, it was a full-size cake with my picture on it. They hit me with hard and rubbed it in and I had cake everywhere. I told to them enjoy, they may never have an opportunity to do this to an Imperial Potentate again. It was all worth it and they enjoyed it so much. Cleaning up was a challenge. We had lunch with most of the Divan and then went back to the hotel for a couple of hours to get ready for the evening's events.

The event this evening was a spectacular production, held at a beautiful private club; there was nothing held back for this 100th Anniversary celebration. Everyone had their picture taken when they arrived and were given a nice gift. The music was playing and videos about Shriners and patients were shown on a large screen. The tables were set beautifully. In attendance were Shriners, the new candidates, all their ladies, donors, community leaders and partners, about 300 in all. A couple of speeches were given, in mine I presented the membership of Abou Saad an Imperial Potentate's MEDALLION for their 100 years of membership and many years of serving and assisting patients. Illustrious Sir Jamie received it on behalf of the entire membership, past and present. Following this all of the new Nobles were Fezzed by their Lady. How exciting!

We then had a delicious dinner and drinks followed by a wonderful band playing into the morning hours. This was certainly a night to remember, one every Abou Saad Shriner, past and present can be proud of.

June 7, 2018 - Thursday

The day did not start until 9 AM today, Wahoo! We were picked up and taken on an open-air double decker bus for a city tour along with many of the Shriners and their ladies. We saw many of the sights and saw them in a much different way than you would in a car. It was very interesting and fun. After the tour, we all went to a restaurant for a late lunch and then returned to the hotel for some rest. During these many trips, valuable time is spent with Shriners and their ladies to build moral and to impress upon them the importance of the outstanding work they do.

That evening was their regularly scheduled Stated Meeting. The new Nobles were present along with a roomful of others. It was a great meeting full of fun and laughter. The Potentate gave out many awards celebrating their 100th Anniversary. After the meeting we joined all of the ladies in the ballroom for dinner. They had been educating the new ladies about the Shrine. We had dinner and celebrated Peters Diaz's birthday. By the time we got back to the hotel it was after ten and we were ready for some rest.

June 8, 2018 - Friday

Up at 5:30 AM today, going on a special trip, a boat ride through the Panama Canal. We all met at Abou Saad Shrine Center. We then boarded a bus that took us to where we got on a boat of about 150 people. We had breakfast and lunch on the boat as we went through three of the locks of the Panama Canal. A great experience in celebration of their 100th Anniversary. Many of the local Shriners riding with us had visited the canal many times but had never actually rode through it on a boat. This was an extraordinary experience.

After the Panama Canal ride we were bused back to the Shrine for dinner and a few drinks. We then proceeded to the hotel to pack and get some sleep. We had an early flight out the next morning to head back home. This has been and incredible experience to attend this well run 100th Anniversary Celebration.

June 9, 2018 - Saturday

We were up at the crack of dawn to catch our flight back home. We arrived back in Orlando in the afternoon and unpacked and had some time to relax back at home. It was nice to be home for a day, lots of mail and other things to catch up on.

June 10, 2018 - Sunday

In the morning we got a few things done at the house. I then spent the afternoon at my office to catch up on business there. Lots to do and of course, the Imperial Session planning and implementation is in full swing now too. Busy - busy days.

David and Marie Angie came over for dinner. We had a nice time and they are also helping with planning for the Imperial Session.

June 11, 2018 - Monday

At work early at J&J Metro, building out the new office space is in full swing. Business is good even with me gone so much, how great is that. By midafternoon I was on my way to Tampa for a meeting the following day.

June 12, 2018 - Tuesday

8 AM start for an all-day Shriners Investment meeting. During the meeting I also met with numerous other departments for planning on the upcoming Imperial Session. I worked in the Membership and Communication & Marketing offices with regards to the Annual Report, Session Reports, and made a couple of short videos.

On a sad note, I began clearing out the office of the Imperial Potentate. I boxed up several boxes of things and loaded my car up. On my next visit back at headquarters in a couple of weeks it will be time to completely clear it out. Where has the time gone? It has just evaporated. I have enjoyed this year to the max, but, it has just gone by way to fast. At the end of the day I made way back to Orlando, arriving home about 9 PM.

June 13, 2018 - Wednesday
Spent a full day at work catching up. Also had a couple of Shriners conference calls. The work on getting ready for the upcoming Imperial Session is intensifying, but things are all falling into place nicely. So PROUD of everyone on our 2018 Imperial Session Convention Committee.

Anne and I met Peter and Vicki for dinner in Mount Dora. They treated us to a wonderful dinner. They then presented us with a stained-glass picture of the Rose Bowl Parade Float we all rode on in the Rose Parade. They hand made this beautiful three-dimensional creation. Anne and I were so touched by this heartfelt gift. In addition, Vickie made 100 stained glass butterflies for Anne's going out luncheon. Again, they were beautiful. The four of us did some great traveling together this year and accomplished some terrific results. It has always been a pleasure whenever we spend time with them.

June 14, 2018 - Thursday
Another partial day at work in Orlando. By midafternoon I was headed to New Smyrna Beach for my first Jesters meeting of the year. It was good to see everyone and on this night the Jesters of Melbourne were also joining us. We had a delicious prime rib meal we all enjoyed.

Also, we received a nice letter from President Carter to be included in our Imperial Session Program Book. The relationship between Shriners and the Carter Center has turned out to be a good one that by working together is helping more kids. Additionally, the personal friendship President Carter and I have, has been inspirational for me. I have learned from him and tried in many ways to emulate his leadership and listening skills.

June 15, 2018 - Friday
The planning has really become important now as we get close to the Imperial Session. The days are filled with calls and emails regarding our upcoming plans. I was in my office most of the day, but the time was spent on Shrine business.

The evening found Anne and I attending an event at Bahia Shriners. This weekend is a busy one there, a Ceremonial and the Potentate's Black and White Ball all rolled into one. This night was a casual one where we got to see many of our friends from around the state of Florida. It was really nice to spend a night with our old friends from Bahia.

June 16, 2018 - Saturday

I was up early and headed to Millard's where the Bahia second section was taking place as part of the Ceremonial that was bringing in 17 new members. This was a good time and I was so pleased my own Temple was also committed to our I AM - RU Committed to Membership Program. After the second section they cooked up some hamburgers and we enjoyed some good fellowship. I stopped by the office to do a couple of things and went home to get packed up for our trip the following day.

By late afternoon we were headed back to Bahia Shriners for a reception and Potentate's Ball. This is the first large event in our new Bahia Shrine building and they had it beautifully decorated. The food and fellowship was great as well with some dancing to follow.

June 17, 2018 - Sunday

The alarm went off at 4 AM, we jumped up to get ready for our flight to Springfield, Massachusetts. It was an early flight to visit the Shriners Hospitals for Children there. Today is also Father's Day, a day for me to be thankful for the wonderful healthy children and grandchildren we have. Peter and Vicki picked us up at the Springfield airport and we checked into our hotel. That evening the four of us had dinner at a local restaurant.

June 18, 2018 - Monday

After breakfast we dropped Anne and Vicki off at the Mall so they could do a little shopping. Peter and I then proceed to Shriners Hospitals for Children - Springfield to visit the newly remodeled areas of the hospital. The new Acute Rehab area was still under construction, but the Fracture Care area was in full swing. This Shriners Hospital has done a real turn around in its patient care by taking on some new missions. The enthusiasm and excitement has reached new levels among the employees and volunteers. This is so great to see.

In the afternoon we visited the "Smith and Wesson" facility in town. They have been donors to the local hospital for the past 29 years. Their cumulative total is approaching a quarter of a million dollars. We were able to give thanks to them. During the tour of their facility we saw first-hand how they produce and assemble their many different products, some completely unrelated to weapons. We were all impressed by the size of the facility, it was huge. We were also impressed with all of the technology and machines that were used to make these products. It was truly an incredible tour.

That evening we had dinner with the hospitals entire board of governors plus, Dr. Guidera, John McCabe, and Jim Doel. We were all gathered for the Ribbon Cutting that would take place the following morning at the hospital. It was also a day for the Board of Governors to have their monthly Board Meeting. At the conclusion of our dinner we learned our waitress was a former SHC - Springfield patient from 29 years ago. We then learned her son was a patient there too.

How amazing, we had to do some pictures with her. This is not unusual, we have met many of our patients during our travels this year, it gives you the greatest feeling.

June 19, 2018 - Tuesday

After breakfast at the hotel we headed to the hospital for the big event. Today at 9 AM the Shriners Hospitals for Children - Springfield, Inpatient Acute Rehab Pre-Opening Ceremony took place. The Ceremony started in the Amphitheater and then moved to the Upstairs Atrium. It was a beautiful ceremony that concluded with a Ribbon Cutting Ceremony.

This was one of the finest days of my eleven years of service on the Joint Boards. I was the liaison at this hospital for three years. During this time this particular hospital went from nearly closing to finding a way to remain relevant. This was special to me as I worked alongside of them and a consultant to find a way to make it work. I was never on a hospital project where a new building was being built. My greatest accomplishments with our hospital system came in Erie and Springfield. While serving as an Imperial Officer during my three-year tenure as a liaison at each we found a way to turn them around in their current building to again become viable in a different way. Much of this was due to the change in the way medical care is delivered. Being here on this day was special.

In the afternoon we had a patient success story with a child from Cyprus that we found when Anne and I were there last October. During the presentation the young boy of eleven years took some of his first steps with a walker. This was so inspiring it brought tears to my eyes. Some individuals were recognized and then I was called to the front by Steve Behe, the Chairman.

I was informed this Pre-Opening was done because they wanted to have me in attendance prior to going out of office. I was then presented with a beautiful plaque that read;

Shriners Hospitals
For Children
Springfield, Massachusetts
Presented to: Gary J. Bergenske, Imperial Potentate 2017 - 2018

In grateful appreciation for the supportive role you played as our Hospital Liaison from 2014 to 2017 and for your ongoing support.
Your encouragement and belief in our five-year Strategic Vision Plan has helped to solidify the future of the Springfield Shriners Hospital. Your dedication to our

facility has left an incredible mark of compassion on the lives of the children and families, we serve.

With deepest gratitude,
Board of Governors, Staff, Patients, & Families

Of course, my eyes were filled with tears as I accepted this recognition and thanked all of those in attendance. I was caught off guard with this special recognition, and I'm sure I did not give proper thanks as I was lost for words. This really expanded on the thoughts I already had about our collective accomplishments here, so honored to have been here on this day.

Isabella, our National Patient Ambassador was up next and gave a nice speech. She ended with how much she appreciated all that Anne and I had done for her by picking her as an International Ambassador. Her words were very touching, and this time had tears in both Anne and my eyes.

Then it was a quick trip to the airport for our flight home, where we will spend 15 hours before flying out again. This was an amazing two days in Springfield. Two days that really made me feel as though I was a small part of something special, something much bigger than myself.

June 20, 2018 - Wednesday

After spending a couple of hours at work, Anne and I headed to the airport again. We were only home for a few hours. We arrived in Raleigh Durham for the first leg of our flight to Washington DC and our flight was delayed for two hours. During this time, we found out our White House visit was still on, but that President Trump would be unable to join us. There was lots going on with the Mexican border immigration policy and how the children were being handled. The news was all over it and many of the Presidents appointments were being canceled as his time was being focused on the needs of the American people.

When we finally took off, the weather was rough. After flying above DC for an hour waiting to land our plane was running low on fuel. We had to head over to Harrisburg, PA to refuel out on the runway. It appeared the airport itself was closed. Once we got back in the air, we finally landed in DC about four hours late. We made our way to the hotel, checking in after midnight. This was a long travel day.

June 21, 2018 - Thursday

After breakfast at the hotel, we proceeded to the United States Capital for a tour by Kathy Hartz who works for the Capital Police and a is a Past Potentate's lady. Kathy gave us a great tour including some places normal tours do not go. Ill Sir Mark, her husband and a good friend of ours joined us for lunch. We then went to the Library of Congress for a very good tour there.

After dinner, Anne and I, along with Jim and Patsy Cain, and Larry Leib, walked over to the White House to take our White House tour of the West Wing. We brought with us the presentation we were planning to give to President Trump for the assistance provided by the United States Military and Government just in case we got lucky and were able to see him.

When we arrived at the security gate, because we had something for the President, it raised the level of security checking in to a higher level. The security dogs and some additional security personnel were called in for checks of the package. This was required for us to proceed and took some extra time, but soon we were on our way.

Matthew Flynn, a Shriner who works as an Assistant to the President was our escort. We dropped off the package for the President at Matthew's office and began our amazing tour of the West Wing including the Oval Office, Cabinet Conference room, Roosevelt Conference room, and White House Rose Garden. There was much more we saw as well, but another area of real interest was the White House Press Room where all Press Conferences are held, currently by Sara Saunders. The press room was small and not vary impressive at all compared to how it looks on TV.

It was decided we would leave the first ever Shriners Hospitals for Children "*Health Advocacy Award*" to be presented to the US Military, State Department, and Embassy, with President Trump receiving it on their behalf of them with Matthew. He could then move it through the proper channels to the President as it was unknown when we would be able to get another appointment. Matthew assured us it would reach the President, but it would take some time. This was an amazing time we all enjoyed. Touring this building makes you proud to be an American, loads of history.

June 22, 2018 - Friday

Another early rise and shine day as Anne and I were up early and off to the airport to catch a flight home for a day. We arrived back home about 2:30, I dropped Anne off at the house, so she could start washing and getting our suitcases repacked while I went to work for a couple of hours.

We ate at home and got everything packed and ready to go for the following morning. Another one of the times we are only home for a few hours with little sleep.

June 23, 2018 - Saturday

The alarm went off at 4:30 AM and we jumped up for what is sure to be a big day. We arrived in Atlanta by 10:30 AM and got a rental car so we could head to Plains, GA. On the way we stopped by daughter Carrie and Bronson's home to see them and the boys. We all went out for some lunch before we continued on our way to Plains to have dinner with President and Rosalynn Carter. We arrived in Plains by 4:30 at Jill Stuckey's home where our friend Andrea Walker lived. Andrea was making dinner for us for the evening and it was smelling really good.

By 6 PM President and Mrs. Jimmy Carter were walking down the sidewalk from their home about a half mile away with Secret Service in tow to have dinner with us. They arrived all smiles and looking fantastic as we exchanged hugs and entered the home. We all had a glass of wine before dinner. We talked of the many places Anne and I traveled during the year where we came across things related to the Carters.

Places like the Naval Air Museum, Annapolis Naval Training, the Panama Canal, the Tomb of the Unknown, the White House and The Paraskadevitas Foundation in Cyprus. I told President Carter it was as if he was traveling with me much of the year. We enjoyed talking about these locations.

We then moved to the dining room for some delicious food. Andrea joined us for dinner while Jill served us and took pictures and videos. We had discussions about several things. One was about the old Victorian boarding house the five of us were eating in. It was built in 1904. Jimmy's parents were married in 1923 and one of the rooms upstairs was their first place to live. The story is Jimmy Carter was conceived in this vary home, isn't that something. There is a brass plaque on the door of one of the rooms upstairs that simply says, "Conceiving Room." We also talked of the doors President Carter has opened up for Shriners Hospitals and of his willingness to do a commercial for us the previous year.

At the conclusion of the dinner, it was my proud moment to be able to present President Jimmy Carter with the first ever, *"Shriners Hospitals for Children Humanitarian Award."* It was being given on behalf of his worldwide humanitarian efforts in addition to his efforts to assist Shriners and the children we care for. We videotaped it so that it could be shown at our upcoming Imperial Session. After that, I also presented another award from me personally, an Imperial Potentate's MEDALLION. We videotaped this as well.

After all of this, the Carters headed home along with their Secret Service, this time riding in their car. Anne and I spent some additional time with Andrea and Jill and thanked them for all of their efforts to put this evening together. We then jumped back into our rental car for the 3-hour drive back to Atlanta, so we could catch our flight the next morning. We arrived at the hotel about midnight. This was another one of those 20-hour days, but we enjoyed it so much. We both always love spending time with the Carters.

As I drove through the darkness of the Georgia night and thought about the day, I felt so blessed for the many people I have been able to meet. My friendship with President Jimmy Carter is one I imagine very few have with a former United States President. To be able to one on one along with our wives have a glass of wine and dinner and discuss how we can help more children in the world is so encouraging to me. President Carter is truly an amazing Humanitarian whose reach is worldwide through his Carter Center. I have learned so many things from him, one of which is to be a good listener. I'm thankful for my friend Johnny Walker, who has since passed away, for introducing the President to me. We have accomplished so much together. And to his wife Andrea Walker who continues to be a great friend.

<u>June 24, 2018 - Sunday</u>

Our alarm went off at 5:30, we had to get the rental car turned in and catch our flight to Cincinnati. We were going to spend a day and a half with the Daughters of the Nile. Our first meeting was with their Foundation to give honor to their top fundraising Temples who raised over $10,000 each. There were 30 Temples in attendance who reached this goal and were there for a light lunch and recognition. I was able to speak and share some hospital patient stories. I was honored to then be asked to participate in handing out the awards. These ladies winning the awards did an awesome job raising over $800,000. The total of all of their Temples raised just under $2,000,000. for Shriners Hospitals for Children. Anne and I were so impressed.

We had a couple of hours to settle into our room and then get into our formal wear. This evening was the Formal Opening of their Annual Session and it was spectacular. I was given an opportunity to address the group and I was honored to do so. After a few opening remarks, I presented an Imperial Potentate's MEDALLION to their entire membership for their extraordinary efforts in raising money to support Shriners Hospitals for Children. This brought every lady in the hall to their feet in applause, they were so appreciative. I actually teared up, I'm so thank for their extraordinary work.

I followed this up with a video, addressed directly to the Daughters of the Nile I had made about our Joint Board visit to SHC - Mexico City. After watching this, I don't think there was a dry eye in the house. Again, the ladies came to their feet in applause.

When the meeting was over, Anne and I walked across the street to a Pizza Place for a light dinner. There were also many Daughters of the Nile members there who just left the Opening, we were thanked many times for coming to their Session, it was very nice.

June 25, 2018 - Monday

Finally, a day without an ultra-early start. We did not have to get up until eight. During the morning there was lots to catch up on. We had to be checked out by eleven. As I had to give a speech on membership to the ladies at 1:30, we had to put our luggage in the bell hop station.

At the opening of the afternoon session I presented a good membership program for them using my Rudy presentation. Following the speech, Anne and I caught our ride to the airport for our flights back home. We had two cars at the Orlando airport as I had to go to Tampa, and Anne was going to be going home. We just had to get there and then go our separate ways.

Well, of course, our flight was delayed. We finally made it to Atlanta but again our flight was delayed due to weather. After a long wait we took off. By the time we got to our cars it was 1 AM. Anne headed home, and I arrived at my hotel in Tampa at 3 AM totally exhausted. I was going to have to sleep fast. But no complaints, it's all been worth it. Anne and I are working to accomplish everything we can to make a difference during our term.

June 26, 2018 - Tuesday

Up and going at 6:30 AM for our 8 AM meeting at headquarters. Actually, I felt pretty good even with so little sleep. Hope it lasts. Today we are meeting with the four hospitals that have legislation submitted regarding their future. Attending were representatives from Spokane, Cincinnati, Boston, and Twin Cities. At the conclusion of all these discussions, we had a Joint Board meeting to discuss other matters. We were done about 7 PM and then went to dinner. Following that I was really ready for bed.

June 27, 2018 - Wednesday

Again an 8 AM start for committee meetings. I attended some but also worked with various departments on preparations for the upcoming Imperial Session. There is lots to do to get ready and it is getting close.

During the day I also emptied out the Imperial Potentate's office of all my personal items. This was sad for me, the year had gone by so fast, it sure did not seem like I had been in office for an entire year. The time just evaporated. As I boxed up the gift items and many pictures I had received over the year, many wonderful memories came back to me that gave me a great feeling of accomplishment. I hope in some small way we were able to move the needle some in a positive way this year.

This was my last dinner in Tampa as the Imperial Potentate, imagine that. After dinner we then all had a drink in the hotel lounge, but again, it was an early night to bed for me. I thought to myself, I'm so thankful for the year the nobility allowed Anne and me to have. It's been an incredible adventure.

June 28, 2018 - Thursday

After spending a few hours at headquarters, I headed back to Orlando for a 12:30 PM dental appointment. This was my last day at headquarters serving as the Imperial Potentate, wow - that was a fast year. I feel good about our preparations for the Imperial Session, but I also know, we have lots to do.

I spent a couple of hours at work in the afternoon and then went to pick up Avery for Jason. Anne, Avery, and I had dinner out and then did some shopping before taking her back to Jason. She is growing up so fast and is talking well.

June 29, 2018 - Friday

Spent the morning at J&J Metro and spent some time with Anne in the afternoon going to some doctor appointments. We have been gone so much we are behind on all personal appointments. We will be home for a few days prior to going back to Daytona Beach for the Imperial Session. Time to start catching up on things.

June 30, 2018 – Saturday

Catch up day at the house, we have lots to do for sure. Working as well on speeches and planning for the Imperial Session. One week from today we will be back in Daytona Beach for the Session and to wind up an incredible year.

"You receive the greatest compliment when you are asked for your opinion."
GARY BERGENSKE

Chapter Thirteen
July 2018

July 1, 2018 – Sunday
Really nice to be home for a few days, we again worked on catching up on things around the house. Even had time to wash the cars. In the evening some of the kids came over for dinner.

July 2, 2018 – Monday
Worked a full day at J&J Metro today. In the evening we had the Amico's, Juett's, Zorians, and Mole's over for Pizza and drinks. We had all of us working on the gift bagging and set up for Anne's Ladies Luncheon. We finished up wrapping the 1300 gifts and 1300 patient pictures to be given out during the lunch. We then loaded all of the items into Mikey's trailer for him to take over to Daytona Beach. Anne and I have been blessed with wonderful friends who are so willing to help and assist with all of the projects and responsibilities we have as Imperial Potentate and First Lady. We certainly feel wonderful for all they have contributed of their time and efforts.

July 3, 2018 – Tuesday
At J&J Metro all day but most of it was taken up with Shrine work as the Imperial Session in closing in fast. Lots of time on the phone confirming activities and functions. Again, we have an incredible team.

Gary Bergenske's Shriners Diary - Our Mission – Our Members – and Me

July 4, 2018 – Wednesday
We worked around the house on this Holiday in the morning. In the afternoon we went over to David and Marie Angie's for dinner. It was really nice. Once it got dark David had a bunch of fireworks he set off. Fireworks were being set off all around. This is the first 4th of July we were home in many years as we are usually at the Imperial Session on this Holiday.

July 5, 2018 – Thursday
I worked during the morning, but we are in full swing packing mode now. Anne and I both are preparing to leave in a couple of days for two weeks at the Imperial Session in Daytona Beach. Packing this year involves much more than just clothing as we also have gifts, planning materials, speeches, etc. that we have to have with us. We will have two cars full of stuff to take in addition to the trailer Mikey already took over.

July 6, 2018 – Friday
Final packing day prior to going to Daytona Beach. Suitcases are full along with numerous boxes. House is being set up for us to be gone for two weeks. It's a bitter sweet feeling to know our year in the top office is almost over; the top position of Shriners worldwide. Anne and I are going to do our best to make this Imperial Session one of the best yet. Our Convention Team and the Daytona Beach CVB have been fantastic and will give it their every effort to be sure all is successful. We are proud of what we were able to contribute this year along with our support teams.

July 7, 2018 – Saturday
Up early to get the cars packed for our trip to Daytona Beach. We got to the Hilton Ocean Resort by noon however our room was not ready. After lunch we were able to get into the room. I immediately left along with Stumpy, Bob, and Mikey for the Daytona International Speedway for the Daytona Coke Zero 400 NASCAR race. We arrived and entered the pit area as we were guests of NASCAR Driver and Shriner David Ragan for the Pit area and for the race. After touring the Pit area along with Shriners Hospital for Children patient Theodore and his family we had something to eat.

It was then time to go on the track where all of the cars for the race were displayed. The Shriners car was right next to the Air Force car and a group of soldiers were there around their car. One of the them was a Three Star General. I made my way over to him to thank him for the assistance of the Air Force in helping to transport children from

Guatemala to Shriners Hospitals who were injured because of the volcano. As I spoke to him he had little reaction, so I asked him if he was familiar with what I was referring to. He replied, "Yes, I signed off for those planes to go." With that we had great conversation and did pictures with the Shriners and the General. General Tuck expressed to me how grateful he was to meet us as often they run missions but never get to see the team on the other side. He then gave me his card with his personal cell number on it and said, "If you ever need assistance again, call me, we are here to help." This was so rewarding to hear. Who would have thought fate would bring us all together like this?

The race was about to begin, and we took our seats on the top of the tool box in David Ragans Pit area right on the track. These were great seats, just inches from the track and we were with the entire Ragan Pit Crew. We watched the race, David was in a couple of big accidents but managed to finish in the fifteenth spot. It was a great night at the track.

July 8, 2018 – Sunday

Today was setup day for the Hospitality Room and to prepare for the upcoming Board meeting prior to the Imperial Session. It was a relaxing day as things moved along good in the Shrine office and Director Generals office as well. We are all ready for the coming two weeks. We had dinner with our Convention Corp Executive team and some Staff and we celebrated on our accomplishments to date. After dinner we stopped for Ice Cream, it was good. We are ready to go.

July 9, 2018 – Monday

Today all of our Board members began to arrive for the upcoming meetings. They arrived at different times and most were present for our first dinner in the evening. We had dinner as a group at the Hilton and everyone was glad to see each other.

It was good for everyone to reunite with the Daytona Beach CVB Staff who are outstanding. We were welcomed back as well by all of the Daytona Beach Police Dept. Police Officers who take such good care of us. It was like old home week as everyone became reacquainted.

July 10, 2018 – Tuesday

The men started their day with a 7:30 breakfast and then began their board meeting to conduct the business of Shriners International and Shriners Hospitals for Children. The ladies left at 8AM for their tour to St Augustine and they had a great time, compliments of the Daytona Beach Convention Bureau.

For dinner we went to 31 Supper Club; everyone was asked to dress in Great Gatsby clothing and about 80% of them did. It was a fantastic evening with everyone dressed up, live music, dancing, and good food and drink. On this evening I presented Stumpy with an Imperial Potentates MEDALLION, he was so appreciative. I also presented Anne with a new diamond necklace that matched my Imperial Potentates ring. This was done to let her know how much I appreciated all of her efforts this past year. She did an incredible job. I really surprised her with this. The ladies all loved it, the men not so much. The men were complaining I started something all of their wives will come to expect. Well, I told them it's up to them what they do, but my wife earned it for all the things she has done to help and assist me.

There was plenty of fun and singing on the bus as we traveled back with a full police escort. What a hoot. During the night Anne woke up several times not feeling good but was able to go back to sleep.

July 11, 2018 – Wednesday

Anne spent the night very sick and woke up in the morning feeling bad. The men started with breakfast and their meeting again. Anne felt so bad she could not go on the lady's trip. I brought Dr. Diaz in to check on Anne and he told me I should take her to the Emergency Room, might be her appendix.

I left our meeting to take Anne to the hospital, we got right in and they checked her out. It didn't take long for them to decide it was her appendix and that she would need surgery, they thought they could get her in by 2:30. The time kept getting pushed back as they had some emergencies coming in. Of course, we missed the dinner at Off the Hook while we continued to wait for her to have the surgery. David and Marie Angie came over to be with us as we continued to wait for Anne to go to surgery.

The Police Dept brought us food from OutBack, how nice was that. Finally, about 10:30 PM they took her to pre-op, but she did not get into the operating room until 1AM. By 2:30 AM we were able to see her and confirm all was well. I headed back to the hotel and went to bed at three. Another 20-hour day.

July 12, 2018 – Thursday

Anne got out of surgery at 1:30 AM, so of course she was unable to go on the lady's day trip again. I was up at 6:30 AM to get ready for our Board breakfast and meeting, it was a short night on sleep. By late morning I was able to talk with Anne, she thought she would get out that afternoon, amazing. As we progressed through our day of meetings, Anne let me know she could be picked up. Bob and Bev went to get her checked out of the hospital and brought her to the hotel. When I met Anne in our hotel room she was getting a shower and said she was going to dinner that night. I could not believe she felt good enough to go out. She was determined to be with our friends and all of those who had supported us all year.

We went in our car along with Bob and Bev with a four motorcycle Daytona Beach Police full escort. We ran every red light all the way to the Dog Track and Card Room and arrived with lights going and sirens blowing. All of the Shriner guests were waiting at the door as we pulled up. A round of applause began as Anne exited the car, everyone was amazed she could leave the hospital and come to dinner. The Police did an amazing job, these guys are wonderful. I believe they had as much fun as we did escorting us through the streets of Daytona Beach.

We had a nice dinner, bet on some dogs, and greeted the many people there. Everyone was so nice to Anne, she was like Super Women tonight after all she has been through the past two days. It was a pleasant evening, and the Police escort, Wahoo! After dinner we returned to the hotel and Anne got some rest.

July 13, 2018 – Friday

Today was technically a free day, but it was full of activities as we got ready for Shriners from around the world to arrive over the next two days. In the morning we had Compliance Training. The Market Place was being set up and venders were moving in. It is going to be another wonderful Market Place.

The Shriners office lead by Chris Harrison was in full swing now. This group also really steps it up for the Imperial Sessions. They have a lot of responsibility. Executive Vice President John Piland is also working hard to assist in every way, working alongside the Convention Corp., the CVB, and his team from the home office.

For dinner we met daughter Jami, Jason, and the family at the Deck Down Under. Anne was feeling better after her surgery but a little week, however no pain. It was nice to see the kids, they are the first of the Bergy Bunch to arrive in Daytona Beach. The rest come in over the weekend.

July 14, 2018 – Saturday

Today things are getting started as many Shriners and ladies are arriving. The Representatives are getting registered and are happy to be "Back at the Beach." The Market Place is now open and doing some good business. The Convention Executive Team is working to assure all is well with the upcoming activities and the Imperial Convention Office is busy with the arriving Shriners.

In the evening the Board members and their families were hosted for dinner by the Daytona Beach CVB at One Daytona. There was great food, drinks, music and fun. Shriners Patients Ambassadors Kechi and Alec and their families also joined us on this evening, it was great to welcome them, they both have some key parts in the coming week.

The ladies of the Daytona Beach CVB, Linda, Lynn, and Amber have done a tremendous job with the planning for all of the events they hosted us for. We can't thank them enough. Again, on this night, as every night, we had a Police escort for our buses provided by the Daytona Beach Police Department. Tonight, we had their entire motorbike unit of nine bikes, they moved us through town back to the hotel without a stop. We enjoyed this so much, I think they enjoyed providing it as well. Local residents have to wonder, who is on those buses?

Upon arrival back at the hotel many of us had a nightcap in the hospitality room. Anne was feeling better, but still weak after her surgery. I can't believe she is able to do as much as she is, amazing. We have a fine group on our board, all so willing to give of their time and talents. I'm so proud to be leading this group through this Imperial Session.

July 15, 2018 – Sunday

Today starts the 144th Shriners Imperial Session, the city is full of Red Fezzes. This is one of the busiest days of the week. The morning started early with the Joint Boards visiting both the Treasurers and the Recorders annual meetings. Then by 9:30 we were all changed into our casual clothes and headed to the Daytona International Speedway for the Walk, Ride, or Drive for Love experience. Of course, we had our Police escort to get there. Kechi sang the National Anthem and then the activities began. There was a good turn out and some media was there covering the activities.

After arriving back at the hotel, we showered and changed again in preparation for the Church Service. The Peabody Auditorium was the place the Church Service was held, and the attendance was large. The committee that planned and implemented this event did a great job. Kechi was the featured singer and she brought the house down with her outstanding voice. She is so admired by everyone as a former Shriners patient and a finalist on "Americas Got Talent."

Next up was the Public Opening in the Arena. Many accolades were given by the local Mayor, a representative from the county, and the Daytona Beach Police Deptartment Chief. In the comments from the Police Chief Craig Capri, he called me to the podium and presented me with an official Daytona Beach Police Department Honorary Police Officer Badge. This was a surprise and a real honor to be recognized in this way. We then had several check presentations, one for Anne's project for $50,000 from Al Aska Shriners. She was so surprised and appreciative. A BIG thank you to our Shriners from Alaska.

The Al Rai'e Saleh Shriners from Puerto Rico then made a presentation of appreciation to myself for the care and compassion I extended to them after the Hurricane that devastated their island. They thanked me for the large amount of money that was raised through an effort I championed to give them help, aid, and assistance. They also had a plaque of thanks from the Grand Master of Puerto Rico they presented to me. They then recognized Anne for the role she played as First Lady and for her unconditional commitment to help me. She was also presented gifts. This was a heartfelt presentation for Anne and I that had us both in tears. The plaque's they gave us read as below:

Ill. Gary J. Bergenske
Imperial Potentate
Al Rai'e Saleh Shriners

For taking out your time, in a very complicated agenda, to be present in our Temple and our Island after Hurricane Maria severely affected us. For contributing to our Nobles and our Island could return to normal as soon as possible. The Nobles of Al Rai'e Saleh Temple of Peurto Rico say:

Thank you, Thank you Very Much! Given today July 15,2018
Ill. Ramón L. Sierra Laporte, Potentate

****

Al Rai'e Saleh Shriners
Lady Anne Bergenske

Congratulations for Having at your side a Special Noble. Who really Loves the principles of our SHRINERS INTERNATIONAL Organization.

Thank you for your supporting this noble charitable endeavor, because every successful Man has an Excellent Lady by his side.

Given today July 13, 2018

Ill. Ramón L. Sierra Laporte
Potentate

I then proceeded to give out a couple of prestigious awards. The first was the Shriners Hospitals for Children Humanitarian Award. Although the recipient was unable to attend, I traveled to his home town a few weeks prior to the Session to present it to him. It was videotaped and played at this time to the entire audience at the Public Opening. It was my pleasure to present the SHC Humanitarian Award to the 39th President of the United States of America, President Jimmy Carter.

Next up was the Shriners Hospitals for Children IMPACT Award. This award is presented to an individual who gives of their personal time and talents to promote the awareness of Shriners Hospitals. I was so proud, to announce that the IMPACT Award recipient this year was Kechi Okwuchi, a former Galveston patient and finalist of Americas Got Talent who has used her fame to create awareness for Shriners Hospitals. She was in the audience and able to personally accept the award. She was so surprised, and it was my honor to present it to her. Kechi is a wonderful person who inspires everyone she meets. She gave a wonderful acceptance speech that touched everyone in the audience.

The afternoon opening finished up with our friend Neomi Wellman singing a beautiful song while pictures of patients were on the screens. She has a beautiful voice and it was a perfect way to close out this program.

Following this we grabbed something to eat with our Executive Team at Sloppy Joe's and called it a day, a long productive day.

July 16, 2018 - Monday

Today started off early with a 6AM breakfast with the Texas Shrine Association. As usual this was a nice time. The food and fellowship were good, and during the event Anne was presented a $6,000.00 check for her First Lady's program.

The Imperial Session started sharply at 8AM. The first hurdle was to get the use of electronic voting devices voted on and approved. It passed, this was important legislation as we had 48 items of legislation to move through. We began knocking them out one by one.

We stepped away from legislation for a moment and it was then my honor to call to the stage members of Bolivia Shriners to receive their Charter. They become our newest Shrine Chapter with the name "Bolivia Shriners." Speeches were given and gifts were exchanged. Congratulations to Bolivia Shriners. What an honor for me to be a part of this after my visit in Bolivia a few months ago as they reached the required number of members.

The most controversy came during the legislation pertaining to the Imperial Recorder, he had hired an attorney during the year with a demand for certain things including to be paid. The boards had honored his request per the bylaws however the amount of the salary was not acceptable to him. The legislation failed.

During lunch I grabbed a sandwich and a coke and went into one of the locker rooms behind the stage all by myself to think. I had not campaigned for the position of Imperial Recorder during the year as in my mind that would not be appropriate while holding the office of Imperial Potentate. Although I felt certain I would do a credible job in that position if elected, was it the right thing to do? After the controversy that transpired during the morning session it seemed the nobility may be looking for a change. I prayed about this, something I don't often do for something like this. I came to the conclusion that because of the controversy the nobility should have an option for the position of Recorder, so I decided to give them that option and run for the position. If I lose, I'm alright with that, the nobility has given me a tremendous opportunity to date and I am appreciative for that. I felt that what I have done in the past and in particular this past year, should make me a qualified candidate if the nobility wishes to make a change.

After lunch the first order of business was to elect our new Imperial Potentate and the remainder of the Divan. Imperial Sir Jim Cain was elected as the next Imperial Potentate, congratulations! We then proceeded down the line. When we got to the election for Recorder, the candidates were Imperial Sir Randy Rudge and myself. Randy won by a large amount, and I gave all of my votes to him, so it would be a unanimous vote in favor of Imperial Sir Randy Rudge. We continued down the line, until the next challenge that was for Imperial Outer Guard. Nomination speeches were given, the vote was taken, and Ill. Sir Mark Hartz from Boumi Shriners in Baltimore was elected as the next Imperial Outer Guard.

We continued calling for legislation the remainder of the day, working through the many pieces we had. By the end of the day we had actually called upon and voted on 31 items in the call. This may be a record for the number of items taken care of in one day. We went to recess at 5 PM and the meeting was dismissed.

Next up was a private party with the Bahia Shriners and ladies along with some special guests at the Peabody. It was a time to thank all of those who worked so hard to put on these two consecutive sessions. We had a rock star attendance of SHC patients and each were given a few minutes to share their story. We had Alec, Kechi, Jessica, Bella, and Riley. They brought the house down with their comments and brought tears to many eyes. Additionally, there were some presentations to Anne for her project. A special one was from the First Lady of Azan Shriners, Patricia Savage, who presented Anne with a check for $5,000.00 she had raised as part of her project. This was so heartwarming to see. A BIG thank you to Patricia Savage.

This event closed out with me presenting my final Imperial Potentates MEDALLION to a Bahia Shriner I admire so much, he gives all he has at Bahia of his talent and time. He is an unsung Hero who just works day in and day out for Shriners. It was a proud moment for me to present my final MEDALLION to Noble Bill Sears. Bill is so humble, he was filled with tears and unable to say much as the crowd erupted in applause. It felt so good to have had the opportunity to recognize him, he is so deserving. The nobles and ladies in attendance from Bahia all expressed I could not have made a better choice.

July 17, 2018 – Tuesday

We started the Imperial Session Meeting at 8:30 AM today. The morning Session concentrated on many of the reports that are required to be given during the meetings. During this time, I called to the stage members of Amal Shriners. They came to receive their Charter as a new Shrine Chapter in São Paulo, Brazil. There was a loud celebration as this Charter was presented and gifts exchanged. Wonderful speeches were given along with a translator. This is the second new Shrine Chapter getting their Charter at this 144th Imperial Session. Something that rarely happens, I'm so happy to be a part of it. I traveled to São Paulo a few months ago and spent time with them as they were working to get enough members to get this Charter. A very proud moment for all Shriners as we continue to experience International growth.

Late morning, we had a few pieces of legislation that were being pulled, so we went through the proper procedure to have them officially withdrawn.

During the lunch break I made a mad dash back to the Hilton to address the nearly 1300 ladies at Anne's Luncheon. The room looked so beautiful and it was full of the most beautiful ladies I know, inside and out. I gave them a warm welcome and thanked them for all they do to assist in helping to take care of children. I also expressed to them the tremendous job Anne had done all year representing each of them in all of her travels. She made us both look good everywhere we went. I also expressed how proud I was of her this week. She had her appendix out just a couple of days ago, yet regardless of how she felt, she is committed to attend every event during the Imperial Session. She did a great job, little did they know that on this day she was really sick and weak from the surgery. This was her special day and she had been waiting for years for it to arrive and now she was feeling so bad she was worried about how she looked and if she could make it to the end. She is a strong lady, she would never complain and did her best not to let it show.

Now another mad dash back to the Ocean Center to attend the Membership Luncheon. After eating a quick lunch, we recognized the successful Temples. I had a chance to speak to them, to thank them, to ask for more from them, and to ask them to influence others. And in closing, we did the final I AM – RU Committed to Membership video, it was soon posted of Facebook.

The afternoon Session started off with the elections for the Trustees for the ensuing year for Shriners Hospitals for Children. There were four running for two positions. Imperial Sir Jerry Gantt and Ill. Sir Paul Poulin, MD prevailed.

I then call on a number of visiting dignitaries for their comments. When I called on the Grand Master of DeMolay, Boyd Patterson of Texas he came to the podium and gave a nice talk on DeMolay. He concluded with presenting one of the highest honors I have ever received, The DeMolay Grand Cross. He was presenting it on behalf of the previous years Grand Master, Ron Minshall, who is the individual who selected me. This came as a total surprise, I was so appreciative. The DeMolay Grand Cross is the highest honor that DeMolay has to present individuals and is based upon their commitment to help, aid, and assist the Order. They began giving out this honor in 2000 and only 2 can be given out per year. Some years no one is recognized as worthy and none are given out. I received the number 24 "DeMolay Grand Cross," what an honor.

The rest of the afternoon was spent calling legislation for the Hospital side. Some of it was serious legislation, however everyone acted in an orderly fashion and we moved through several items. We adjourned at 4:30 PM so everyone could begin to prepare for the Imperial Session Parade.

The parade stepped off at 7PM and proceeded down A1A from Splash Park and ended at the Ocean Center. Again, we had a great parade in Daytona Beach that lasted over 2 hours with many participants. A couple of Super Star patients were in the parade too, Alec and Zion. In addition, this was the first parade in the 144 years of having an Imperial Session that non-Shriners could be in the parade. This turned out to be a hit as some local entries were included, some antique race cars, Masonic Ladies Organizations, DeMolay, and more.

After the parade a large fireworks display took place over the Boardwalk on the ocean. It was a great way to end a busy day. Anne was not feeling well from her surgery a couple of days ago, so we ordered some food from room service and ate in our room. I can't believe all she continues doing after surgery, but she needs to rest as well.

July 18, 2018 – Wednesday

The morning started with an early morning breakfast starting at 6:30 AM with the Cabiri. (Past Potentates) Here I also had a chance to address the audience. I spoke to them about the need for their assistance to help, aid, and assist their Temple Leadership. I expressed they are the most important asset a Temple has if used accordingly. I asked for their help in building leaders and in building membership and thanked them for their assistance.

The Session started with the Pageant for Imperial Potentate Elect Jim Cain and his Lady Patsy. It was a great pageant that took us back to Nashville and the Grand Ole Opry. A lot of work was put into this and everything was exceptional. They received many gifts from friends and other Temples. Lady Patsy then gave her First Lady's presentation for her project called "Little POPS." Following the presentation, she had several checks presented to her to kick off the 2018-2019 year. The morning wrapped up with the public installation of 2018-2019 officers on stage.

After lunch the meeting was called back to order at 1:30 PM. We started off by recognizing those from the Iowa and Colorado Corporations who had earned their Emeritus status this year. Imperial Sir Jerry Gantt and I called them to the stage and made the presentations.

Next, I had the opportunity to recognize a special person in my life, my wife Anne. Anne came to the stage so I could present her an award for her program, *"Love Grows Miracles."* After she spoke, Zion, one of our patients from Philadelphia and his Mother Patti came out to speak on the importance of research at Shriners hospitals. When 8 years old Zion received the first bilateral pediatric hand transplant at the Children's Hospital

of Philadelphia, along with Penn Medicine, Gift of Life, and hand surgeons from the Philadelphia Shriners Hospital, he became an inspiration to many. Zion was Anne's patient ambassador helping to promote her program during the year. He is an energetic amazing child you instantly fall in love with.

I then presented Anne with an Award on behalf of Shriners Hospitals for Children for her dedication as the First Lady to raising funds and awareness. I'm so proud of her, she represented us all in an excellent fashion all year. Thank you, Anne.

Following that I had the opportunity to make some awards, the following is the exact script used to make these prestigious awards to recognize extraordinary men.

BEGIN ACTUAL SCRIPT WEDNESDAY AFTERNOON - BERGENSKE

Last month, I had the honor of visiting White House with Imperial Sir Jim Cain and Lady Patsy along with Imperial Sir Larry Leib. Unfortunately, President Trump was unable to meet with us, but we did leave behind an award that will be given to him. It was my great pleasure to present the first-ever Shriners Hospitals for Children Health Advocacy Award in appreciation of our government's concern for the health and well-being of children around the world. We are especially grateful for the actions of the Department of State, embassy officials, the U.S. military and others in the federal government who help ensure that children receive the compassion, concern and care that Shriners and Shriners Hospitals for Children are committed to providing. We especially appreciate the U.S. military being willing and ready to provide transportation assistance, when approved, for our efforts.

Our hope is that this award will one day reside in the presidential library, a unique honor and privilege for Shriners Hospitals for Children and Shriners International.

At the end of each Imperial Year, the Imperial Potentate has the honor and privilege of presenting extraordinary nobles with the highest honor our fraternity can bestow upon a Shriner, the Award of Merit. Recipients of this award have demonstrated a deep commitment to the missions of both Shriners International and Shriners Hospitals for Children and have made a great impact.

Choosing only a few to honor with this prestigious accolade is a very challenging task, as there are many remarkable and dedicated men in our fraternity.

However, there are five nobles I have particularly noticed throughout this past year, and whose outstanding achievements and accomplishments have made them especially well-deserving of this great honor.

These five exceptional Shriners truly embody the heart and soul of Shriners International, and the essence of the Award of Merit. They are not only devoted to our fraternity and Shriners Hospitals, but also to their communities, careers, and families, and I am very pleased to be able to honor them here today.

The first noble I have the privilege of introducing has been a steadfast champion for our health care system since 2008. He has become an amazing ambassador for both Shriners International and Shriners Hospitals for Children on the public stage, raising awareness and funds through various campaigns and activities, and we are so grateful for his support.

This noble was born on December 24, 1985, in Unadilla, Georgia, and currently resides in Kannapolis, North Carolina.

He first hit the racetrack at age 11, beginning a racing career in the Bandolero Series in 1997 under the guidance of his father Ken, a former Winston Cup driver.

After winning two national championships within three years, he progressed to full-size cars, advancing through the Goody's Dash Series and Legends Pro-Division.

As soon as he turned 18, this noble made his first foray in NASCAR, running Camping World Truck and XFINITY series events, along with a limited ARCA schedule.

His hard work paid off when Jack Roush selected him in 2007 to be the driver of the No. 6 Ford in what is now called the Monster Energy NASCAR Cup Series.

He proved Roush had made the right decision, finishing the 2007 season as runner-up for the Rookie of the Year title in the Cup Series and winning Rookie of the Year in the NASCAR XFINITY Series.

His Cup Series career hit its first major milestone in 2011. After nearly winning the season-opening Daytona 500, he finally earned his first Cup Series victory in July at Daytona International Speedway with his No. 6 Roush Fenway Racing team.

After a move to the No. 34 Ford of Front Row Motorsports, he made the sports world take notice in 2013 when he scored an upset victory at Talladega Superspeedway – a last-lap surge to the checkers while being pushed by teammate David Gilliland. The win was the first ever for Front Row Motorsports and, with a second-place finish by Gilliland, became the most memorable and celebrated day in the team's history.

After racing for BK Racing in 2016, he returned to Front Row Motorsports – the team where he celebrated his last win – for the 2017 season behind the wheel of the No. 38 Ford.

Now in his 12th season, he has amassed two premier series wins, 15 top-five and 39 top-10 finishes, and two poles, and is looking for more.

In 2008, this racecar driver named Shriners Hospitals for Children his official charity of choice. Since then, he has worked to increase awareness and raise funds for our health care system, and his race car now displays a Shriners Hospitals logo.

At the 2012 Imperial Session in Charlotte, North Carolina, he became a member of Oasis Shriners. During the induction ceremony, Imperial Potentate Alan Madsen presented him with his fez. He was raised a Master Mason at Williams Lodge in Cornelius, North Carolina, on May 22, 2012.

During race season, this noble visits Shriners Hospitals and invites patients to the track for once-in-a-lifetime experiences.

He also raises awareness and funds for Shriners Hospitals for Children through various campaigns, public service announcements, events and activities.

This is the third consecutive year that Shriners Hospitals for Children has partnered with this noble for the design of his Front Row Motorsports' No. 38 Ford Fusion for several races.

He recently contributed his Bell Racing USA Shriners Hospitals for Children racing helmet, signed for display, to Shriners International Headquarters' memorabilia collection.

This noble is also a dedicated family man. His wife's name is Jacquelyn, and the couple has two children – Julia and Meredith.

We are so honored to have this great Shriner and NASCAR driver as a member of our fraternity and are incredibly thankful for his efforts and support.

Please join me in congratulating Noble David Ragan, Oasis Shriners.

David Ragan slide appears on screen.

David, please join me on stage!

Keep David's slide on screen until he walks off stage.

After applause award slide appears on screen.

****

The next noble I would like to recognize with the Award of Merit was born in Cuba and graduated high school at age 16. He has had a long career in medicine and has used that experience to benefit Shriners Hospitals for Children in countless ways.

He came to the United States when he was 6 years old, and currently lives in Orlando, Florida.

He received his bachelor's degree from the University of Madrid, and graduated medical school in San Diego, Spain, at age 22.

He completed his residency at the Orlando Regional Health Center.

For 35 years, he has managed his OBGYN practice and has served as the Medical Director and a Board Member for Humana Hospital Lucerne in Orlando.

He was also the Chairman of the OBGYN department at the hospital, and a member of the American Medical Association.

In addition, this noble is a professor of laparoscopic surgery, and has taught the procedure in the U.S., Central America and South America.

He is a member of Mokanna Lodge #329 F & AM in Orlando.

In 2002, he became a member of Bahia Shriners, also in Orlando, and has been involved with the temple in several different capacities.

He served as the Divan physician, translator for the paper crusade magazine and director of the Antique Car Show.

He is also a member of the Royal Order of Jesters Court #166, and the Order of Quetzalcoatl, Lagos de Orlando, Teocalli #36.

Re-elected during the Shriners' 2017 Imperial Session, he is currently serving his third three-year term on the Shriners Hospitals for Children Board of Trustees.

This noble is an energetic and dedicated Shriner with a strong desire to use his medical experience to benefit our health care system.

He and his wife, Vicki, have been married for 20 years. They have five children – Marie, Peter, Cristina, Carolina and Lindsey, and seven grandchildren.

He also likes to fish, and has gone fishing in Brazil with his father-in-law, George.

Please join me in congratulating Noble Dr. Peter Diaz, Bahia Shriners.
Dr. Peter Diaz's slide appears on screen.
Peter, please join us on stage!
Keep Dr. Diaz's slide on screen until he walks off stage.
After applause award slide appears on screen.

****

The next noble I would like to recognize with this award is a highly successful lawyer with considerable experience in both private practice and as a state's attorney. Prior to joining our staff, he practiced law in Texas, and has been a Shriner for nearly 30 years.

This noble is a graduate of the University of Illinois College of Commerce, earning a bachelor's degree in Business Administration.

He earned his Juris Doctor degree from the University of Illinois College of Law.

He was named a Truman Scholar by the Harry S. Truman Scholarship Foundation based on demonstrated leadership, scholarship and commitment to public service. The Foundation is the official US government memorial to President Truman.

He is licensed to practice law in Illinois and Texas.

This noble was elected State's Attorney for Champaign County, Illinois, for ten years. He also served as President of the Illinois State's Attorney's Association.

He has also served on a number of law-related statewide Boards and Commissions, including the Board of Governors of the Illinois State Bar Association, the Illinois Truth-In-Sentencing Commission and the Illinois Children's Justice Task Force. He was also a member of the Illinois Criminal Justice Information Authority.

In 2000, the Law Bulletin Publishing Company, publishers of the Chicago Daily Law Bulletin, named him one of "Forty Illinois Attorneys Under 40 to Watch."

He was appointed to serve on the National Advisory Committee of the U.S. Small Business Administration during the Reagan Administration, and was also appointed to serve on the Illinois Small Business Advisory Board.

He was also appointed as a delegate to the White House Conference on Small Business.

On August 30, 2005, he was coroneted a 33rd degree Mason.

He is also a Companion Adept of the Temple of the York Rite, a member of Western Star Lodge No. 240 of Champaign, Illinois, and Krum Lodge No. 1453 of Krum, Texas.

He is a member of the Scottish Rite Valley of Danville, Illinois, and is a member of the Scottish Rite Valley of Fort Worth, Texas.

He is also a member of York Rite Bodies in Fort Worth, Texas, and is a Certificate Holder for the Chapter and Council.

This noble has been a member of Ansar Shriners for nearly 30 years.

One of the reasons he became a Shriner was because he was aware of the important work of the Shriners in his community, and he wanted to be a part of it.

In July 2015, this noble became the Executive Vice President of Shriners International, and has been serving loyally in that role ever since.

His goal as Executive Vice President has been to do everything in his power to encourage high quality men of character to become Shriners.

He is married to Debra, and is the proud father of adult children, Jackie and David.

Please join me in congratulating Noble John Piland, Ansar Shriners.

John Piland's slide appears on screen.
John, please join me on stage!
Keep John's slide on screen until he walks off stage.
After applause award slide appears on screen.

****

The next noble I would like to recognize is also an accomplished attorney, with over 49 years of legal experience. He became a Shriner in 1980 and has used his legal background to serve our fraternity for many years.

He was born in Chicago, Illinois, and currently lives in Park Ridge, Illinois.

This noble received his bachelor's degree from North Park College in 1965, and his Juris Doctor degree from Loyola University in 1969.

Professionally, he is an Attorney at Law. He and his son, William, who is also a Shriner, are partners in a law firm, and his daughter, Natalie, also practices law there.

He was raised a Master Mason at Edison Park Lodge No. 974 in 1980.

He is currently a member of Medinah Masonic Lodge No. 1182UD, in Addison, Illinois.

He is a member of both the Scottish and York Rites.

He joined Medinah Shriners on May 12, 1980.

He served as Legal Counsel for his temple from 1986 to 1994.

He served on Medinah Shriners' Divan beginning in 1995 and served as Potentate in 2000.

He has served as Chairman and Past Chairman of Medinah Shriners' Finance/Investments/Insurance Committee.

He has served as President of the Country Shrine Club at Medinah Country Club and is a member of the Maine Shrine Club.

He is a member of the Scottish Rite Valley of Chicago; Red Cross; Crabs; Jesters Court 48; York Rite, Chapter No. 253, Forest C. McDaniel Council No. 115, Austin Commandery No. 84; DeMolay, Frank S. Land Honorary Legion of Honor; and Royal Order of Scotland.

He served as Chairman of the Board of Governors of the Chicago Shriners Hospital from 2006 to 2009, and as a Member from 2001 to 2010.

He served as General Counsel for Shriners International and Shriners Hospitals for Children from 2011 to 2013, and from 2015 to present.

In 2008, this noble was awarded the 33rd Degree.

He also is a Former Director and First Vice President of The Board of Scottish Rite Cathedral Association; Former Chairman of Finance/Investments/Insurance Committees for the Scottish Rite; Puissant Sovereign of Red Cross (2005); and served on the Board for Scottish Rite Children's Learning Center.

He also served on both the Jurisprudence and Laws Committee and Grievance and Appeals Committee for Shriners International.

He and his lady, Natalie, have been married for 50 years.

The couple has three children, William Raymond, Natalie Marie, and Elizabeth Marion Cichy.

He also has many grandchildren – Sophia Marie, Michael Oscar, Natalie Rose DeVooght, Katherine Fay, Lily Claire DeVooght, Nathan Keith Cichy, Andrew Robert DeVooght, Daniel Thomas Cichy, and Robert David Cichy.

His hobbies include being an "Avid Grandchildren Activity Spectator," playing golf, traveling, wine collecting, playing cards, and Corvettes/classic cars.

This noble's longtime dedication to Masonry and Shriners International shows his sincere concern for those less fortunate, especially children.

Those who know him best say he has strong ethical principles and is fair-minded, reasonable and kind in his approach to complex situations.

He is very devoted to his family and friends, is always available to "help out," and rarely misses any activity involving his family.

Please join me in congratulating Illustrious Sir Robert O. Kuehn, Medinah Shriners.

Robert O. Kuehn's slide appears on screen.

Bob, please join me on stage!

Keep Robert's slide on screen until he walks off stage.

After applause award slide appears on screen.

****

The last noble I would like to recognize is also a lawyer and has been practicing in Florida since 1966. He is widely recognized for his ardent support of the University of

Florida and its athletic program, along with his community and the Shriners organizations.

He was born in Atlanta, Georgia, was raised in Jacksonville, Florida, and currently lives in Winter Park, Florida.

He is a Senior DeMolay.

He graduated from the University of Florida in 1961, where he earned a math degree.

He went on to teach algebra and geometry at his former high school, Robert E. Lee High School, for two years, before beginning law school.

He graduated from the University of Florida College of Law, third in his class of more than 200, in 1965.

He taught at Florida's Law School for one year before joining the predecessor firm of Holland & Knight in Bartow, Florida, in 1966.

In 1970, he became a founding partner of an Orlando law firm, which grew to 130 lawyers with locations in six cities, and in 2003, he founded a new firm to practice with his son in the field of eminent domain and civil trial law.

Today, he is an AV-rated trial attorney with extensive experience in a broad spectrum of property rights issues. He has handled hundreds of eminent domain parcels, ranging in value from a few hundred dollars to more than $60 million.

This noble is especially well known for his enthusiastic support of the University of Florida.

He serves, or has served, in leadership capacities in numerous advisory boards that serve the University and its Athletic Program and has been very generous with his time and money.

He is a member of the University of Florida Hall of Fame, Florida Blue Key, a former President and Life Member of the University of Florida National Alumni Association, a Legacy Director of Gator Boosters, a former President and Life Member of Gator Boosters, and a Member of the Real Estate Advisory Board of the Center for Real Estate Studies for the UF Warrington College of Business.

He has also served on the University of Florida Foundation and the UAA Boards.

In addition to his love of the University of Florida, this noble is a huge supporter of Shriners Hospitals for Children, and a very active Shriner.

He became a Master Mason at age 24 by joining Riverside Lodge #266 in Jacksonville.

He became a member of Bahia Shriners on June 26, 1971 and has served his temple faithfully ever since.

He has also served his Blue Lodge and York Rite on numerous committees.

He is a Past Potentate of Bahia Shriners in Orlando, and a former president of the Florida Shrine Association.

He is a member of the Board of Governors of the Tampa Shriners Hospital.

He has served on Shriners International's Jurisprudence and Laws Committee and Grievances and Appeals Committee.

He is also Past Regional Director and Deputy Director of Shriners International's Endowments, Wills and Gifts Committee, a past international championship clown, Past President of the Southeastern Shrine Clown Association, and the founder and Past President of the Florida Shrine Clown Association.

Perhaps one of his most significant fraternal accomplishments was in 1982 when he arranged for Shriners Hospitals for Children to be the charitable sponsor of the Florida Citrus Bowl football game, formerly the Tangerine Bowl. This was the only NCAA sanctioned post-season Bowl game played for the benefit of Shriners Hospitals.

The 1982 game was a sellout, and provided national recognition for our philanthropy, and a $50,000 first-year contribution.

He served as the Director General of both the 2017 and 2018 Imperial Sessions here in Daytona Beach. He also served as Deputy Director General of the 1982 Imperial Session in Orlando.

In his community, he is the past Chairman of the Board of Trinity Preparatory School and has served on the Board of Visitors of Lake Highland Preparatory School.

He has also been the Senior Warden at St. Michael's Episcopal Church.

His biggest hobby is – you guessed it – University of Florida Gator Football.

He is married to Ruthie, and they have three children – Routledge, Bruce and Sarah.

He also has nine grandchildren – Katie, Danny, Jimmy, Lilley, Graham, Emme, Sarah, Ford and Agatha.

This noble is distinguished by his dedication to his family, his church, his university, and to being a Shriner.

Please join me in congratulating Illustrious Sir Gordon H. "Stumpy" Harris, Bahia Shriners.

Gordon H. "Stumpy" Harris' slide appears on screen.

Stumpy, please join me on stage!

Keep Stumpy's slide on screen until he walks off stage.

Congratulations slide on screen

****

Congratulations to the 2018 Award of Merit recipients! I commend these outstanding men for their many achievements and congratulate them for receiving our fraternity's highest honor. I would also like to recognize everyone in the audience here today – we appreciate each of you, and everything you do for our organizations.

Serving as your Imperial Potentate has truly been the experience of a lifetime. I personally would like to thank all of you for your overwhelming kindness and support.

END ACTUAL BERGENSKE SCRIPT

I now introduced Imperial Sir Jim Cain to give the Marketing and Communications Report. Jim had several areas of success to present to the audience with many videos to back them all up. This is always one of the highlights of the entire Imperial Session. I was presented the 2018 Harris Pole First Place Trophy for name brand recognition for Children's Hospitals. I received this on behalf of all Shriners and all Shriners Hospitals for Children employees. What an honor this organization has received because of our consistent hard work of taking care of children. This was a highlight for sure.

Imperial Sir Jim then proceeded to show a video that introduced our two new International Patient Ambassadors for the 2018-2019 year. These two will represent us well, they are Lily and Riley. I have known Riley for several years; he and Lily will do a tremendous job for us as they travel extensively promoting Shriners Hospitals for Children.

We wrapped up by 4PM so the Oak Ridge Boys band could get set up for our evening concert. It was time to go to the hotel, change, grab something quick to eat and head to the concert.

By 5:30 we were back at the Ocean Center to eat at the VIP Reception prior to the concert. The Oak Ridge Boys made an appearance and did pictures with some of us. I asked the four Oak Ridge Boys if any of them were Shriners, they all said no. However, one of them confirmed with me he would like to be. He told me he was already a Mason. I said to him, "We might just be able to make that happen if you're serious."

We were then escorted in to the arena and the concert began. They were fantastic and had the crowd up on their feet dancing much of the time. They did a song about children and invited all of our patients up onstage with them to dance as they sang the song. This was a hit with everyone, and the kids loved it.

After the Concert I was approached and told that one of the band members wanted to talk with me. I went back stage and it was William Lee Golden of the Oak Ridge Boys, he expressed to me he would like to become a Shriner. I asked him if he was a current Mason, and he replied he was, for 54 years. I told him I would need to see his dues card. He said, "I'll be right back, I need to go to the bus and get it." A few minutes later he returned with his perpetual membership dues card from JAY Lodge 176 in the panhandle of

Florida. He currently lives in Nashville, so I got Imperial Sir Jim Cain as he would become a member there. Jim and I interviewed him for a few minutes, he agreed to fill out a petition. He then asked if he could become a Shriner tonight because of his time schedule of traveling and doing 150 shows per year. Jim and I agreed.

So back stage at the Daytona Beach Ocean Center with about 20 people in attendance, I had the pleasure of swearing in our newest member. William Lee Golden of the Oak Ridge Boys would be the final new member of my 2017-2018 I AM – RU Committed to Membership program. What a great way to end it. We Fezzed him and did Pictures, this made for the perfect ending of a great day.

July 19, 2018 – Thursday

As we began the last day of this 2018 Imperial Session, the first message to the audience was the news of our newest member we created the evening before, William Lee

Golden of the Oak Ridge Boys who has been a Mason for 54 years. The crowd erupted in applause.

We then began to move through the 6 pieces of legislation we still had left to finish up this Imperial Session. They went rather quickly.

We then moved into the final remarks, and I thanked the Nobility for the honor and privilege of serving as their Imperial Potentate. It is truly one of the highlights of my life. We had the opportunity to travel to many places, meet many people and to represent our great fraternity and philanthropy on behalf of our many members, employees, and patients. I could not express my gratitude enough for the confidence they placed in me to hold such a prestigious position. I again thanked them on behalf of my wife Anne and myself.

We then moved to the official installation of the newly elected Boards of Directors and Trustees. I was honored to serve one more year as a Trustee and as the Jr. Past Imperial Potentate.

Imperial Sir Jim, our new Imperial Potentate then announced some of his plans, announced some of his appointments, and then proceeded to close the 144th Imperial Session.

Anne, still not feeling up to par from her surgery, headed back home in the afternoon. She needs to get some rest. I cannot express how proud I am of her. After having surgery to have her appendix out during our visit here she did not miss one Imperial Session event, I don't know how she did it. Guess she is a super woman. She was happy to be heading home to relax and rest now.

The Board members all went back to the Hilton to have our official pictures done for the new year and then went to lunch in the hospitality room. Following that we had a Joint Board meeting in the afternoon. That evening was the first dinner honoring our new Imperial Potentate and First Lady, Jim and Patsy Cain at the Daytona Yacht Club on the Intercoastal waterway. It was a really nice event and well attended. Great start to a new year.

After dinner I spent the evening packing things up to leave in the morning.

July 20, 2018 – Friday

Now as a Past Imperial Potentate, I finished up my packing, called a bell hop and loaded up the car. On the way out of town I stopped at my favorite Daytona Beach breakfast place, Mike's Galley, by myself to have something to eat. Here I had a chance for the first time to reflect back on an incredible year. How will I ever be able to thank all of the people that helped Anne and me the past 11 years? There is no way we can thank them enough for all they did, and for all they allowed us to do. Friendships, we are so fortunate to build so many incredible lifetime friendships. Wow, what a journey.

As I proceeded out of town, I stopped by the Daytona Beach Police Dept to thank them for all they did for us during our stay, especially all of the police escorts and helping with Anne while she was sick. While there, they took my picture and provide me the credential to go with my Honorary Daytona Beach Police Department Badge to make it official, another great honor. We made many friends within the Department, they all work so hard, they are true Hero's for what they do.

As I drove down I-4 on this hot July day back to Orlando, this brings us to the end. I'm so glad I kept this journal, without it we would forget so much of what we had the opportunity to do. As time goes on I will treasure it even more. It will also be my pleasure to share it with others, so they will know just what it is like to be the Imperial Potentate of Shriners International.

I also want to again, thank my friend, President Jimmy Carter for encouraging me to keep this journal, he has been an inspirational mentor to me, and I appreciate his friendship more than he will ever know.

A Year as the Imperial Potentate of Shriners International

Chapter Fourteen

Imperial Potentate MEDALLIONS
Presented by
Imperial Potentate Gary Bergenske
2017 - 2018

    The office of the Imperial Potentate brings with it certain privileges, one of which is having the ability to present **Imperial Potentate MEDALLIONS**. In recent years I felt this privilege had not been used enough to recognize the good deeds of others. I set out to use this privilege as best I could from the beginning, always having one or more with me wherever I traveled to.

I recognized individual Shriners, employees, groups, and celebrities throughout the year. Having the honor to present these small Medallions brings with it a wonderful personal satisfaction of recognizing others when they least expect it. I will tell you these medallions bring with them such a significance, that I do not believe there was one that did not involve tears. The tears came from either the recipient, or me, or both. There were some who received it who were so choked up they could not even respond as the tears flowed. You can never say thank you to much.

It was my pleasure to present the list below of **37** Imperial Potentate Medallions that were presented in the 2017 – 2018 Shrine year. These MEDALLIONS were presented in 7 different countries; United States, Canada, Cyprus, Philippines, Panama, Germany, and Mexico. A tip of the Fez to these individuals and groups who I hold in the highest regard, Congratulations!

"Compliments and recognition of others should become an everyday item on your agenda."
GARY BERGENSKE

A Year as the Imperial Potentate of Shriners International

Imperial Potentate MEDALLIONS

7-13-2017
1) Linda McMahon, Daytona CVB
2) Lynn Miles, Daytona CVB
For loyal support to the Shriners Daytona Convention

8-4-2017
3) Ill. Sir Don Holiday, Almas Shriners
Over 500 Hospital Trips

8-28-2017
4) Dr. Stephen Blount, Carter Center
5) Phil Wise, Carter Center
For collaboration with the Carter Center

9-8-2017
6) Honorable John James Grant
Lieutenant Governor, Halifax.
Appointed by Queen Elizabeth

9-9-2017
7) Ill Sir Mike Schmid
Potentate of Philae Shriners
Halifax, Nova Scotia

9-14–2017
8) Craig Kent
Noble at Ansar Shriners.
Pays for SHC ad in every Sunday Paper

9-27–2017
9) Shrine Guild of America
Presented at Annual Session in Dayton.
For many years of contributions to SHC.

10-9- 2017
10) Thelma Paraskevaides
11) Costas Paraskevaides
For the Paraskevaides Foundations 36 years of helping kids   At
Shriners Hospitals – Springfield
Nicosia, Cyprus.

10-10- 2017
12) MW GM Machalepis
Grand Master of Cyprus

11-18-2017
13) David Ragan, NASCAR Driver and Shriner
14) Dr. Ray Novak, Retiring from SHC
15) Charlene Hanes, Retiring from SHC

12-2-2017
16) Joe Harper, ZOR Shriners
Past GM, ZOR Chief of Staff

12-14-2017
17) Laurie Spieler
VP of Legal, Shriners

1-30-2018
18) Vicki Beck
Shrine Public Relations writer

2-10-2018
19) Greg McEwen PP
Texas Shrines Assoc. Sec - Tres

2-18-2018
20) Larry Tipton P.P.
Pacific North Shrine Assoc. Exec Director

2-20-2018
21) Simon LaPlace PGM from Connecticut
Masonic Service Association, Executive Secretary

3-2-2018
22) Alec Cabacungan
National Patient Ambassador
Featured in many SHC Commercials

3-11-2018
23) Brad Paisley
Singer, Entertainer, Shriner
In concert in Lakeland, FL

3-22-2018
24) Ill Sir Bob Amico
25) Ill Sir Mikey Juett
Deputy Director Generals, 2017 and 2018
Presented in Europe on riverboat

3-27-2018
26) River Melody Crew
GCCL Riverboat trip, Imperial Trip
Cruising -France to Switzerland

4- 16- 2018
27) George Barfield
Mexico Board of Governors
57 trips Orlando to Mexico Hospital

4-17-2018
28) Dr. Philippe Hacis
Mexico SHC Dr., 30 years
SHC Chief of Staff, 20 years

4-28-2018
29) Richard Wright PP
Khedive Treasurer 32 years
Past Mid Atlantic Shrine Assoc. President

5-5-2018
30) Mabuhay Shriners
For Membership TOP results of the year
Manila, Philippines

5-15-2018
31) Ladies Oriental Shrine of North America
Presented at Annual Session in Honolulu
For many years of contributions to SHC

6-2-2018
32) Tunis Shriners, Ottawa
Presented for bringing in new
Members equal to 10% of their total membership

6-7-2018
33) Abou Saad Shriners
Panama City, Panama
100th Anniversary Celebration

6-23-2018
34) President Jimmy Carter
39th President of the United States
Presentation made in Plains, GA
For promoting awareness of SHC

6-24-2018
35) Daughters of the Nile
Presented at Annual Session in Cincinnati
For many years of contributions to SHC

7-9-2018
36) Stumpy Harris PP
2017 & 2018 Director General

7-16-2018
37) Noble Bill Sears
Longtime loyal Bahia Shriner

A Year as the Imperial Potentate of Shriners International
Thank You Letter

This "Thank You" letter was sent out individually by US Mail a couple of weeks after the Imperial Session to thank all of the Chairman and Vice Chairman along with their committees for their exemplary work.

Gary J. Bergenske and his wife Anne
Imperial Potentate 2017 – 2018

To all Convention Corporation Chairman & Vice Chairman

Dear_____

Seventy years ago, that's before Bahia was even formed yet, was the last time a city held two consecutive Imperial Sessions. They took place in Atlantic City in 1947 and 1948 in the Civic Auditorium. Harry S. Truman, a Mason and a Shriner was President of the United States. My guess would be there are very few Shriners who attended those

Imperial Sessions that are still around. Those who are would have to be at least 91 years old.

When we say, "Bahia Shriners did the unthinkable by hosting two consecutive Imperial Sessions in a manner that has set the bar so high, others are pondering if they can match it. We are saying Bahia Nobles and Ladies did an incredible job." We have so much to be proud of; we had a destination that was family friendly, we had more extra fun events than anyone in recent memory, the parade and competitions exceeded everyone's expectations, and our church service and Oak Ridge Boys Concert were so good people could not believe it. Collectively everyone did a wonderful job.

So you have to ask yourself, "How were we able to pull the unthinkable off, how were we able to be so successful?" The answer is simple, we used the greatest asset that Bahia Shriners has, it's people, it's membership, and their families, who worked together to take on this challenge in a professional way that found great results. Everyone worked with pride, passion, and commitment. Our results were awesome, thanks to you.

When Anne and I set out on this journey eleven years ago, we had no idea how much work and travel was in our future. We did have a comfort of knowing that Bahia was behind us and that we could count on our friends to help us. Today we both know, our friends at Bahia stepped it up more than we could ever imagine. When we were asked to do the Imperial Session two years in a row, everyone replied with, "Let's do it." How can Anne and I ever thank you enough? I don't know that we can, we owe each of you so much, but, please know how appreciative we are for your time, efforts, and friendship.

Anne and I thank every person who gave their time to make the two consecutive Imperial Sessions in Daytona Beach a success. We thank you for your support and we thank you for making Bahia a shining light in all of Shrinedom for your exemplary work. We have so much to be proud of after serving a year as your Imperial Potentate and First Lady; however, it's the people of Bahia we are proud of the most. Please share these thanks with all members of your committee and those who assisted you. It's an awesome TEAM.

With best wishes and the warmest regards,

Gary and Anne

About Anne Bergenske

Anne Bergenske "Healthy Births"
Research Fellowship Endowment

Lady Anne Bergenske, who served as the First Lady of Shriners International in 2017 - 2018, promoted a program called "Love Grows Miracles" to raise money for research that focused on Healthy Births. Bergenske, who lost a grandchild 7 1/2 months into the pregnancy knows the pain and sorrow a family feels in the loss of an unborn child. It was because of this loss she spent her time and energy while serving as First Lady to raise money to provide scholarships for medical students to research ways to give children healthier lives even before they are born.

"There are many people who have experienced the shock and sadness that comes with losing a child before birth," said Anne. "Research is developing ways to prevent and treat medical conditions that can cause such heartache."

"Many of us have experienced the joys of having a healthy newborn child. However, others experience the unbearable pain of losing a child or are coping with challenges some children are born with." Anne continued. "We are inspired and comforted by the fact that doctors and scientists at Shriners Hospitals for Children are developing innovative new ways to prevent and treat many medical conditions before children are born. The cutting-edge research in this area will prove to give many children healthier lives in the future."

Anne Bergenske's "Love Grows Miracles" video can be seen on YouTube

> *When dreaming of charity work, ask "What if" and think of how lives can be changed.*
> **GARY BERGENSKE**

Conclusion

The fuel that kept us going all year on our fast-paced agenda was the many patients we met along the way. Every time you spend time with one of these amazing children who overcome great challenges with tremendous confidence and a smile on their face, you become more and more energized. Zion was one of those children who Anne and I became attached to. He along with his family's support overcame the unthinkable and is now charging forward in life with no limits. Zion, is the first child to undergo a successful pediatric double hand transplant; he is in the Guinness Book of World Records. He moves around on his two prosthetic legs as any child would do with a personality that will melt your heart. Today; baseball, basketball, swimming and more are all part of his daily activities. It is truly a miracle, he is an inspiration to everyone he meets.

What a year, to be able to serve as the Imperial Potentate and Chairman of the Board of Directors for both Shriners International and Shriners Hospitals for Children; I would have never thought this to be possible. It was a dream come true. The blessings Anne and I had to meet and to interact with so many wonderful patients and people was outstanding. It was my desire from the beginning to share as much of what we were able to do with everyone. This book was one of the ways I knew of to give everyone the true feeling of how much work our members do, and how important our mission is. I hope it has created some additional awareness.

In the beginning I mentioned old traditions. Shriners are an old tradition, an old tradition of fellowship; of "making good men better." It then stretches far beyond that, as these fine men go above and beyond helping others, making their lives better too. It's been carried out further than our founders could have ever imagined. Personally, I'm so proud to be a part of this old tradition that brought more value to my life and inspires me to do more every day.

People often ask me what I enjoyed most about being Imperial Potentate, the answer may surprise you. Yes, the many people and patients we met, the travel, and of course seeing how we changed lives were all up near the top. But what I enjoyed most was recognizing others and thanking them for their fine work. Every time I did this with the different awards I was able to give, tears were involved, either from me, or the recipient, or both. The emotions that genuine recognition and thanks bring, especially in a volunteer organization, are unmeasurable. People become emotional when they know they and their work have value. It is the greatest form of motivating people. I encourage you to inspire others, thank them, and let them know how much you appreciate them. You will get the greatest feeling. I can also tell you being on the receiving end is great too, it's good for everyone.

Gary

> *"There is nothing like a dream,*
> *A dream can create the future.*
> *If you BELIEVE in it.*
> *A dream can take you anywhere."*
> **GARY BERGENSKE**

About the Author

Gary J. Bergenske

Gary J. Bergenske was born in Madison, Wisconsin in 1954 and raised in Pardeeville, a small nearby town. After graduating from Portage High School, he and his family moved to Jacksonville, Florida. Bergenske and his family have lived in the Orlando, Florida area for over 35 years where he has been the owner of J&J Metro Moving and Storage Company.

As a motivational speaker, he has delivered his inspirational message on leadership, teamwork, and mentoring at engagements throughout the world. For twelve years he served on the Boards for Shriners International and Shriners Hospitals for Children. He served as Imperial Potentate, the highest office in the entire Shriners organization worldwide in 2017 – 2018.

Bergenske was raised a Master Mason in 1994 at Eola Lodge #207 in Orlando. He became a member of Bahia Shriners in Orlando in 1994, where he is now a lifetime member. He served as *Potentate of Bahia Shriners,* Orlando in 2005. Bergenske is the

Founder of the Bahia Historical and Educational Museum in Orlando. He is an associate member of Zor Shriners in Madison, Wisconsin. He is also a perpetual lifetime member of the Orlando Scottish Rite where he was invested with the rank of **_Knight Commander of the Court of Honor_**. Additionally, the Scottish Rite Supreme Council conferred upon him the **_33° Inspector General Honorary_**. This Degree is conferred upon those who have been outstanding in their contributions to Freemasonry, the Scottish Rite, or who have shown in their communities the leadership which marks them as men who exemplify in their daily lives the true meaning of the Brotherhood of man under the Fatherhood of God.

Bergenske currently serves as a certified member of the Advisory Council of Florida for DeMolay International; has received the **_DeMolay Honorary Legion of Honor Award_**, is an **_Honorary Member of DeMolay's International Supreme Council_**, and has been presented the prestigious **_DeMolay International Grand Cross,_** its highest honor. Bergenske was the founding President of the Shriners International Educational Foundation, an endowment set up to provide education on leadership. Bergenske is also an emeritus member of Shriners International, an emeritus representative of Shriners Hospitals for Children, a lifetime member of the Cabiri International, and a member of the Royal Order of Jesters, The Order of Quetzalcoatl, Lions International, and the Loyal Order of Moose.

Bergenske had the honor to be inducted into the **_"Hall of Fame"_** of his High School in Portage, Wisconsin. The "Hall of Fame" is the highest honor granted by the school and is presented to alumni who have shown their worthiness to serve as a model of success and character that the schools' students will admire and emulate. Recipients serve to inspire future graduates to perform and serve in the same spirit.

Bergenske served three successful years as Chairman of the nationally televised Shriners International all-star college football event, the East-West Shrine Game®. During his years as a member of the Shriners Boards of Directors, he served on numerous committees, including as chairman of the Research, Public Relations, Fraternal Strategic Planning, Information Services, Insurance, Protocol, and Capital Evaluation committees. In addition, he has served as the Liaison Officer to the Shriners Hospitals for Children locations in Erie, Springfield, Houston, Galveston, Portland, Honolulu, Boston, and Spokane. He served on the Executive Committee of the Imperial Membership Committee for 14 years and was a charter member of both the TRAC and PACE teams. He has also been an inspirational keynote speaker and presenter at Imperial conferences for Oriental Guides, Assistant Rabbans, public relations, donor relations and membership.

During the time Bergenske was a member of the Imperial Membership Executive Committee, he came up with the idea of having a Shriners mascot to not only promote the fraternity but to also attract younger generations, which resulted in the development of Fez Head Fred. While serving as Membership Chairman of Bahia Shriners, Bergenske created and developed the Mentor Program to get new members involved. Shriners now use this program throughout the world. While serving as Imperial Potentate, he championed the most aggressive Shriners International Membership program in recent memory, called *"I AM – RU Committed to Membership."*

In 1985, Bergenske purchased J & J Metro Moving and Storage, which he has owned and operated for the past 34 years. In addition, Bergenske is a motivational speaker and has written five books. His other books discuss ways to "Build a Better Life" and "Become a Better Leader" and are available in more than 10 countries, where they are making a positive difference in people's lives.

In his down time, he loves traveling, the outdoors, hunting, old cars and Harley-Davidsons. Bergenske and his wife, Anne, have six children – Carrie, Lisa, Jason, Jami, David and Jared – and are often referred to as the "Bergy Bunch." They have 12 grandchildren who regularly brighten their days.

**Visit YouTube.com and search Gary Bergenske
To watch some of the activities described in "Shriners Diary"**

Picture Index

Cover and Page 3
"SHRINERS" logo

Page 2
2017 Imperial Convention Logo

Dedication
Imperial Potentates pin

Foreword
President Carters letter

Introduction
Gary's signature

Acknowledgements
Gary and Anne official portrait

Chapter 1 - July 2017
July 12 - Pageant pictures (3)
July 15 – Anne's Program
July 15 – Anne's Program Tie
July 22 – DeMolay picture

Chapter 2 - August
Aug 3 – White House
April 4 – Anne at Jefferson Memorial
Aug 6 – Boumi visit, Baltimore boat trip
Aug 8 - Fort McHenry flag raising
Aug 28 – Jimmy Carter Library visit
Aug 28 – Yarrab visit, I AM - RU

Chapter 3 - September

Sept 8 - Governors Home
Sept 9 - Philae Shriners visit – Lobster
Sept 22 – Making of a video, Greenville
Sept 24 - Greenville SHC 90th
Sept 27 - Shrine Guilds, Medallion Award

Chapter 4 - October

Oct 5 - Membership Seminar
Oct 9 - Cyprus visit, Clinic
Oct 10 – Cyprus Grand Master
Oct 11 - Cyprus visit, Pres of Parliament
Oct 12 – US Embassy invitation
Oct 13 – Costas and Moro in Cyprus
Oct 20 – Anne presents "Love Grows Miracles" program
Oct 31 - Shriners Open- Las Vegas, Oct 31

Chapter 5 - November

Nov 2 – Gary and Alec in Las Vegas
Nov 4 - Tomb of Unknown wreath laying
Nov 5 – SHC Golf Trophy presentation to Patrick Cantley
Nov 25 - Bolivia Shriners Ceremonial
Nov 25 – Bolivia Shriners w/ Red Nose

Chapter 6 - December

Dec 2 - Zor Shriners, Cheese Head
Dec 5 – Philippines patient
Dec 8 - Philippines visit, Masonic Lodge
Dec 13 - Henry Rifle in Museum
Dec 19 – Eola Lodge Recognition
Dec 25 – Christmas Card of Imperial Potentate

Chapter 7 - January

Jan 1 - Rose Bowl Parade float
Jan 1 – Gary on Rose Bowl float
Jan 8 - DeMolay Headquarters visit
Jan 12 - Puerto Rico visit
Jan 19 - EWSG Hall of Fame, Brett Favre
Jan 26 - Mexico SHC patient

Chapter 8 - February

Feb 9 - Texas Association visit
Feb 12 – Gift from David Ragan
Feb 17 – Pacific Northwest Shrine visit
Feb 19 – Murat Shriners visit
Feb 21 - Panama Clinic visit
Feb 22 – Panama patient
Feb 23 – Panama Shrine event

Chapter 9 - March

March 3 – SHC Baseball Classic, Houston
March 5 - DeMolay groundbreaking, Kansas City
March 9 – The New Bride at Conference
March 12 – Brad Paisley, Medallion presentation
March 17 - Imperial Potentates Cruise, Gary and Anne
March 18 – Dinner on the Cruise at Imperial table
March 20 – Bunch of Shriners Fez's
March 25 - Emirat Shriners, Germany
March 28 - End of Cruise with Bahia Shriners

Chapter 10 - April

April 1 - Washington Masonic Memorial
April 13 - Western Assoc, Las Vegas
April 16 - Mexico Hospital visit (2)
April 19 - Mexico visit, dinner Eduardo
April 27 – Medallion presented to Richard Wright PP

A Year as the Imperial Potentate of Shriners International

Chapter 11 – May

May 4 – Ceremonial Lunch - Philippines
May 4 - Mabuhay Ceremonial Parade – Philippines
May 4 – Mabuhay Fire Truck Spray down
May 7 – Mabuhay Shrine office
May 12 - Honolulu Gala, Coach becomes a Shriner
May 14 – Doing the Hula
May 15 – Past Imperial Potentates grave,
May 27 - Murat Shriners, Indy 500

Chapter 12 – June

June 6 - Abou Saad 100th Anniversary
June 6 - Abou Saad 100th Anniversary, Plaque
June 6 – Gary takes a pie to the face
June 16 – Bahia visit
June 18 – Smith and Wesson visit
June 19 - Springfield SHC ribbon cutting
June 23 - Anne and Jimmy Carter
June 23 - President Carter visit
June 23 – President Carter Award
June 24 – Daughters of the Nile visit

Chapter 13 – July 2018

July 7 - Lt General Tuck meeting
July 9 – 2018 "Back to the Beach" logo
July 10 – Great Gatsby
July 15 - Walk for Love, Daytona Speedway
July 16 – Bolivia gets Charter
July 17 – Anne at Ladies Luncheon
July 17 – Imperial Shrine Parade
July 18 - Award of Merit Awards (5)
July 18 – Anne receives recognition with Zion
July 18 - Oakridge Boy becomes a Shriner
July 19 – Oakridge Boy announcement

Chapter 14 – Awards

Imperial Potentate Medallion

Conclusion

Gary and Zion

Greatness develops by;
Having made a difference in the past,
Making a difference in the present,
And by being willing to be different.
- GARY BERGENSKE

A Year as the Imperial Potentate of Shriners International

Contact the Author, Gary Bergenske
1101 West Kennedy Boulevard
Orlando, Florida 32810

Phone: 407-875-0000
FAX: 407-875-0480
GBergenske@aol.com

To arrange a speaking engagement with Gary Bergenske, please write him at the above address, or call 407-875-0000, or visit GaryMotivations.com Requests can also be e-mailed to Gary Bergenske at GBergenske@aol.com

Visit YouTube.com and search Gary Bergenske To watch some of the activities described in "My Shriners Diary"

To purchase additional copies of "My Shriners Diary" contact your favorite bookstore or go on line to amazon.com or Advbookstore.com. Also available in eBook an Amazon.com or at Advbookstore.com.

Be sure to get other books by Gary Bergenske

"Campaign for a Better Life"
20 Tools to Enrich Your Life and Everyone Around You

"Campaign to be a Better Leader"
12 Essential Keys for Unlocking Leadership Excellence

"Quotes for Leadership Success"
365 Little Quotes for Optimizing BIG Opportunity

Discounts are available for multiple book purchases by contacting Gary Bergenske at 407-875-0000

A Year as the Imperial Potentate of Shriners International

"The true value of a leader is not judged while serving, but is determined by how those he has influenced perform once he is no longer there."
— GARY BERGENSKE

GARY BERGENSKE

GaryMotivations.com

www.ingramcontent.com/pod-product-compliance
Lightning Source LLC
Chambersburg PA
CBHW050103170426
43198CB00014B/2437